Anglican Slavery
in New Jersey

Anglican Slavery in New Jersey

An Initial Accounting

Jolyon G. R. Pruszinski

Foreword by Elaine H. Pagels

CASCADE *Books* • Eugene, Oregon

ANGLICAN SLAVERY IN NEW JERSEY
An Initial Accounting

Copyright © 2025 Jolyon G. R. Pruszinski. All rights reserved. Except for brief quotations in critical publications or reviews, no part of this book may be reproduced in any manner without prior written permission from the publisher. Write: Permissions, Wipf and Stock Publishers, 199 W. 8th Ave., Suite 3, Eugene, OR 97401.

Cascade Books
An Imprint of Wipf and Stock Publishers
199 W. 8th Ave., Suite 3
Eugene, OR 97401

www.wipfandstock.com

PAPERBACK ISBN: 979-8-3852-1606-2
HARDCOVER ISBN: 979-8-3852-1607-9
EBOOK ISBN: 979-8-3852-1608-6

Cataloguing-in-Publication data:

Names: Pruszinski, Jolyon G. R., author. | Pagels, Elaine H., foreword.

Title: Anglican Slavery in New Jersey : an initial accounting / Jolyon G. R. Pruszinski.

Description: Eugene, OR: Cascade Books, 2025 | Includes bibliographical references and index.

Identifiers: ISBN 979-8-3852-1606-2 (paperback) | ISBN 979-8-3852-1607-9 (hardcover) | ISBN 979-8-3852-1608-6 (ebook)

Subjects: LCSH: Slavery and the church—Episcopal Church | Slavery—New Jersey—History | Slavery and the church—United States—History

Classification: HT913 P78 2025 (paperback) | HT913 (ebook)

VERSION NUMBER 10/24/25

To all those harmed,
and to all who received the inheritance built on harm
without understanding it.

Contents

List of Illustrations | ix
Foreword by Elaine H. Pagels | xi
Preface | xiii
Acknowledgments | xxiii
Abbreviations | xxv
Introduction | xxvii
A Timeline of Slavery in New Jersey | xxxi

Part I: An Outline of Anglican and Episcopal Slavery in New Jersey | 1

1. Slavery in New Jersey in the Colonial Era | 3
2. The Church of England in Colonial New Jersey | 7
3. New Jersey Anglicans and Slavery in the Colonial Period: A Brief Sketch | 11
4. The Revolutionary Period and Early Black Estrangement from the Episcopal Church | 18
5. Gradual Abolition and the Persistence of Slavery in New Jersey | 25
6. The Development of the Episcopal Church and Its Relation to Slavery in Antebellum New Jersey | 31

Part II: Historical Documents | 41

7. George Keith's Anti-Slavery Sermon of 1693 | 43
8. Correspondence with the SPG: Letters from Sharpe (1712), Haliday (1717), and Holbrooke (1727) | 49

Contents

9   Rev. Thomas Thompson's "The African Trade" Tract in Defense of Slavery (1772) | 58

10 Bishops Addressing the Afterlives of Slavery | 67

Part III: Vignettes and Afterlives | 75

11 Congregational Histories | 77

12 Black Believers in and out of the Episcopal Church in Antebellum New Jersey | 96

13 White Episcopalian Rejection of Black Participation | 108

Part IV: Conclusions and Next Steps | 121

14 Conclusion | 123

Epilogue: How Can I Research My Congregation? | 133

Appendix 1: Further Recommended Reading | 147

Appendix 2: Questions for Discussions | 150

Appendix 3: The Anglican Church in New Jersey *by Nelson R. Burr (1954), a Review* | 152

Appendix 4: Colonial (Anglican) and Antebellum (Episcopal) Parishes, Missions, and Preaching Stations in New Jersey | 156

Appendix 5: Congregational Giving to the American Colonization Society (ACS) in the Diocese of New Jersey (through 1865) | 165

Appendix 6: Congregational Giving in the Diocese of New Jersey to the Africa Mission of the Episcopal Church (through 1865) | 166

Selected Bibliography | 169

Index | 183

List of Illustrations

Figure 1: Map of Colonial Anglican Churches and Preaching Stations in New Jersey | 6

Figure 2: Col. Lewis Morris | 12

Figure 3: Rev. John Jea | 20

Figure 4: Rev. Alexander Crummell | 27

Figure 5: Map of Antebellum Episcopal Churches in New Jersey | 30

Figure 6: Bishop John Croes | 33

Figure 7: Rev. Absalom Jones | 37

Figure 8: Rev. Peter Williams | 39

Figure 9: Rev. George Keith | 44

Figure 10: The Plantation Imaginary | 54

Figure 11: Cape Coast Castle | 59

Figure 12: Bishop George Washington Doane | 68

Figure 13: The Original St. Philip's Church, Newark | 69

Figure 14: Slave Galleries of Trinity Cathedral, Newark | 87

Figure 15: Jacob Van Wickle | 92

Figure 16: T. Thomas Fortune | 114

Figure 17: Carrie Fortune | 115

Foreword

THOSE OF US WHO are White Christians like to think that we stand for justice, for human equality, compassion, and kindness; certainly we oppose slavery and racism. That is why we owe a great debt to Jolyon Pruszinski for offering us this initial investigation of the history of slavery in the Episcopal Diocese of New Jersey.

At the start, he acknowledges his own previous ignorance of this history, an ignorance shared by most of us who have not personally been targets of racism. Those who grew up in public schools like mine, in the California town of Palo Alto, learned in history class that long ago in the past, Abraham Lincoln freed the slaves; now we could proudly endorse the "liberty and justice for all" that our Pledge of Allegiance celebrates. Never mentioned in our history class, however, was what preceded that event: two hundred and fifty years of horrific human trafficking in chattel slavery that helped build and enrich the towns and institutions familiar to us, most of them entirely dominated by White people like ourselves. The history we learned gave only a passing mention to the political struggle to maintain slavery and the horrors of the Civil War. Instead, at the time, our complacency seemed natural—almost our birthright. There was also East Palo Alto, where Cornel West, who later would become my colleague at Princeton, grew up, but I knew little of that, since most Black students were funneled into other school districts.

But since the 1960s and 1970s, when intense conflict over issues of race increasingly broke into the open, some educators have brought much more of that hidden history to light, while others, to this day, are fighting hard to suppress it. Only more recently have Christians of many denominations

Foreword

begun to acknowledge, much less to reckon with, their part in this tangled and contested history.

So I deeply appreciate the great service Jolyon Pruszinski has done for members of the Episcopal Church in New Jersey, and especially to members of Trinity Church, Princeton. In this current report, he shows the results of having investigated how, and in what ways, members of the Episcopal Church in New Jersey have engaged slavery and racism, from the first founding of Anglican churches in colonial times to the outbreak of the Civil War. His work is also ongoing, as he now intends to document what has happened from that time to the present.

The report now before us, more than a history, comes as a manifesto. Pruszinski challenges us to stop avoiding painful truths, and to find freedom instead in acknowledging them, recognizing that the Episcopal churches in which we participate have reaped enormous benefits in wealth and influence from centuries of practicing slavery, segregation, and racism, often armed with scriptural justification. The facts he documents here challenge us not only to recognize what happened, but also to begin the process of repairing the harm in every way we can.

Pruszinski ends with a call for each one of us to rediscover one another, echoing the prophet Micah's call to "do justice; love mercy, and walk humbly with your God"—and with your neighbor, and mine.

Elaine Pagels,
Professor of History of Religion, Princeton University

Preface

I DIDN'T BECOME EPISCOPALIAN because I wanted to confront racism. Perhaps you didn't either. But here we are.

I grew up in Massachusetts in the 1980s and nineties, in essentially White spaces, being taught implicitly (but sometimes explicitly as well) that the advances of the civil rights era had "solved" racism. Overt racism was considered a thing of the past (or the South), and slavery a thing of the distant past. This understanding was a product of the White liberal biases of the largely White spaces I inhabited, including my home, the classrooms in my public schools, my sports teams, my Boy Scout troop, and my church.

If I had ever asked the adults in my life if racism was still a problem, some of them probably would have said "yes," but the problem did not loom large enough for them to ever really mention it themselves. If I had ever asked any of my few Black friends if racism was still a problem, they might have said "yes," but they might not have felt comfortable admitting as much to me. Had I been adequately thoughtful or sensitive, I would have perhaps been more aware that a White sixth-grade peer calling a Black peer the "n-word" indicated that things had not progressed quite as much as my progressive state would have had me believe. When this White peer was pummeled as a result of his insult, many of us thought he deserved it, but I'm not sure that we wondered why he had felt free enough to say it in the first place, or whether this indicated if things needed to change any further. Playground justice had been done. At the time I didn't think about what it would take to change our society to the point that such an anti-racist response might no longer be necessary.

My own awakening to the ongoing problems of racism occurred slowly, and was in no way special or unique. There was no epiphany. It came as the result of the steady trickle of facts that found their way into my largely White, sheltered experience. I conducted environmental justice analyses for my job. I saw demographic data on persistent wealth gaps. I read reporting on unequal policing, and unequal racialized treatment of those harmed by the [in]justice system.

But more than through data, and reporting, and reason, in many ways, my awakening to the persistence of racial injustice, in spite of my White silo, was the result of being a part of the church.[1] I became aware of the racism that Black people experience because I was part of the church, and so were they, even though we were mostly in different parts of it. And the church, in spite of all of its many sins in this regard, has yet always somehow somewhere managed to preserve the witness that *all people* are children of God, that *these same people* can continue to do evil, and that *anyone* may have legitimate testimony about it on account of the indwelling of Holy Spirit. It is as a result of these convictions that a door in my awareness was cracked open wide enough for the reality of Black suffering to sneak its way in. It is to my shame that it took as long as it did, but I am thankful that I have begun to become aware. If the reality of Black suffering has not yet entered into your awareness in earnest I hope you will allow it to do so. I hope this book will help.

As a White person, I know that most White people are not terribly comfortable talking about racism. Even those of good will are often afraid of accidentally saying something offensive, or of being misunderstood. The result is typically avoidance. And here we are talking about the White people who are, at least, amenable to supporting the fight against racism. If even these, the most likely White allies, are largely avoidant, that wouldn't seem to bode well for efforts to address racism publicly. And yet, White people have an obligation to reckon with the racist system they have created, cooperated with, and benefited from.

White churches are perhaps even less likely to want to address racism openly, but have perhaps even more reason to do so. White priests, pastors, and parishioners, of overwhelmingly White churches and denominations, were those predominantly responsible for providing moral cover for the project of slavery. It was their words and actions that legitimated White-supremacist logic and justified Black enslavement, Black exclusion, Black disenfranchisement, and Black suffering. That moral cover allowed, and has continued to allow, systemic anti-Black patterns of behavior and

---

1. I mean in the universal, small "c" catholic, sense.

effect to continue to thrive in our society. The legacy of slavery casts a long shadow and often White Christians are afraid to admit it. And the culture of not discussing anything controversial or "impolite" in certain parts of the church (I'm looking at us, Episcopalians) continues to provide cover for still-operating racism.

This White resistance to admit to this history, or to engage with it, or even to allow the subject to be broached, is itself, however, a kind of admission. Often this resistance is voiced as a concern that broaching such a subject will drive people away. But this leaves us with a question begging to be asked: If one is concerned that talking about, or admitting to, a history of racism will turn White people away from the church, is that not, at root, an admission that the church as it is currently constituted, depends for its very existence on leaving racism unexamined and unchallenged? Is that not an admission of reliance on racism for one's very existence? I think that when White Christians will not allow the subject of slavery or racism or reparations to be discussed in their churches, it is a kind of admission that their churches continue to depend on the preservation of undisturbed, unexamined racism.

Allow me, for a moment, a direct admonition: "Don't fear the data." When I was in college, a dear friend of mine, Dr. Michael Pirozzi, said this to me and it stuck with me ever since. "Don't fear the data." We may have made decisions, or lived our lives, or built our institutions on certain data. But unless we are willing to admit new data, or different data, or corrections to flawed data, we will live a lie, or perhaps more generously, only a partial truth. For centuries, White churches have systematically excluded certain data from their reckoning. But if the church is to be founded upon truth, it has nothing to fear from the data. Don't fear the data.

Admitting new data, though, always requires change. It requires turning from the old arrangements toward new arrangements that more adequately handle the new data. And this turning often involves repentance. But turning from evil that had not previously been admitted should not be something that the church is afraid of. Repentance is at the core of Jesus' message and was integral to his earliest, and perhaps most memorable proclamation: "The kingdom of God has drawn near, *repent* and believe the good news" (Mark 1:15). This should not be something Christians shy from. It is at the very heart of what it means to be Christian. We should not be afraid of repenting.

Preface

By now, though, if you are a White Christian reader, you may be thinking to yourself, "What about the rest of Jesus' proclamation? Where is the good news in all of this? We are a good news people. Why should we give attention to something that is not good news?" This is an understandable question. Many of us have been trained to block out bad things. Many of us have been trained to focus only on the good. My question in response to this question is: "Good news for whom?"

For centuries White Christians have forged the immediate circumstances of their privilege, their "good news" in this life, through forcing "bad news" upon Black people.[2] They have gained their ill-gotten "White blessings," to use the phrase of Atlanta megachurch pastor Louie Giglio,[3] through the enslavement of, rape of, marginalization of, and theft from Black people, all the while pretending to be paragons of virtue, innocence, and morality. Owning up to this appalling history—finally admitting to it—may not immediately sound good to White Christians, but it is clearly good news to Black people. Would you withhold that good news from them?

To suggest that dealing honestly with a history of racism is "not good news" is to suggest that the church is only for White people. Even though for much of its history, much of the Episcopal Church has been willing to live based on that lie, it remains a gross rejection of the reality of the true catholicity (universalism) of the church, a lie of which our Black brethren have been trying to disabuse us for centuries. It is long past time that the reality of White-imposed Black suffering be acknowledged by the predominantly White churches that have done the harm. And this harm needs to be not just acknowledged but repented for and repaired.

But, this disclosure and acknowledgment is not only good news for Black Christians. It is in fact good news for White Christians as well. It is an opportunity to stop living a lie. You may have heard it said that "you will know the truth, and the truth will set you free" (John 8:32). There is spiritual freedom in the truth, just as there is spiritual enslavement in falsehood. That's why the phrase "toxic positivity" exists. Insisting on a positive framing of things that are horrifically negative is poisonous. It kills. And it's

---

2. For many examples see Lauren Winner's *Dangers of Christian Practice*, and the words of US Senator Theodore Frelinghuysen who, in 1824, said "survey your comfortable habitations, your children rising around you to bless you. Who, under Providence, caused those hills to rejoice and those valleys to smile? Remember the toils and tears of black men." As quoted in Gigantino, *Ragged Road to Abolition*, 189.

3. Bailey, "Atlanta Megachurch Pastor Louie Giglio Sets off Firestorm by Calling Slavery a 'Blessing' to Whites."

Preface

not just affecting you. The poison spreads. Sometimes you spread it. Be free of the poison.

The freedom that comes from this truth is, however, not a one-time catharsis. It comes with the responsibility to make things right, and that is a long, long road. But the yoke of truth is lighter than the burden of falsehood.

And now, in the aftermath of years of protests against police brutality toward Black Americans, and as a result of the work of the Black Lives Matter movement, a space has begun to be carved out to address this history. In spite of a long-established White church culture of denial, a culture of politesse, a culture of toxic positivity, there has begun to be some movement on addressing racism in earnest.

The Episcopal Diocese of New Jersey has made a start.[4] In the wake of the George Floyd protests, and under the leadership of then-bishop William H. Stokes, in November 2020 the Diocese took up the charge of General Convention Resolution A143 ("Extend 2006 Resolution to Examine and Repent for Complicity in Slavery"), and approved the formation of a year-long Reparations Task Force to begin to investigate its history with slavery and racism. Years of running anti-racism trainings had worked to build diocese-wide support for the effort. This broad support was clear from the rapid affirmation by the diocesan convention of converting the task-force into a formal commission following its initial work in 2022. The first members of the commission considered their most pressing initial goal to be establishing how the church had participated in the early days of New Jersey's development of a slavery economy. Bits and pieces were known (an early bishop had been a slaveowner)[5] and a few congregations had begun to reckon with their histories with enslavement (e.g. Christ Church, Shrewsbury[6] and Trinity Church, Princeton[7]), but a more complete accounting was necessary to support diocesan educational efforts. The commission hired me to facilitate this research and we began a systematic investigation in earnest. I created the *Diocese of New Jersey Racial Justice Review*[8] to document the research, which provided the initial basis for this book.

---

4. For a more expansive description see Pruszinski, "Public History in the Diocese of New Jersey Racial Justice Review." Some text from this paragraph comes from this article.

5. John Croes (1762–1832).

6. Their report is entitled "Anglican Slavery in New Jersey: A Focus on Christ Church Shrewsbury."

7. Research had been conducted by parishioners Abigail Edwards and Kyra Pruszinski.

8. See https://dionj-racialjusticereview.blogspot.com/.

Preface

In the meantime, reparations initiatives have gained steam throughout the United States. Evanston, Illinois has begun making payments to African American residents.[9] California's reparations study determined that a total of over $1 million is owed to each long-time Black resident for the effects of redlining, mass incarceration, and other forms of discrimination,[10] and deliberations regarding additional action steps are taking place. As of June 2024 a bill to study reparations efforts has also been passed by the legislature in New York,[11] and others are under consideration in a number of other states, including New Jersey.[12]

Hundreds of local research efforts have been begun. The New Jersey Reparation Council has just released an excellent report documenting the pressing issues confronting our state and providing robust policy recommendations.[13] And of the many educational institutions that have conducted slavery audits, some like Georgetown University, Virginia Theological Seminary, and Princeton Theological Seminary have instituted or announced modest reparations programs. The Justice League of Greater Lansing (JLGL) is a church-initiated regional Michigan program that "aims to address the impact of slavery" by "fostering relationships and reparations to boost wealth equity for African Americans in Lansing."[14] And even as The Church of England Church Commissioners[15] recently announced that they had set aside £100 million for reparative initiatives,[16] church lead-

---

9. See City of Evanston, "Evanston Local Reparations."

10. See Fry, "California Reparations Task Force to Recommend 'Down Payments' for Slavery, Racism." Redlining is the practice of refusing to loan money or insure a property purportedly because the transaction is viewed as too risky for the lender or insurer, but either the refusal or the perceived risk or both are due to racism.

11. Khan, "New York Will Set up a Commission to Consider Reparations for Slavery."

12. Bills A602/S3164 would establish a state task force to study the case for reparative justice for the lasting harms of slavery.

13. The *Diocese of New Jersey Racial Justice Review* is the exact kind of faith-institution-based research initiative called for in the report (New Jersey Reparations Council, "For Such a Time as This," 187). However, the report also calls for many additional reparative steps beyond research for majority-White faith institutions.

14. See https://www.justiceleagueglm.org. See also Saliby, "Grassroots Effort in Michigan Is Raising Reparations—While the Government Lags."

15. The charity that runs COE investment funds.

16. Church of England, "Church Commissioners Publishes Full Report Into Historic Links to Transatlantic Chattel Slavery and Announces New Funding Commitment of £100m in Response to Findings."

ers subsequently insisted, rightly, that the number was too small by at least an order of magnitude.[17]

Church Pension Fund research recently determined various overt links to slavery in donated funds for the Episcopal Church, but emphasized that *all* funds were inextricably tied to racist systems of White wealth accumulation.[18] Recent polling suggests that an increasingly large percentage of Americans[19] favor reparations for slavery, and an outright majority of young Americans are not actively opposed.[20] Moreover, recent work by Harvard scholars Linda J. Bilmes and Cornell William Brooks suggests that reparations for slavery would be neither unprecedented, nor infeasible, having shown in their paper "Normalizing Reparations"[21] that various similar programs already exist within our society to provide redress for harms done, and that the federal government already has the resources and capabilities in place for accomplishing a robust reparative program. Moreover, multifaceted plans like that proposed by William Darity and Kristen Mullen[22] would address many of the systemic issues involved, including long-standing household wealth discrepancies between Black and White households.[23]

As I said at the outset, I did not become Episcopalian because I wanted to confront racism. Like many other White people, I was confirmed as an adult without any awareness of the Episcopal Church's sordid history. This is a testament to how well the overwhelmingly White parts of the Episcopal Church have buried their history of slavery and racism. But the more I

---

17. Sherwood, "C of E Hoping to Create £1bn Fund to Address Legacy of Slavery."

18. See Church Pension Group, "Report by the Church Pension Group on the Origins and Sources of Its Assets." See also Church Pension Group, "Church Pension Group Releases Report on the Origins and Sources of Its Assets."

19. Pew Research polling suggests 30 percent of Americans support cash reparations for the descendants of enslaved peoples: Blazina and Cox, "Black and White Americans Are Far Apart in Their Views of Reparations for Slavery."

20. A Berkeley Institute of Government Studies poll (DiCamillo, "Majority of Voters Believe Black Californians Continue to Be Affected by the Legacy of Slavery, Yet Cash Reparations Face Headwinds," 5) found that 53 percent of respondents who were eighteen to twenty-nine years old were not opposed to cash reparations for the descendants of the enslaved.

21. Bilmes and Brooks, "Normalizing Reparations," 30–68.

22. Darity and Mullen, *From Here to Equity*.

23. In 2019 the average White household was approximately 700 percent wealthier ($983,400) than the average Black household ($142,500). Bhutta et al., "Disparities in Wealth by Race and Ethnicity in the 2019 Survey of Consumer Finances."

Preface

have learned about my church, and the more I have learned from Black Episcopalians, the more I am convinced that confrontation of racism is utterly necessary and that all White Episcopalians have a responsibility for it.

Is it the place of a White person to presume to write on this subject? Some might say "no." But the fact is that our Black sisters and brothers have resisted racism and horrific treatment for centuries and it is wrong to expect them to continue to do this work for us while we sit idly. Would not that be yet another form of Black service we White Episcopalians inappropriately expect? White churches and White wealth were built through imposing suffering on Black people. This history is White church history, and White people need to take responsibility for what we have done. Moreover, we need to take responsibility for what still remains to be done to fix it.

I am not a "cradle Episcopalian." I am the first Episcopalian in my family. Neither am I wealthy.[24] But just because I am not wealthy does not mean that I have not benefited from White privilege. My life has been easier because I am White.[25] As an inheritor of that unjust privilege I have an obligation to deal with it. Similarly, because I have been confirmed in the Episcopal Church, I am an inheritor of its history even if I did not make that history. Even though I didn't realize it at the time, by becoming part of the Episcopal Church I became, in part, responsible for its history and for how the church responds to that history. This will require work.

Rather than pretending everything is fine, that racism is "solved," which would be a continuing insult to the experiences of our Black sisters and brothers, we need to deal with our horrific past and our unjust present. I am not interested in being a spiritual "trust fund baby," blithely enjoying a spiritual inheritance based on ill-gotten gains and predicated on Black suffering. That would be neither responsible nor loving. Being an adult means taking responsibility, and, in this case, taking responsibility requires repentance for both "the evils we have done, and *the evil done on our behalf*."[26] Moreover, true repentance requires working to make right what has been done wrong. I want to be part of that work and I hope you do too.

---

24. My children have been enrolled in the public school free lunch program for almost a decade. I do indeed mean "not wealthy."

25. If you, as a White American, would not immediately be willing to trade places with a Black American, you instinctively recognize that you have benefited from White privilege. And until such a thought experiment of trading places yields different results, there is still work to be done to address the systemic racism of our nation that disproportionately harms Black Americans and privileges White Americans.

26. The Church Pension Fund, "Confession," 19.

Preface

This book is subtitled *An Initial Accounting*. That it can be understood as no more than a beginning of the research and reckoning for the history of slavery and racism in New Jersey in the colonial era Anglican Church, and the pre-Civil War Episcopal Church, will no doubt become clear by the end. There is so much that remains to be done to document the church's awful history of slavery and racism. And as it is only an *initial* accounting, it is my hope that this book will spark further research, reckoning, education, repentance, and repair in the churches of the Episcopal Dioceses of New Jersey and Newark, in the Reformed Episcopal Churches (ACNA) of the Diocese of the Northeast and Mid-Atlantic, in these dioceses themselves, in the Episcopal Church and the Anglican Communion as a whole, and in the church universal.

But research and education themselves are just two early steps in the process of reparation, steps that Episcopal priest Rev. Peter Jarrett-Schell, in his recent book *Reparations: A Plan for Churches*, calls "truth finding" and "truth telling."[27] The full work of reparation for the wrongs done and for the ongoing effects of these wrongs involves much more, as is already well known by our Black sisters and brothers who have been engaged in this work for centuries. But even as the scope of the task of justice may seem daunting, as Rabbi Tarfon once said, "Do justly, now. Love mercy, now. Walk humbly, now. You are not obligated to complete the work, but neither are you free to abandon it."[28] Thank you for reading, and thank you for your willingness to share in the work that history and justice require.

Jolyon Pruszinski
Princeton, New Jersey
Juneteenth 2024

---

27. Jarrett-Schell, *Reparations*.

28. This is a popular rendering of *Pirkei Avot* 2.16, commenting on that great justice text Micah 6:8. Quoted here from Chaim Harrison, "Three Jewish Reminders for When the World Seems Overwhelming."

Acknowledgments

I WANT TO OFFER my very great thanks to the members of the Reparations Commission of the Episcopal Diocese of New Jersey for inviting me into this field of research and for their support and funding of this project. A special thanks to the co-conveners, Canon Annette Buchanan and Canon Barbie O. Bach, and the members of the history working group, including the Rev. Beth Rauen Sciaino, the Rev. Jack Zamboni, Vernon Anthony, Patrick Milas, and Alice Vassar. Thank you also to the Rev. Cn. Clive Sang, The Rev. Cn. Leroy Lyons, and the Rev. Cn. Terry Roshuevel for your willingness to speak with me and share your wisdom and experience. Thank you to my priest, the Rev. Joanne Epply-Schmidt, who has been utterly supportive of this work, and the Rt. Rev. William Stokes, who as twelfth Bishop of New Jersey presided over the founding of the Reparations Commission and supported this work wholeheartedly. And thank you to the Rev. Cn. Richard Wrede, diocesan archivist, for facilitating access to the diocesan archives and for his helpful research suggestions.

Thank you to my colleagues at Princeton University, New York University, and Princeton Theological Seminary for your kindness and support, especially Jonathan Henry, Jonathan Gold, AnneMarie Liujendijk, MK Bodnar, Kerry Smith, Jack Tannous, Adam Becker, Wendy Li, Cayla Delardi, Janine Paolucci, the United Auto Workers Local 7092, Andrew Scales, Mark L. Taylor, and Dale Allison. Thank you to George Parsenios, Steve Bohannon, Tim Neuschwander, Dan Lundquist, Nate Johnson, Stacey Hoffer, Mike Pirozzi, the Most Rev. Michael Curry, and Sheryl Kujawa-Holbrook for your support and advice. And to the inimitable Elaine Pagels: thank you for your unfailing kindness over the years, for your constant thoughtfulness, for your resolute commitment to support justice in your

Acknowledgments

teaching, and for your insistence on speaking the truth. You are an inspiration to us all.

Thank you to the editing and production staff at Cascade for your hard work to bring this book to publication. Thank you to the Mercer County Board of Social Services for indirectly funding this research. And to my fellow scholars doing good work and relying, in part, on public assistance: a Fulbright is public assistance too. It just sounds fancier. Don't be afraid to admit to all your sources of funding. People need this assistance. Do what you can to destigmatize it.

To my parents Ellen Rivoir and Glenn Pruszinski: Thank you for your unwavering love. I am so fortunate to have such utterly kind and supportive parents.

To my children Kyra, Teddy, Joseph, and Balian: Thank you all for helping me do this work. It would not be possible without you, and I am grateful for the ways you have contributed. A particular thank you to Kyra for your research on Trinity Church, Princeton and to both Kyra and Teddy for producing many of the figures for the book. Thank you for sharing your gifts. I love you all so much.

To my wife, Emily: How can I offer any kind of thanks here that even remotely approaches the scope of the thanks you deserve? I only hope that I can support you and your scholarship to the degree you have supported me. I love you with my whole being.

And though it is not yet customary when making acknowledgments, I would also like to extend a special thank you to the priests and diocesan officials in the Diocese of New Jersey who have indirectly proven that this work is utterly necessary through their attempts to undermine, discredit, and otherwise hamper my work and the work of the Reparations Commission. I am not naming names here, but I am keeping receipts. Particular thanks goes to those who have pretended to support our work in public while privately undermining it. A further "thank you" goes to all the Episcopalians who have cowered in fear and avoided publicly supporting our work even though you know it is necessary. It's not too late to grow a spine.

Abbreviations

ACS	American Colonization Society
AEH	*Anglican and Episcopal History* Journal
aka	also known as
AME	African Methodist Episcopal
C.C.C.	Cape Coast Castle
Cn.	Canon
COE / C of E	Church of England
Co.	Company
Co.	County
Col.	Colonel
d.	died
Deut.	Deuteronomy
diss.	dissertation
DNJRJR	*Diocese of New Jersey Racial Justice Review*
ed(s).	editor(s)
ENS	*Episcopal News Service*
E.g.	*exempli gratia* (for example)
et al.	et alia (and others)
Exod.	Exodus
G.A.	General Assembly
Geo.	George
HMPEC	*Historical Magazine of the Protestant Episcopal Church*
Ibid.	*ibidem* (reference to the same source as the previous note)

Abbreviations

ID	Identification (number)
Id.	*idem* (reference to the same author just mentioned)
I.e.	*id est* (in other words)
Institut.	Justinian's *Institutes*, one of four parts of the *Corpus Juris Civilis*
Isa.	Isaiah
LEVAS	Horace Clarence Boyer, ed. *Lift Every Voice and Sing II: An African American Hymnal.* New York: Church Publishing, 1993.
Lib.	George Sandys's Library Now in America (multi-volume manuscript collection)
M.A.	Master of Arts
MSS	manuscript
NAID	National Archives ID
NESRI	Northeast Slavery Record Index
N.J.L.	New Jersey Law
no.	number
pp.	pages
SPG	Society for the Propagation of the Gospel in Foreign Parts
Rev.	Revelation
Rev.	Reverend
RSF	*The Russell Sage Foundation Journal of the Social Sciences*
Skinneri etymol. ling. Angl.	Stephen Skinner, *Etymologicon Linguae Anglicanae* (London: Typis T. Roycroft, & prostant venales apud H. Brome [etc.], 1671).
TEC	The Episcopal Church
Tho.	Thomas
Twp.	Township
viz.	videlicet (in other words)
Vol(s).	Volume(s)
WPA	Works Progress Administration

Introduction

ANGLICAN SLAVERY IN NEW Jersey: An Initial Accounting is a primer on the history and prehistory of slavery and racism the Episcopal Diocese of New Jersey through the Civil War. The information presented here is, for the most part, not new, but has never been drawn together in one place from the various research fields involved. There are a number of reasons that this history has been left siloed in various non-church fields and repositories, and even locked away and often forgotten in church archives, but the time is long past due for it to be collated and made better known.

It is not exactly a secret that most majority-White institutions have not been very good at, or interested in, accurately portraying their role in the history of slavery and racism in the United States. The result has been that most White people, White Christians included, are almost entirely unaware of their own history, and certainly also unaware of much of what is commonly called Black history. This is, of course, a very self-serving pattern of behavior on the part of White institutions, and contributes to the culturally ingrained (and well documented) White self-perception of innocence. That this innocence is an ill-founded perception, and cannot be defended from historical data, is also not disputed by legitimate historians. Nevertheless, the result of the institutional production of this sense of White innocence is the broad lack of awareness among White people, including White Christians, regarding their history, and especially their persistently harmful role in Black suffering.

Because of the long-standing patterns of White avoidance of the subject, even as the data are readily available, the facts presented in this book should not be understood as "discoveries" or "findings." The information presented here, at least in its general outline, has been known by historians, and certainly also by many Black communities, for decades, except when it has been known for centuries. This book then should be understood, not as presenting "findings," but as a project designed to de-silo this information, and to undo White Christian—and particularly Episcopalian—historical and cultural amnesia.

The Episcopal Church is not in fact a White Church, but its White members have often acted as if it is. Its White leaders and members have, at best, ignored and marginalized, and at worst enslaved and persecuted Black people, including Black Episcopalians. Black Episcopal historians, such as George F. Bragg, Robert E. Hood, Robert A. Bennett, D. Elwood Dunn, and James T. Yarsiah, have regularly shown that there is a much larger history to the Episcopal Church than the White hagiography known and popularized by White people. Harold T. Lewis' *Yet With A Steady Beat: The African American Struggle for Recognition in the Episcopal Church* is a particularly important contribution.

In light of these White patterns of doing harm, and avoiding admitting to the harm, it unfortunately bears repeating that Christians should understand that they have very good biblically based reasons for attending to "the truth," whether regarding historical realities or contemporaneous events.[29] Similarly, and again unfortunately, it also bears repeating that Christians should understand that they have good, biblically based reasons for adopting an attitude of willingness to admit to wrongdoing (e.g., Sirach 20:3), willingness to repent of it (e.g., Luke 13:3–5), make reparation (e.g., Exodus 22, Luke 19:8), and seek to do right (e.g., Micah 6:8, James 2:14–17). Being amenable to correction for wrongdoing is a frequent theme throughout the biblical canon, and this includes willingness to be held responsible and make reparation for wrongs done by previous generations.[30] As will become clear from the historical information presented in this book, *if you consider slavery and racism to be wrong,* White Episcopalians in the Dioceses of Newark and New Jersey, White Reformed Episcopalians (Anglican Church of North America [ACNA]) in the New Jersey region of the Diocese of the Northeast and Mid-Atlantic, and their White Anglican and Episcopal forebears, have a good deal to repent of and, as a consequence, a good deal to work to repair.

29. See, for example, John 8:32.

30. According to biblical paradigms, descendants are still responsible for restitution for crimes committed by ancestors (e.g., Leviticus 26:40–42) and reparation can be made to next of kin (e.g., Numbers 5:8) even across generations, as suggested by the Jubilee Year laws (Leviticus 25–27, Luke 4).

Introduction

The first six chapters of this book (Part I) briefly lay out the broad outline of the history of the Anglican Church in colonial New Jersey and the Episcopal Church in antebellum New Jersey with respect to slavery and racism. These chapters should not be understood as an exhaustive treatment, but as a primer on the basic dynamics at play, described with illustrative examples. No colonial-era or antebellum-era church is given an exhaustive treatment with respect to its responsibility for slavery, nor is any particular historical figure. That historical work remains to be done, and should be conducted in order to approach a more complete reckoning with the history presented in this book. Consider this book a prompt. I invite you, readers, to take up the work.

Part II, "Historical Documents," presents several important primary historical documents, in part or in full, in order to give the reader a deeper sense of how early and how fully the Anglicans and Episcopalians involved with slavery were aware of the gravity of their actions. A persistent falsehood about the actions of historical personages is that "they didn't know any better." Chapters 7 through 10 dispel this notion entirely. At times it has been necessary to preserve some of the archaic racialized language from early sources that is now considered offensive. This has only been done when necessary to give an accurate sense of these early sources and is not in any way an affirmation of the use of such language in modern parlance.

Part III, starting with Chapter 11, "Congregational Histories," presents a series of vignettes of particular congregations and individuals, giving a somewhat deeper sense of some of the troubling events in the history of the diocese. The operation of the Van Wickle Slave Ring is a particularly appalling episode. Many of these vignettes are based on presentations produced for the first "Stations of Reparations" service of repentance, organized by the Reparations Commission of the Diocese of New Jersey, and held on March 25, 2023 at St. Peter's Episcopal Church in Freehold, New Jersey. The liturgy for this service was designed to be widely replicable, and a recording of the service is available if you would like to learn more about it.[31]

Chapter 12, entitled "Black Believers in and out of the Episcopal Church in Antebellum New Jersey," explores some of the patterns of treatment of Black Christians in the diocese before the Civil War. Among these patterns were exclusion from leadership, segregation in worship, opposition to residency as freedmen, support for ongoing enslavement, and rape. Many Black Christians left the Episcopal Church as a result, but, even in

---

31. See the recording at https://www.youtube.com/watch?v=K1x6bEZOmGU.

Introduction

spite of these horrific experiences, some stayed and continued to insist upon the catholicity of the church, that is, its universal nature and its necessary inclusion of all peoples. The content from this chapter is paired with that of Chapter 13, "White Episcopalian Rejection of Black Participation."

The epilogue, "How Can I Research My Congregation?," is a resource for acting on the prompt provided by the information presented in this book. Much more research needs to be done at a congregational level. Indeed, much more remains to be done than can be accomplished by any single researcher. This chapter points to useful resources available to the congregational researcher and provides important warnings regarding pitfalls to avoid in the process.

Because this book is intended, in part, as a resource for congregations, Appendix 1 includes a guide for further reading, and Appendix 2 includes a number of generative questions to prompt discussion on the key themes of the book. In general, the book is designed so that individual chapters can be read one at a time for this purpose. And, as it is the most widely held account[32] of much of the history addressed in this book, Appendix 3 provides a review of *The Anglican Church in New Jersey* by renowned historian Nelson Burr, with an emphasis on its very inadequate treatment of slavery and racism.

As you will see as you read, the Anglican Church in colonial-era New Jersey, and the Episcopal Church since then, including her White parishioners, priests, and bishops, typically supported slavery, worked to establish and protect it, and sought to (and did) benefit from it. Much research remains to be done to establish the details of this general picture on a church-by-church basis, but the overall picture is very clear. Nor is the effect of these patterns of behavior confined to the past. The dramatic negative effects on Black Americans of this horrific history have been generational and continue to this day, including everything from persistently great disparities between Black and White household wealth to continuing marginalization of Black Episcopalians in the Episcopal Church. As you read, I invite you to consider not only what wrongs have been done in the past (as described here), but what effect these wrongs have had on our present, and what actions might be required to remediate them.

---

32. Most New Jersey Episcopal church libraries hold at least one copy.

A Timeline of Slavery in New Jersey

1665 Colonial proprietors issue governing directives to grant additional land to settlers bringing enslaved people to New Jersey. The incentives put in place in various areas during the settlement period were as high as 150 acres per additional enslaved person.

1694 The East Jersey legislature passes "An Act Concerning Slaves." Citizens could punish enslaved persons found traveling without written permission more than five miles from their residence.

1704 An omnibus slavery bill, based on draconian East Jersey precedent, is passed for all of New Jersey prohibiting free and enslaved Black people from owning property and disallowing baptism as grounds for manumission.

1713–14 More draconian slavery laws are passed, making manumission so expensive as to prevent it almost entirely.

1786 Trans-Atlantic import of enslaved persons is made illegal, but the domestic slave trade is allowed to continue. Free Black people are not allowed to leave or enter the state without formal written permission.

1793 The federal government passes the "Fugitive Slave Act" requiring interstate cooperation in the retrieval of enslaved persons by enslavers.

1793 The New Jersey Society for the Promotion of the Abolition of Slavery is formed.

1798 New Jersey passes "An Act respecting Slaves" adding further constraints on the allowed actions of the enslaved.

1804 The "Gradual Abolition Law" is passed in New Jersey, requiring the release from bondage of all enslaved persons born after the passing of the law upon completion of a term of service: twenty-one years for women, and twenty-five years for men. No enslaved persons are immediately freed. Consent of the enslaved is required for sale out of state.

A Timeline of Slavery in New Jersey

1807	New Jersey passes legislation taking away free Black people's right to vote.
1809	The New Jersey Society for the Promotion of the Abolition of Slavery disbands.
1816	The American Colonization Society (ACS) is founded with significant support from influential New Jersey residents.
1820	The New Jersey legislature passes an omnibus slavery bill reaffirming laws on the books.
1825	The first enslaved persons begin to gain their freedom as a result of the Gradual Abolition Law.
1826	A New Jersey personal liberty law is passed, adding modest protections for free Black people.
1836	The New Jersey Supreme Court overturns precedent, no longer allowing the presumption that Black people are enslaved until proven otherwise for the purposes of law enforcement. At this time New Jersey also begins to require trials by jury for "escaped slaves."
1839	The New Jersey Anti-Slavery Society is founded.
1842	The US Supreme Court decision in *Prigg v. Pennsylvania* voids most New Jersey personal liberty provisions that had provided modest protections for freed Black people.
1846	"An Act to Abolish Slavery" is passed in New Jersey but only recategorizes the enslaved as "apprentices for life" whose involuntary service is still owned by their enslavers.
1857	The US Supreme Court decision in *Dred Scott v. Sandford* further undermines legal rights for Black people throughout the country, including New Jersey.
1863	The Emancipation Proclamation does not free slaves in the North and "apprentices for life" in New Jersey remain enslaved during the Civil War.
1865	The Thirteenth Amendment to the US Constitution, abolishing most forms of slavery, is rejected by the New Jersey legislature and becomes the law of the land without the consent of New Jersey. Slavery still remains legal as a punishment for a crime.
1866	New Jersey, under a new legislature, ratifies the Thirteenth Amendment after it has already become law. Again, slavery still remains legal as a punishment for a crime.

PART I

An Outline of Anglican and Episcopal Slavery in New Jersey

1

Slavery in New Jersey in the Colonial Era

THE EARLIEST LEGAL ESTABLISHMENT of slavery in the land that would become New Jersey can be dated to the Dutch presence in the area prior to its English annexation. English settlement of the region only began in earnest following the annexation in 1664 of "New Netherland," which to that point had been settled mostly by the Dutch in the vicinity of New Amsterdam (modern-day New York City) and by Swedes in the region along the lower Delaware River (formerly "New Sweden"). By the time the British took over, hundreds of enslaved people were already held against their will in both of these settled areas. The slavery set up by the Dutch in these areas was not legally racialized,[1] but it was widespread, with approximately one-eighth of Dutch settlers in New Netherland owning slaves.[2] Once taken by the English, the territory was established as a proprietary colony, sold to Sir George Carteret and Lord Berkeley of Stratton, and split into East Jersey and West Jersey, dividing the region according to its two primary established areas of European settlement.

---

1. "Like in other colonies, New Jersey's charter generation lived in a society that had neither firmly delineated laws on slavery nor used race to determine enslaved status." Gigantino II, *Ragged Road to Abolition*, 12.
2. Goodfriend, "Burghers and Blacks," 142–43.

Part I: An Outline of Anglican and Episcopal Slavery in New Jersey

At this time the English continued to allow slavery throughout their colonies. In fact, before the annexation, the Crown was already directly profiting from the Atlantic slave trade. From 1660 it had operated a transportation monopoly in the Atlantic as the sole legal provider of enslaved peoples to British colonies.[3] British settlement in New Jersey after the annexation mainly came from migration between colonies, including plantation owners from the British colonies of the West Indies, who came for the promise of land granted in proportion to the number of enslaved persons brought.[4] These largely Anglican settlers moved to East Jersey, while much of West Jersey became increasingly dominated by Quaker influence. Ultimately, West and East Jersey were unified in 1702 into a single royal Province of New Jersey; however, the legal statutes regarding slavery adopted for the whole colony were based mostly on East Jersey precedent.

Barbadian settlers especially had brought with them to East Jersey the legal precedents of the English colonies of the West Indies. There, under the seventeenth-century colonial plantation system, the English had developed both racialized chattel slavery and the new linguistic-legal conventions of "Black" (associated with "slave" and "pagan") and "White" (with "free" and "Christian").[5] The legal statutes of East Jersey, formalized in 1694 and 1695,[6] replicated and perpetuated these particularly English (and by extension, Anglican) systemic developments. After the unification of East and West Jersey, the Barbadian plantation owners of East Jersey, through their political influence in the legislature,[7] managed to extend these laws to the entire unified province by way of the 1704 omnibus slavery bill.[8] Among the provisions of this bill were the prohibition of property ownership for both slaves and free Black residents, and the formal disqualification of Christian

---

3. Pettigrew, *Freedom's Debt*, 22–23. The monopoly was initially called the "Company of Royal Adventurers Trading to Africa" but was reorganized and renamed "Royal African Company" after 1672, continuing to operate as a monopoly until 1712 when the Crown began to allow other merchants to profit from the trade as well.

4. Gigantino II, *Ragged Road to Abolition*, 13: "each settler received 150 acres and an additional 150 acres for each male slave and 75 for each female slave."

5. Rugemer, "Development of Mastery and Race in the Comprehensive Slave Codes of the Greater Caribbean during the Seventeenth Century," 446–47.

6. Which in Monmouth County *required* landowners to own slaves: Boyd, ed., *Fundamental Laws and Constitutions of New Jersey, 1664–1964*, 51–67.

7. The so-called Anglican "ring." See Burr, *Anglican Church in New Jersey*, 373–75.

8. See "An Act for Regulating Negro, Indian, and Mallatto Slaves within this Province of New Jersey," 2:28–30.

baptism as legal grounds for manumission.[9] This latter provision was passed with full approval of the Archbishop of Canterbury.[10]

These harsh laws were amplified in an even more draconian slave code, passed by the legislature in 1713–1714 in response to anxieties over "slave conspiracies" in the state. The codes effectively ended manumission, as those who desired to free persons they had previously enslaved would be required both to pay the Provincial government a bond of £200 upon manumission and then to render to each freed slave a further £20 every year.[11] The effect of these laws was both to control and to grow the enslaved population in the state and, by extension, to strengthen the role of slavery in the state economy. As a result, through the middle of the eighteenth century, slavery took on an increasingly important role in the economy of New Jersey, becoming the "primary labor supply" in rural areas, but in truth, "[operating] in almost every imaginable locale and time."[12] The enslaved population of New Jersey also rapidly increased as a result of increased direct importation of enslaved Black Africans, and on the eve of the Revolution enslaved persons made up more than 7 percent of New Jersey's population, while in some east New Jersey counties the figure stood at as much as 15 percent.[13]

Summary: Slavery was first introduced to the New Jersey region by the Dutch, but the English expanded and codified the enslavement of Black people. English Barbadian enslavers settled in New Jersey and brought with them the brutal racialized legal structures that had begun to develop in the Caribbean. Slavery became especially well established in East Jersey, but was employed throughout the state as part of a plantation economy.

---

9. Manumission at baptism had been a rather well-established European custom, in part, as a result of the Doctrine of Discovery.

10. The administration of the archbishop had drafted a law "For Converting the Negroes &c In the Plantations" that specifically stated that baptism did not in any way change the property status of a slave. This was sent to various authorities in the colonies to influence the legislative process. See "1st draught." Also Burr, *Anglican Church in New Jersey*, 225.

11. "Act for Regulating of Slaves," 2:136–40.

12. Gigantino II, *Ragged Road to Abolition*, 17, 3.

13. US Bureau of the Census, *Historical Statistics of the United States*, 2:1168. See also Gigantino II, *Ragged Road to Abolition*, 17.

Part I: An Outline of Anglican and Episcopal Slavery in New Jersey

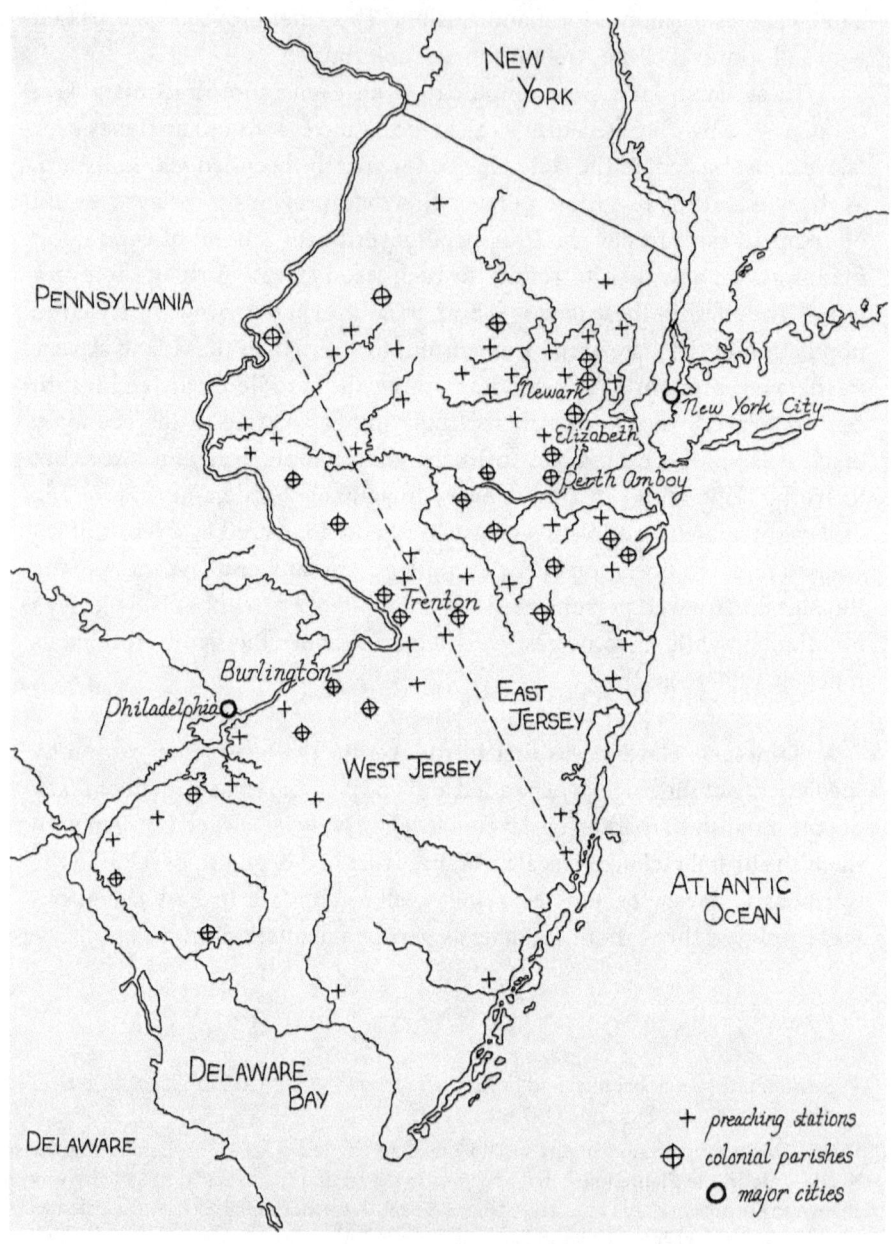

Colonial Anglican churches and preaching stations. By Kyra N. Pruszinski. Used with permission.

2

The Church of England in Colonial New Jersey

EVEN BEFORE THE FOUNDING of the first Anglican churches in New Jersey, the influence of the Church of England there was significant. Such influence should probably be dated to the first British settlement, but certainly at least to the period after annexation in 1664. It is true that most European-descended settlers to New Jersey were not expressly devoted to the Church of England. Presbyterians, as a result of prior Dutch settlement, and Quakers, as a result of movement of settlers from other North American English colonies, were more numerous. Members of other Christian sects, including Baptists and Congregationalists, migrated to New Jersey as well, in part because there was no established church.

Nevertheless, the Anglican heritage of and influence upon many of the English settlers can be easily seen within a few decades through the settler interest in organizing worshipping Anglican communities.[1] This

---

1. E.g., the promptings of Colonel Lewis Morris recorded in Hawks, ed., "Memorial of Col. Morris Concerning the State of Religion in the Jerseys, 1700." Another typical example is the petition from the laity of Salem, New Jersey in 1704: "A poor unhappy people settled by God's Providence, to procure by laborious Industry a Subsistance for our Familys, make bold to apply ourselves to God, thro' that very pious and charitable Society . . . our Indigence is excessive, and our Destitution deplorable, having never been so bless'd as to have a Person settled among us, to dispence the August ordinances of Religion . . . Be pleased to send us some Reverend Clergyman . . . to whom we promise

Part I: An Outline of Anglican and Episcopal Slavery in New Jersey

interest was prompted neither by a significant presence of ordained Anglican priests, nor by Anglican missionaries, who did not come to New Jersey in any numbers until after 1702. The first Anglican parish in New Jersey, St. Peter's at Perth Amboy, dates its founding to 1685, even as the ecclesial authorities in England viewed this early self-organization by the laity rather dimly. The opinion of George Keith that the inhabitants of the region were afflicted by "little else but . . . heathenism"[2] is indicative of the general feeling among Society for the Propagation of the Gospel in Foreign Parts (SPG)[3] clergy toward the colonial settlers before their coming. But such perspectives should be taken with a grain of salt.

The Anglican church in the American colonies was marked by more prominent empowerment of the laity than in England proper, in part as a result of the modest early presence of formal representatives of the church hierarchy and the absence of a local bishop until after the Revolutionary War. As such, the descriptions of the woeful state of affairs of "religion" and the Anglican Church in the colonies given by members of the church hierarchy, including the SPG, should not be taken literally. Such negative statements are perhaps more accurately indicative of a failure to *establish* the Church of England in New Jersey.[4] While they accurately describe the absence of ordained clergy, such comments should not be taken as fully accurate regarding the state of the influence of the Church among the laity. This latter influence is certainly evidenced by the repeated urgent requests from the colonies for priests to minister locally.[5] Such interest hardly indicates a land bereft of the influence of religion generally, or the influence of the Anglican Church in particular. In fact, many of the English settlers had an affinity for the Church of England and her particular approach to religion.[6]

Thus, the development of the Anglican Church in New Jersey began during this period before a significant presence of priests, and involved the

---

all Encouragement according to our Abilities . . ." See "Laity of Salem."

2. Keith, *Journal of Travels*, 47.

3. The Society for the Propagation of the Gospel in Foreign Parts (SPG) was a voluntary association within the Church of England, founded in 1701.

4. It was never established.

5. And the conditions were described by some devoted Anglicans in America in particularly negative terms with the specific goal of inducing the Church to send priests. Some of the communications of Colonel Lewis Morris Sr. in particular fall into this category.

6. And this Anglican influence played a significant role in shaping slavery in the region.

early organization of a few local meetings in homes and, in some instances, construction of church buildings.[7] These groups of laity did want the ministration of priests, and petitioned the newly formed SPG to send them, promising support in various forms. The SPG answered the call according to its means and began a campaign of support for the growth of the Church in New Jersey. This mostly involved sending a few priests, providing a large portion of their stipend, and providing books and pamphlets.

Most of the establishment of church buildings, rectories, and glebes came from the contributions of the laity of nascent New Jersey congregations.[8] Many of the missionary priests sent to New Jersey were assigned more than one parish, and some to several. It was the minority of locations with a quorum of Anglican sympathizers who could fund a church building, a partial salary for a priest, and a rectory and/or glebe. Many locations that were visited by clergy for preaching and administering the sacraments never built a church in the colonial era, not for lack of Anglican sentiment, but more due to the subsistence nature of the economy, and the understandably inconsistent visitation from the limited number of clergy the SPG did send.

In short, during the colonial period, the church grew significantly, as did the population of the state, but well-established parishes were the minority, and the coverage and support the SPG could provide for the province was limited. By 1775 there were eleven SPG missionary priests operating in New Jersey, twenty-four churches built and operating, and an approximately equal number of "occasional preaching stations" being visited by the clergy.[9] When the attentions of the SPG began in 1702 the

---

7. Burr notes "unorganized" (read: lay-organized) congregations in Shrewsbury, Middletown, Toponemus, Perth Amboy, Woodbridge, Piscataway, Elizabethtown, Crosswicks, Burlington, and Salem. Burr, *Anglican Church in New Jersey*, 19.

8. Though, more often than not, what was promised was never made good, as may be readily seen in the highly complainant missionary correspondence (summarized in Burr, *Anglican Church in New Jersey*, 128–41).

9. Burr, *Anglican Church in New Jersey*, 114–15. Churches or chapels were to be found in Newark, Second River, Elizabethtown, Newton, Delaware, Kingwood, Amwell, Trenton, Allentown, New Brunswick, Piscataway, Woodbridge, Perth Amboy, Spotswood, Freehold, Shrewsbury, Middletown, Burlington, Mount Holly, Waterford, Berkeley, Salem, Greenwich, and Boonton. Of these, Newark, Second River, Newton, and Boonton were in the region that became the Diocese of Newark in 1874. There were also several (non-ordained) preachers active on the three preaching circuits of New Jersey commissioned by the colonial volunteer Methodist society, who at least until after the revolution, considered themselves under the authority of the Church of England.

Part I: An Outline of Anglican and Episcopal Slavery in New Jersey

population of the state was likely no more than 20,000,[10] and by the time of the first US census in 1790 it had grown to over 184,139.[11]

Summary: Prominent lay Anglicans laid the foundation for the Church in New Jersey, but much of its formal expansion can be credited to the priests sent by the Society for the Propagation of the Gospel in Foreign Parts (SPG), a voluntary organization of the Church of England founded in 1701. The SPG provided a large percentage of the funding for New Jersey priests, but the building of churches was mostly funded by wealthy locals. By the end of the colonial era over twenty churches had been built, many of which shared priests.

---

10. Burr, *Anglican Church in New Jersey*, 9.
11. Wu, "New Jersey Population," 1. This figure is likely an undercount.

3

New Jersey Anglicans and Slavery in the Colonial Period
A Brief Sketch

IN GENERAL, THE RELATION of the Anglican Church to slavery in New Jersey during the colonial era was a product of the Church as an arm of the state. Of course, the Church of England was never formally established in New Jersey, but her authorities and adherents were acculturated to her operation as a support to the Crown and Crown policies. Rather than a possible force for significant moral accountability in the direction of political power, church authorities viewed the role of the Church as bringing morality and order, in addition (of course) to spiritual nourishment for the people. As such, slavery was generally viewed as a scheme that prospered the state,[1] its power and authority, and her most faithful subjects—a state

---

1. The language used for SPG missionaries' commission was generally that they were being sent "into the plantations," which is to say, to the British lands run as plantations using enslaved labor, for the benefit of the Crown and her supportive elite. For instance, in 1727, Bishop Gibson of London gave several addresses and wrote letters to promote the work, a few of which were titled: "An Address to Serious Christians among ourselves, to Assist the Society for Propagating the Gospel, in carrying on the Work of Instructing the Negroes in our Plantations abroad," and "Letter to the Masters and Mistresses of Families in the English Plantations abroad; Exhorting them to encourage and promote the Instruction of their Negroes in the Christian Faith," and "Letter to the Missionaries in the English Plantations; exhorting them to give their Assistance towards the Instruction of the Negroes of their Several Parishes, in the Christian Faith," as recorded in Pascoe, *Two Hundred Years of the S.P.G.*, 1:8.

Part I: An Outline of Anglican and Episcopal Slavery in New Jersey

of affairs that most Anglicans either viewed as salutary, or with which they were entirely willing to cooperate.[2]

"Governor Lewis Morris" by John Watson (1685–1768). Held at the Brooklyn Museum (courtesy Wikimedia Commons).

The earliest prominent lay booster of the Anglican Church in New Jersey was Lewis Morris. He was likely named for his uncle, who had moved to the American colonies from Barbados to care for Lewis when his father died. When he emigrated, Morris's uncle capitalized on the plantation land grants available in New Jersey for those who brought slaves, bringing forty enslaved Black people in 1677.[3] He established a mine at Tinton Falls that by 1690 enslaved at least sixty-seven Black people.[4]

---

2. Thomas Bray, one of the primary founders of the SPG, described this goal as being: "To reduce whole Provinces under the Obedience of God . . . to reduce them to the just and happy Government of their rightful Lord and Master Jesus Christ . . . to instruct those Dark Corners of the Earth, in which the Light of the Gospel has not yet shone . . . to render them obsequious servants to a just and holy God, whose Service is perfect Freedom." Bray, *Rev. Thomas Bray*, 82.

3. Strassburger, "Origins and Establishment of the Morris Family," 67. See also Hodges, *Slavery and Freedom in the Rural North*, 9.

4. Freiday, "Tinton Manor." There were "60 or 70" enslaved Black people there according to Scot, *Model of the government of the province of East-New-Jersey*, 128–29. See

New Jersey Anglicans and Slavery in the Colonial Period

The younger Lewis Morris inherited his uncle's holdings when he died in 1691. The younger Morris heavily supported the Church of England as a "staunch patron" and "shining light,"[5] contributing to the establishment of St. Peter's (Perth Amboy),[6] Christ Church (Shrewsbury),[7] St. Michael's Church (Trenton), and even attempting to establish the Church of England through the New Jersey legislature.[8] He was an early member of the SPG in New Jersey, served on the first vestry of Trinity Church (now known as Trinity Church, Wall Street), and ultimately became governor of the Province of New Jersey. He was one of the most influential lay Anglicans in New Jersey during the colonial period and may have been the most prolific enslaver in the American colonies at the time.[9]

Lest we think that the Morrises' practice of enslavement was somehow enlightened by a significant moral sensibility, we should note that his cousin (and business partner) of Passage Point, also named Lewis Morris,[10] was murdered in 1696 in revenge for abusing one of the Black people he had enslaved.[11] The baptism records of the enslaved during this period in Monmouth County similarly show that Anglican "masters" were not above raping the Black women they enslaved.[12]

Another celebrated[13] East-Jersey Anglican layperson, Colonel Peter Schuyler, derived a large portion of his wealth from enslaved labor. He inherited a large share in the Schuyler copper mine in Belleville, which was

---

also Hodges, *Slavery and Freedom in the Rural North*, 9.

5. Burr, *Anglican Church in New Jersey*, 8, 216.

6. McGinnis, *History of St. Peter's Church in Perth Amboy*, 21.

7. Keith, *Journal of Travels*, 34, 46; Humphreys, *Historical Account of the Incorporated Society for the Propagation of the Gospel*, 57.

8. Burr, *Anglican Church in New Jersey*, 157, 10.

9. The mine at Tinton Falls accounted for approximately half of the enslaved Black population of Monmouth County at the time (Hodges, *Slavery and Freedom in the Rural North*, 12).

10. Passage Point was a location within Shrewsbury.

11. Weeks, *Not for Filthy Lucre's Sake*, 113.

12. The parish register of Christ Church Shrewsbury shows evidence of baptisms of four "bastards" and twelve "mulatto" "servants," suggesting impregnation by Anglican heads of household. See Christ Church, Shrewsbury, *Parish Register*. See also Kelley, "Slavery Evidenced in the Parish Register."

13. Described in Society for the Propagation of the Gospel in Foreign Parts, *Abstract of Proceedings, 1750*, 50, as having a name held "very deservedly in high Esteem." This estimation is repeated uncritically by Burr, *Anglican Church in New Jersey*, 149.

Part I: An Outline of Anglican and Episcopal Slavery in New Jersey

operated for decades in a state of heavy dependence on enslaved labor.[14] His large plantation (over 700 acres) also operated with enslaved labor. The mine was so prosperous that Schuyler's father, before he died, was probably the wealthiest British subject in the American colonies.[15] Peter Schuyler was the primary donor responsible for giving the glebe and rectory for Trinity Parish, Newark,[16] helped establish the church there,[17] served as a warden,[18] and supported the parish at Second River.[19]

Such examples are indicative of the state of affairs in eastern New Jersey, which was home to a robust slave economy, but the Anglican churches of western New Jersey were also implicated in the enslavement of Black people even as slavery was less firmly established there. A cursory look at some of those involved in the establishment of St. Mary's Church in Burlington provides an illustrative example. One of the largest early benefactors of the Church was Governor (then of Virginia) Francis Nicholson, who not only enslaved Black people himself, but helped establish the legal system that supported slavery in Virginia. His largesse to the church was made possible through his profit from slavery. Queen Anne was also a significant benefactor, giving "lead and glass, a silver chalice and salver, a pulpit cloth, and a brocade altar cloth."[20] As her wealth was significantly derived from the profits of slavery, these gifts must be considered encumbered.

A later benefactor in the colonial period who also enslaved Black people was Governor William Franklin (son of Benjamin Franklin). He committed a "handsome subscription" for the rebuilding and repairing of the church in the early 1770s.[21] Without doubt, many of the other forms of support the church in Burlington received in the colonial period were given by enslavers, even as a significant portion of the critical mass for the parish came from early followers of George Keith, perhaps the most anti-slavery Anglican priest of the era in New Jersey. The first SPG priest stationed at

---

14. Young Jr., "Origins of the American Copper Industry," 121–22.
15. Latrobe, "Description of the Schuyler Copper-Mine in New Jersey."
16. Burr, *Anglican Church in New Jersey,* 111–12, 129, 149.
17. Burr, *Anglican Church in New Jersey,* 537.
18. Burr, *Anglican Church in New Jersey,* 216.
19. Burr, *Anglican Church in New Jersey,* 233.
20. Burr, *Anglican Church in New Jersey,* 493–94.
21. Burr, *Anglican Church in New Jersey,* 495.

New Jersey Anglicans and Slavery in the Colonial Period

Burlington, Rev. John Talbot, often known as "the apostle of New Jersey," enslaved several people during his long tenure as rector there.[22]

Such dynamics however were not limited to the establishment of particular parishes. George Whitefield, the traveling Anglican priest who fostered much of the spirit of the so-called "Great Awakening" in the colonies, spent a good deal of time in New Jersey, though he was affiliated with no particular parish. As the highest profile Anglican priest in the colonies at the time, he had a significant popular influence in all areas, and certainly on attitudes toward slavery among them. His perspective was indicative of that of many Anglicans at the time,[23] including many of those who would later become Methodists when that denomination formed immediately after the Revolutionary War.

In a letter[24] written in New Brunswick on April 27, 1740, Whitefield describes how he purchased slaves to use for his mission, seeing no problem with this practice. He viewed Black people as human, but criticized SPG attempts to reach them, remaining dubious that those who "converted" were in earnest in their profession when preparedness for conversion was measured "only" in knowledge of the Lord's Prayer, the Ten Commandments, and the Nicene Creed.[25]

More convinced of the legitimacy of the conversion of Black Americans' was the influential Anglican priest Thomas Thompson. He was a highly educated and respected missionary of the SPG who served in New Jersey for five years (1745–1750) before leaving the state to become the first formally commissioned Anglican missionary to West Africa, where he served as the chaplain to the slave-trading corporation headquartered at Cape Coast Castle. While in New Jersey he served as the SPG missionary to Monmouth County, ministering to the parishes in Shrewsbury, Middletown, Freehold, and Allentown, and baptizing dozens of enslaved Black people (including his own),[26] most of whom were the domestic slaves of parishioners.

---

22. In her last will and testament, which came into effect only three years after the death of Rev. John Talbot, the widow Mrs. Talbot bequeathed to her children at least seven enslaved persons. Talbot, "Will of Mrs. Talbot."

23. Even if his attitudes toward "enthusiasm" were not shared by many other Anglican priests.

24. Whitefield, *Three Letters from the Reverend George Whitefield*, 16–20.

25. See letters from George Whitfield (sic.) to the Bishop of Oxford from the summer of 1741 (June 9, June 18, July 28—in my bibliography under "Geo. Whitfield . . .") and the bishop's response (September 17—in my bibliography under "Bush of Oxford . . ."), all held in the Robinson Collection.

26. Christ Church, Shrewsbury, *Parish Register*, 1:166–71.

Part I: An Outline of Anglican and Episcopal Slavery in New Jersey

In Thompson's opinion, slavery was not inherently wrong. He wrote a very influential treatise, *The African Trade for Negro Slaves Shewn to be Consistent with Principles of Humanity and with the Laws of Revealed Religion*,[27] arguing in favor of the use of slavery for the purpose of converting Black people to Christianity. This proslavery position no doubt accounts for his popularity in a parish like Christ Church Shrewsbury, which was home to dozens of churchgoing, enslaving Anglicans.[28] After its publication (1772) the treatise circulated widely in New Jersey, due in part to his preexisting reputation in the state, and was influential enough that the nascent abolitionist Quaker movement felt the need to respond to it in print.[29]

Such a brief survey can only depict aspects of a general picture, but of this general picture several key elements emerge. While it may be true that average Anglicans did not account personally for a very significant level of enslavement, influential elite Anglican laity were prolific enslavers who participated fully in the "plantation economy" of New Jersey.[30] As a result, the best-established churches inevitably had significant ties to slavery as a result of this support from wealthy Anglicans. Further, as previously mentioned, these elite Anglicans had a significant early role in establishing the legislative codes related to slavery for the province.

Beyond these factors we must remember that all the colonial-era Anglican churches have significant ties to slavery through their connection with the SPG. The organization provided essentially all of the clergy for New Jersey in the colonial era and the bulk of the financial support for that clergy. That support was made possible in part through profits derived from the direct SPG ownership of the Codrington Plantation in Barbados, starting in 1710.[31] The plantation enslaved hundreds of Black people at any given time and operated in SPG hands for more than one hundred years. And, as the second bishop of New Jersey, George W. Doane, wrote in his

---

27. Thompson, *African Trade for Negro Slaves* (reproduced in full in chapter 9).

28. As evidenced in the early parish registers. See, e.g., Christ Church, Shrewsbury, *Parish Register*.

29. See Sharp, *Just limitation of slavery in the laws of God*.

30. But in general, the most common pattern of enslavement in this period was for a household to enslave one or two Black people. See Gigantino II(*Ragged Road to Abolition*, 14) and Hodges (*Slavery and Freedom in the Rural North*, 8). There is no reason to believe that this was not also the most common pattern among Anglicans in New Jersey.

31. See Glasson, *Mastering Christianity*, 141–70. To say nothing of the private donations to the organization, many of which were made possible through the labor theft inherent to enslavement.

New Jersey Anglicans and Slavery in the Colonial Period

1851 convention address, "To no other Diocese, was the hand of the venerable Society more constantly and freely opened, than to this."[32]

Further, the SPG missionary priests sent to New Jersey during the colonial period, almost without exception,[33] supported the enslavement of Black people, and often enslaved Black people themselves,[34] even as several of these priests encouraged their baptism. In general, however, the priests did not push this baptism agenda for enslaved Black people hard enough to result in the baptism of plantation field hands (the majority of the enslaved). Rather, Black baptisms were largely confined only to enslaved Black domestics in elite households, and even the extent of these was limited.[35]

Summary: The Anglican Church in colonial New Jersey supported and sought to benefit from slavery. Many wealthy Anglicans were prolific enslavers and used their financial gains from enslaved labor to establish churches. Many New Jersey priests enslaved Black people as well. The SPG funding for priest salaries in New Jersey was derived in part from the profits of its Codrington Plantation in Barbados. And while the Anglican church did teach and baptize some Black people enslaved by Anglican parishioners, for the most part field hands were excluded, Black Christians were not treated as equals, and they were typically segregated in worship.

---

32. This is perhaps a slight exaggeration, but is nevertheless accurately indicative of the level of dependence of the Anglican Church in New Jersey upon direct SPG support. See Doane, *Episcopal Address to the Sixty-Eighth Annual Convention*, 19.

33. George Keith being the primary exception. He is most explicit in his views before becoming Anglican, as evidenced in *An exhortation and caution to Friends concerning buying or keeping negroes* (reproduced in full in chapter 7). But his most prolific co-worker in initiating the work of the Anglican Church in New Jersey, and especially in Burlington, Rev. John Talbot, enslaved several people, as mentioned above.

34. Such as Rev. Samuel Cooke at Shrewsbury, who baptized his own Black slaves, Rev. Thomas Thompson (as mentioned above), and Rev. Alexander Innes, unassigned priest resident in Monmouth County, owned a sizeable plantation (150 acres) which he managed via enslaved labor. A large proportion of the SPG priests either owned plantations themselves (including at least Innes, Cooke, Beach, Vaughn, Skinner, Keith, and Lindsay) or received income from glebe or Church-owned plantation land (e.g., Blackwell, Ogden, Odell, Frazer) often worked by enslaved Black people. Sporadic, brief references to these situations occur throughout Burr's *Anglican Church in New Jersey*. Rev. Thomas Haliday did not think the state of affairs adequate and suggested a more regularized and comprehensive plantation funding scheme employing enslaved Black people to better ensure the comfort of the SPG priests assigned to New Jersey (see chapter 8 of this volume).

35. Hodges, *Slavery and Freedom in the Rural North*, 69.

4

The Revolutionary Period and Early Black Estrangement from the Episcopal Church

EVEN AS ANGLICAN PRIESTS in New Jersey largely avoided directly addressing the issue of the enslavement of Black people,[1] the effects of SPG missionary attention to the enslaved were not insignificant, and "undermined the authoritarian power of the master in important ways."[2]

> As a transatlantic faith, Anglicanism stressed the importance of international and imperial bonds over local governance. Anglican instructors accentuated the importance of sacred power over the temporal authority. Although Anglicans vigorously denied that baptism mandated emancipation, folk customs held that refusal of this rite placed slave masters in opposition to God, instilling among blacks a critique of slavery. Finally, Anglican educational efforts constructed genuine English establishment ties to blacks, which made African American choices in the American Revolution very easy.[3]

---

1. Hodges, *Slavery and Freedom in the Rural North*, 75.
2. Hodges, *Slavery and Freedom in the Rural North*, 71.
3. Hodges, *Slavery and Freedom in the Rural North*, 71.

The Revolutionary Period and Early Black Estrangement

While many Anglican parishes in New Jersey[4] certainly allowed both free and enslaved Black Christians in worship,[5] and the opportunities available to some enslaved Black people through participation in Anglican parishes in New Jersey were not insubstantial, nevertheless these attentions to the enslaved on the part of the SPG missionary priests did not translate into large-scale affinity among Black Americans for the Episcopal Church in New Jersey after the Revolutionary War. .

Though the Anglican churches may have afforded one of the most robust opportunities to Black Americans to participate formally in church life before the war, this reality did not overcome the problems associated with this avenue of institutional religious participation. Among the reasons for hesitancy was the problem that there was no avenue authorized by Church of England authorities for Black religious leadership in Anglican parishes in New Jersey in the colonial period. Ordination was effectively impossible.[6] Gifted, knowledgeable, and earnest Black Christian leaders in the region like John Jea and George White, who had experience and training with the Anglican Church in their background, found the need to express their calling outside the Episcopal Church, in part because it was too limiting of their free expression of their faith and leadership.[7] The Methodist split, and the further formation of what would become independent African Methodist Episcopal churches in the region after the war, offered readier opportunities for Black church leadership. A further reason for the hesitancy of Black Americans to embrace the Episcopal Church after the war may be seen in the military policy developments that occurred during the war itself.

---

4. Burr (*Anglican Church in New Jersey*, 224–28) collates much of the priestly correspondence on this issue, suggesting that there was probably at least partially integrated worship in several parishes, though Edgar Pennington ("Thomas Bray's Associates and Their Work among the Negroes") strangely leaves New Jersey out entirely in his treatment of the SPG efforts to reach enslaved Black people in the American colonies.

5. Unlike many other denominations, notably the Quakers, who, though more vocal about the abolition of slavery were *less* willing to extend fellowship to Black Christians. Gigantino II, *Ragged Road to Abolition*, 71.

6. Certainly during the colonial era, but also after. Absalom Jones proved otherwise in Philadelphia in 1802, though his career shows it remained incredibly difficult for Black Episcopalians to become ordained for decades after the Revolutionary War. See also the experience of Alexander Crummell at General Seminary in 1839, detailed in Wilder, "Driven . . . from the School of the Prophets."

7. Hodges, ed., *Black Itinerants of the Gospel*.

Part I: An Outline of Anglican and Episcopal Slavery in New Jersey

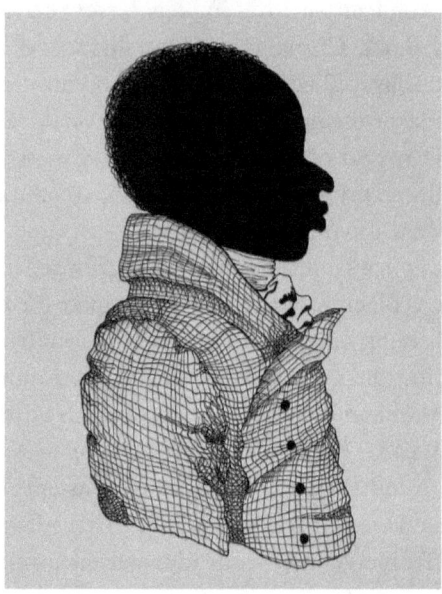

"John Jea." Artist's rendering by Kyra N. Pruszinski of portrait
(artist unknown) appearing in John Jea, *The Life*, i.

The British military policy toward slavery, which arose during the conflict, could be understood as an about-face from their previous colonial policy. While the colonies had been viewed as a useful source of plantation income, slavery was facilitated. But as soon as the colonies were in rebellion, British commanders saw an opportunity to undermine the rebellion by offering freedom to any enslaved Black people who would fight for the Crown. Even before the Declaration was signed (1775), the Governor of Virginia, John Murray, had declared that any slave or indentured servant who would serve in the British military to put down the rebellion would be freed.[8]

A steady stream of Black volunteers fled to the British lines, particularly from New Jersey to New York City, to fight for their freedom. Ultimately this fiat manumission was extended even to those who did not fight, when the British general for New York, David Jones, declared free any enslaved Black people who left rebel-occupied territory, saying "no person whatever [could] claim a right to them."[9] These military policymakers were Anglicans, and no doubt much of their motivation came from military concerns

8. Berkeley Jr., *Dumore's Proclamation of Emancipation*.
9. Egerton, *Death or Liberty*, 84.

The Revolutionary Period and Early Black Estrangement

rather than moral or scriptural conviction. Nevertheless, the British stuck to their promise, offering passage out of the United States and confirmed freedom to those who had made it behind British lines before the cessation of hostilities.[10]

However, rather than viewing the wartime British policy toward enslaved Black people as an about-face, it should probably be viewed in continuity with the previous policy. Certainly the previous proslavery policy was intended to benefit the Crown. The Anglican Church support for the state policy can be viewed as a function of its role as a state church "loyally" working to benefit the economic and political power of the Crown. The SPG attention to enslaved Black people can be seen in a similar light. Graham Hodges has suggested that these proselytizing attentions were intended as "the strongest bulwark against disloyalty and insurrection," which were seen as particularly necessary in a land full of "Dissenters" whose loyalty was questionable and who could not be expected to become ready converts to the Church of England.[11] These attentions were part of a full-spectrum effort which included "secret Crown instructions to royal governors"[12] requiring special efforts to "encourage the Conversion of Negroes . . . to our Christian religion."[13]

Seen in this light, the Anglican concern for the conversion of enslaved Black people in New Jersey was clearly not disinterested, nor motivated purely by humanitarian or spiritual concern. The concerns of the Anglican Church, as an arm of the state, were in inculcating loyalty wherever possible to God, the Church, and the Crown. Loyalty to one of these entities was expected to affect loyalty to the others positively. The Church of England's concern for conversions among the enslaved was an extension of a geopolitical concern, one which bore fruit for the British during the Revolutionary War in the fealty, even if opportunistic, shown by enslaved Black people seeking freedom under temporarily instituted military policy.

---

10. See Birch, *Inspection Roll of Negroes*, created by Brigadier General Samuel Birch (1783), held in the National Archives. However, this initial freedom experienced by many of these formerly enslaved Black people did not always translate into permanent freedom or full welcome elsewhere in the British Empire. Many were not welcomed where they were resettled and in some instances were re-enslaved.

11. Hodges, *Slavery and Freedom in the Rural North*, 28.

12. Hodges, *Slavery and Freedom in the Rural North*, 27.

13. "Extract from the Instructions to Earl Clarendon when Lord Cornbury & Governor of New York, January 1, 1702/3."

Part I: An Outline of Anglican and Episcopal Slavery in New Jersey

Following the War, the Anglican Church in New Jersey was in utter disarray—services had been disrupted, and priests had mostly fled.[14] In no position to make further political waves,[15] the enfeebled Church continued its previous policy supporting slavery. Its previous proslavery sentiments remained consistent with then-current popular opinion in the state. Some New Jersey priests even sought reparations for the loss of their runaways.[16] Since it was Anglicans who had, through military policy, freed "loyal" Black people during the war (and then left), but also Anglicans who continued to support slavery in New Jersey, it was clear to Black New Jerseyans that the Anglican Church in New Jersey did not have their deepest interests at heart. Anglican institutional interest in Black people had been largely a function of economic and political self-interest, pious protestations aside.

Of course the most obvious reason for Black abandonment of the Anglican Church in New Jersey after the Revolutionary War was the fact that the Church had been, and continued to be, fully cooperative with Black enslavement.[17] The ideological, legal, and financial responsibility of the Anglican Church for slavery in what became the Diocese of New Jersey was very significant, and went well beyond accounting for the dollar value of gifts given from slavery-encumbered wealth.[18] If Church hagiography,

---

14. As a result of the aforementioned connected loyalties, which were represented even in the mandatory prayers for the king offered during Church of England worship services. The inclusion of these prayers in the required liturgy was what made Anglican Church services too dangerous to conduct during much of the war in New Jersey.

15. And not seeing any reason to do so when most Anglicans were viewed as loyalist traitors to the new nation.

16. E.g., Samuel Cooke of Shrewsbury. Hodges, *Slavery and Freedom in the Rural North*, 96.

17. As evidenced by the Van Wickle slave ring.

18. There are various reasons why such calculations are unhelpful, or even counterproductive. Among them is the fact that this kind of calculation only attends to the value of available "priceable" labor. It does not attend to the "missing value" of the destroyed and disappeared lives of those enslaved persons who did not survive the transatlantic trip, or who were murdered, or who died young due to abuse. This "economic value" is destroyed by enslavers and is irretrievable, but in general is a "disappeared" or "externalized" cost in any system that permits slavery, and in most forensic accounting. This problem makes any accurate calculation of responsibility effectively impossible. Accounting for such gifts cannot consider them partially encumbered, or even entirely encumbered as a result of enslavement profiteering. Rather, such donations should most accurately be understood to be *supersaturated with encumbrance*: the market value of the gift drastically understates the vast toll of human destruction wrought on countless people in order to extract that small amount of "profit," which is then, by donation, converted to "charity." For this and other reasons, basic forensic accounting cannot accurately determine a

The Revolutionary Period and Early Black Estrangement

which emphasizes concern for and education of enslaved Black people, were the only story to be told,[19] clearly Black Americans would have been more involved in the Episcopal Church in New Jersey after the Revolutionary War. While there was not a wholesale abandonment,[20] there was a clear movement to other institutional expressions of Christian religion.[21] This movement came partly as a result of freer opportunities in these other contexts for the expression of Black leadership and Black faith, and it came partly as a result of the previous and continued support for enslavement by Anglican leadership[22] and laity.[23]

However, perhaps the most significant reason for Black disengagement from the Anglican Church was that it was likely very clear that attention paid them by the Church[24] was primarily the result of self-interested economic and political concern and not predominantly concern for them as human brethren. Though not formally a "state church," and in spite of even its predecessor (the Church of England) never having been the officially established church of New Jersey, the Episcopal Church in New Jersey operated toward Black Americans out of its prior broader Anglican identity as a state church and its concerns over political clout and stability, even well after the separation of the American colonies from England.

As such, the British military policy enacted during the war should not be seen as a reversal exactly, but rather indicative of a larger—consistent—*instrumental* view of enslaved Black people on the part of most Anglicans. Black people were viewed as either means to more important ends, or as a concern of lesser importance than other, more pressing economic and

---

dollar value for responsibility for slavery. See chapter 14 for more on this.

19. As suggested by Burr, *Anglican Church in New Jersey*, 224–28.

20. As evidenced by, for example the "Samson Adams Papers," the will from which indicates a significant connection between Adams and St. Michael's Church, Trenton. Though it is possible that the bequest to St. Michael's was made only in order to ensure that the will would be honored by the court system and interested White parties, and that, by extension, this would ensure that the bulk of the estate went to his sister, the primary beneficiary.

21. Including most notably, Methodist churches, the nascent African Methodist Episcopal (AME) movement, Baptist churches, and denominationally independent Black churches.

22. As previously mentioned, the first Episcopal Bishop of New Jersey, Bishop Croes, enslaved Black people.

23. Influential laity like Robert Stockton continued to enslave Black people well into the gradual abolition period, and worked to remove free Black Americans to Africa.

24. Particularly the attentions of the SPG in the colonial period.

Part I: An Outline of Anglican and Episcopal Slavery in New Jersey

political concerns. As a result, when allowed the option to leave slavery during the war, many enslaved Black people *left*, and when choosing their religious affiliation after the war, Black Americans generally *left* the Episcopal Church *alone*.

Summary: During the Revolutionary War, the British freed all enslaved Black people who defected to their side, including a large percentage of the enslaved from New Jersey. The Revolutionaries sought to continue the practice of slavery and the fledgling Episcopal Church participated in this practice postwar. In spite of prewar White Anglican (self-serving) attentions to some Black people, for the most part Black Americans sought postwar outlets for religious expression that were more affirming of their experience, leadership, and humanity than the Episcopal Church was at the time.

5

Gradual Abolition and the Persistence of Slavery in New Jersey

AFTER THE REVOLUTIONARY WAR many New Jersey residents clearly saw the problem with continuing legal slavery in an ostensibly "free" nation, but many more insisted that the fledgling nation needed every economic advantage it could leverage to recover from the war. Meanwhile, most Americans held very racist views of Black people. The influence of these latter two perspectives prevented any dramatic action in New Jersey on the issue of slavery.

That New Jersey bore the brunt of the destruction from the war as the chief locus of military action provided a heavily deployed excuse for legislative inaction in freeing slaves. Nevertheless, Quaker pressures toward manumission and abolition began to take effect, and many private manumissions occurred in the years following the war. Quaker influence in western New Jersey resulted in diminishing levels of enslavement in the region, while in eastern Jersey the institution remained entrenched.[1] In the early days following the war (1786) the legislature passed an act[2] preventing

---

1. The number of enslaved Black people in East Jersey grew significantly in the decades after the war. See Gigantino II, *Ragged Road to Abolition*, 67.
2. "An Act to prevent the Importation of Slaves into the State of New-Jersey, and to authorize the Manumission of them under certain Restrictions, and to prevent the Abuse of Slaves."

Part I: An Outline of Anglican and Episcopal Slavery in New Jersey

further importation of slaves from Africa. However, intrastate trade was still allowed.[3]

The New Jersey Society for Promoting the Abolition of Slavery was formed during this time and worked to protect freed Black residents, lobby for liberalization of slavery codes, and minimize the abuses of the institution. Following the Revolution, at least in theory, free Black people in New Jersey could own property and vote; in fact, New Jersey was the only state in which these were legal rights. However, the constraints on Black residents, and especially on enslaved Black people, were very slow to lessen. Following Caribbean revolts, in 1793 the federal government passed the Fugitive Slave Act, which required interstate cooperation in the return of escapees.

In 1798 the New Jersey legislature passed a slave code[4] that reaffirmed the institution and strengthened constraints on the behavior of enslaved persons. Then, in 1804 the New Jersey legislature passed a law (the Gradual Emancipation Act) for the gradual abolition of slavery,[5] but no enslaved persons were immediately freed through the bill. Children born to enslaved persons after July 4, 1804 would be freed upon a term of service of twenty-one years for women and twenty-five years for men. New Jersey was the last northern state to pass such a law, and few viewed the act as a dramatic development.

This modest advance was accompanied by significant losses. Masters were allowed to abandon babies born to their slaves to the care of the state, but generally took the children back with state compensation, making their enslavement more profitable. Free Black people lost the right to vote in New Jersey in 1807.[6] The New Jersey Society for Promoting the Abolition of Slavery considered its work done and disbanded in 1809. The population of free Black residents grew, but at least in east Jersey, so did the population of enslaved Black people.

In 1820 the legislature passed an omnibus slavery bill codifying and reaffirming existing slavery laws on the books.[7] The New Jersey supreme court,[8] in spite of the significant population of free Black people in the state,

3. This act also removed some of the onerous existing barriers to manumission.
4. "Act respecting Slaves."
5. "Act for the Gradual Abolition of Slavery."
6. "A Supplement to the act entitled 'An act to regulate the election of members of the legislative council and general assembly, sheriffs and coroners in this state,' passed at Trenton the twenty-second day of February, one thousand seven hundred and ninety-seven." November 16, 1807, §1, *Acts* 32nd G.A. 1st sitting.
7. Gigantino II, *Ragged Road to Abolition*, 150.
8. Known as the "New Jersey Court of Errors and Appeals."

Gradual Abolition and the Persistence of Slavery in New Jersey

continued to defend the default assumption by law enforcement that Black residents were *prima facie* enslaved until proved otherwise.[9] As such, Black New Jerseyans could not expect just application of the law.

This legal presumption was only finally overturned[10] after significant numbers of Black people began to gain freedom through gradual abolition starting in 1825.[11] During the following decades the balance of enslaved versus freed Black residents in New Jersey shifted permanently toward freedom. There were still major obstacles, but the power of freed Black people to shape their own destiny grew inexorably greater. White anxiety over the increasing numbers of free Black people in the state led to the founding and support for the American Colonization Society (ACS),[12] the purpose of which was to facilitate the removal of Black residents from the United States.

Rev. Alexander Crummell (1819–1898). From Crummell, *The Greatness of Christ* (courtesy Wikimedia Commons).

---

9. This formal decision was made in 1821: *Gibbons v. Morse*, 7 New Jersey Law 20, Court of Errors and Appeals, November term, 1821.

10. Not overturned until 1836.

11. Women began to be freed in 1825, and men in 1829.

12. Founded in 1816.

Part I: An Outline of Anglican and Episcopal Slavery in New Jersey

A few Black Americans, upon sizing up the ugly state of affairs in the United States, cooperated with the ACS, but for the most part ACS overtures and initiatives were met with hostility by Black people. Black newspapers of the time are full of articles denouncing the aims and tactics of the ACS.[13] Ultimately the ACS was successful in establishing Liberia as the proposed colony, but was very unsuccessful in winning broad cooperation among stateside Black Americans.

The legal landscape for Black Americans during these decades was constantly shifting. Hard won protections at the state level required constant effort to maintain, but could still be threatened by federal actions. The 1826 New Jersey personal liberty law added protections, and a 1836 state Supreme Court case required trials by jury for purported "escaped slaves" in order to prevent corrupt decisions supporting enslavers.[14] However, the federal Supreme Court decision *Prigg v. Pennsylvania* of 1842 overturned all such state decisions.[15]

Due to the various difficulties free and enslaved Black people were experiencing in the state, and the increasing awareness and concern among White residents regarding these conditions, in 1839 the New Jersey Anti-slavery Society was founded. Further lobbying resulted in the passing of an 1846 law[16] that ostensibly ended slavery in the state, but euphemistically still required former slaves to remain bound "apprentices" for life. Practically, New Jersey slavery proved very hard to stop. The *Dred Scott v. Sandford* US Supreme Court decision[17] of 1857 in particular undermined even the meager[18] legal rights that had to that point been won by Black New Jerseyans.

New Jersey, as a state near the Mason–Dixon line, developed into a key transit point, and even destination, for formerly enslaved Black people escaping from the South. Towns along the east banks of the lower Delaware linked Black escapees moving by boat to the corridor to New York City. Several free Black towns sprung up in this area, offering temporary protection to those moving farther north, and longer-term shelter to those willing to risk proximity to the South and active slave-catching operations. Towns such as Timbuctoo, Colemantown, Snow Hill, Guineatown, Saddlertown,

---

13. Hodges, *Black New Jersey*, 65–66.
14. Gigantino II, *Ragged Road to Abolition*, 219.
15. Gigantino II, *Ragged Road to Abolition*, 222.
16. "Act to Abolish Slavery," passed April 18, 1846.
17. See "Dred Scott v. Sandford (1857)."
18. And haltingly acknowledged, yet hard won.

Gradual Abolition and the Persistence of Slavery in New Jersey

Springtown, and Gouldtown were critical stops on the New Jersey section of the Underground Railroad.[19] However, as seen by the modest growth in the Black population of New Jersey at this time, most Blacks people were looking to head somewhere safer and more hospitable.

In this period New Jersey authorities generally cooperated with slave-catchers. Discrimination and segregation made property ownership and wealth building difficult for Black residents of New Jersey. There were some jobs available in service industries, but for the most part White people worked to keep free Black people employed in the same roles in which they had worked when enslaved.[20]

Once the Civil War broke out, New Jersey was, in many ways, a reluctant member of the Union. The persistence of slavery in the state meant that while technically New Jersey was a Northern state in many ways, it maintained significant Southern sympathies. When in 1865, at the conclusion of the war, the US Congress passed the amendment banning slavery in all states (except as punishment for a crime), the majority Democrat New Jersey legislature did not ratify it. It was not until a new, more Republican, congressional class took office in 1866 that the New Jersey legislature ratified the Thirteenth Amendment.

Summary: In the period after the Revolution some positive legal changes in New Jersey affected enslaved Black people, including ending the importation of slaves and removing some of the obstacles to manumission, followed eventually in 1804 by the Gradual Emancipation Act, but in other ways the situation for Black residents worsened. Free Black New Jerseyans were stripped of their right to vote in 1807 and White racism prevented the Black exercise of many freedoms that White people took for granted. The free Black population grew every year, especially following the late 1820s when gradual emancipation finally began to take effect, and throughout the mid-1800s Black New Jersey residents managed to carve out a difficult existence in a state where racist attitudes were so established that even the ratification of the Thirteenth Amendment after the Civil War was initially rejected by the state legislature.

19. Hodges, *Black New Jersey*, 81.

20. Exceptions existed of course, but these were the predominant patterns. See Gigantino II, *Ragged Road to Abolition*, 111, 117; Hodges, *Black New Jersey*, 63–64.

Part I: An Outline of Anglican and Episcopal Slavery in New Jersey

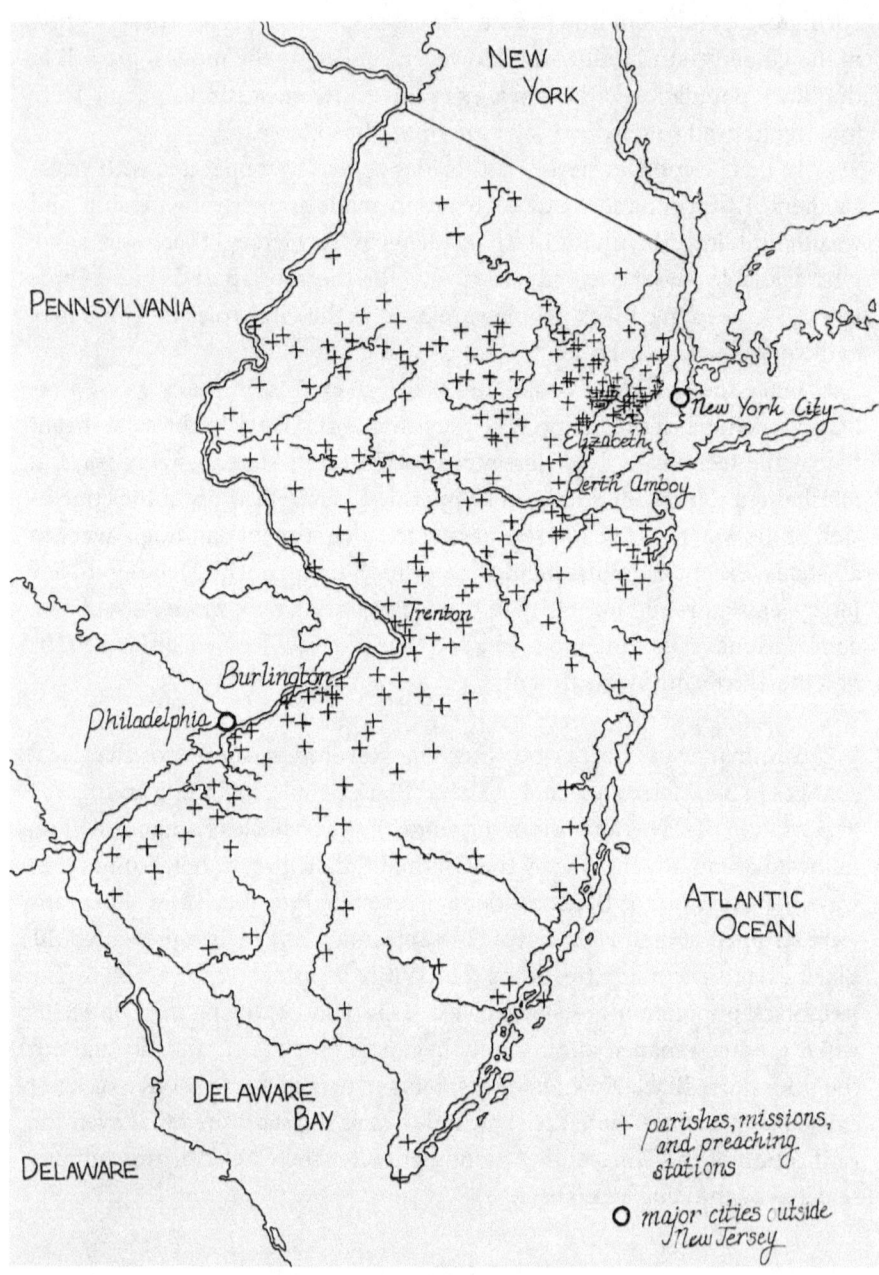

Antebellum Episcopal Churches in New Jersey. By Kyra N. Pruszinski. Used with permission.

6

The Development of the Episcopal Church and Its Relation to Slavery in Antebellum New Jersey

WHEN LOOKING BACK AT the nineteenth-century history of the Episcopal Church in the Diocese of New Jersey some of the data regarding its treatment of Black Americans can be surprising to a modern reader. This may be especially true if one views the Church through its modern reputation of being one of the most progressive Christian denominations in the United States.[1] To such a reader the picture of the diocese during the period of gradual abolition in New Jersey may seem unfamiliar: As a founding member of Trinity Church in Princeton Robert Stockton not only himself enslaved hundreds of Black Americans, but was instrumental in the American Colonization Society efforts to rid the nation of Black people.[2] The first bishop of the diocese, John Croes, not only enslaved Black people,

---

1. One might be similarly confused if one took the knowledge that the (Anglican) Society for the Propagation of the Gospel was ostensibly founded for the catechism and baptism of Native American and Black slaves in colonial American to mean, like Nelson R. Burr did, that "The Church cherishes the Negro." See Burr, *Anglican Church in New Jersey*, 224–28.

2. Society of the American Colonization Society in New Jersey, *Proceedings of a Meeting Held at Princeton, New Jersey, July 14, 1824 to Form a Society in the State of New Jersey to Cooperate with the American Colonization Society*.

Part I: An Outline of Anglican and Episcopal Slavery in New Jersey

but freed them just before he became legally liable for their care in old age.[3] St. Peter's Church, Spotswood welcomed and affirmed the participation of Jacob Van Wickle who, as a judge in Middlesex County, was the central enabler of a notorious interstate slave trading ring designed to circumvent gradual abolition law.[4]

The precedents formed in the colonial era shaped how the diocese handled issues related to slavery and the treatment of Black Americans during the gradual abolition period in New Jersey. While the Church of England was never formally established in New Jersey, its role as a state church in England set the tone for how its priests and laity handled the issues of slavery. The role played by the Church of England in sanctioning the plantation economy in New Jersey as a legitimate enterprise, and enslaved Black people as instrumental to its success, influenced the treatment of Black Americans in the diocese long after the Crown had ceased oversight, and even well after England and other northern states had rejected slavery. These influences and their afterlives following the American Revolution, likely served to estrange many Black Americans from the Episcopal Church in the early days of the Diocese of New Jersey and helped set the tone for a widely acknowledged[5] alienation from the denomination.

Following the Revolutionary War, the few remaining Anglican clergy who had not fled the colony sought to restart public worship and to repair what had been lost and destroyed during the War. The process, however, was slow, as friends of the Church of England generally were viewed as traitors to the American patriot cause. Rebuilding would also involve organizing the Church apart from the efforts of the SPG.

Dioceses were organized by state, but the speed at which a bishop was finally appointed in New Jersey (not until 1815) indicates the state of organizational and financial disarray at the time. The Church of England had never been established in New Jersey like it had been, for instance, in Virginia, so it had little to lose from disestablishment, but it had been very dependent on its financial connections to Britain, and in particular to the SPG. Of the forty or so parishes and preaching stations active before the war, only eight[6] sent a representative to the first diocesan state convention

---

3. Bayker, Blakley, and Boyd, "His Name Was Will," 80.

4. Gigantino II, *Ragged Road to Abolition*, 157–60.

5. See for example Hood, "From a Headstart to a Deadstart." The alienation was not universal, but significant.

6. Christ Church, New Brunswick (the host church); Trinity Church, Newark; St.

The Development of the Episcopal Church and Its Relation to Slavery

after the war (at Christ Church, New Brunswick in July 1785), and among the delegates were only three priests.[7]

That is not to say that the Anglican Church was bereft of supporters at this time. There had been plenty of SPG activity in New Jersey before the war and the effect of those efforts laid an ample groundwork for the Episcopal Diocese of New Jersey. In general, the Church in New Jersey grew with the state during this period. By 1810 the number of active parishes had recovered from its postwar nadir to twenty-six and ministering clergy to fifteen.[8] There was steady growth under Bishop John Croes, such that at the end of his tenure (1832) there were thirty-two congregations, eighteen clergy, and approximately eight hundred communicants.[9]

"Right Reverend John Croes, D.D." From Perry, *The Bishops of the American Church*, 36 (courtesy Wikimedia Commons).

John's Church, Elizabethtown; St. Peter's Church, Perth Amboy; Christ Church, Shrewsbury; St. James Church, Piscataway; St. Mary's Church, Burlington; and St. Andrew's Church, Mount Holly.

7. Rev. Abraham Beach, Rev. Uzal Ogden, and Rev. John-Hamilton Rowland.
8. WPA, *Inventory of the Church Archives of New Jersey*, 48.
9. In a state with a population of approximately 320,823 people. At the end of his tenure the proportion of Episcopalians in New Jersey was still quite low: Less than 0.25 percent of residents were communicants. Burr, *Anglican Church in New Jersey*, 478.

Part I: An Outline of Anglican and Episcopal Slavery in New Jersey

Under the second bishop, George Washington Doane, the diocese experienced dramatic growth, due not only to his intense, and at times less-than-legal, "energetic episcopate,"[10] but likely also due to the fact that the Revolutionary generation had passed, and living generations did not harbor the same distrust of the Church of England. At his death in 1859, the diocese had ninety-eight clergy, eighty-four churches and chapels, several missions, and approximately five-thousand communicants.[11]

William H. Odenheimer was the third bishop of the diocese, serving through the Civil War, until 1874 when the diocese split into the Dioceses of Southern New Jersey (now called the Diocese of New Jersey) and Northern New Jersey (now called the Diocese of Newark), a split occasioned by significant growth. Odenheimer continued his tenure with the Diocese of Northern New Jersey after 1874. Under Odenheimer, and before the split, the diocese grew to include 152 clergy, 129 parishes and missions, and 12,176 communicants, representing approximately 1.2 percent of a state whose population had exploded in the intervening years to approximately one million residents.[12]

In general the Episcopal Church in New Jersey during this period did not make waves politically.[13] Few Episcopalians became abolitionists, and many more supported the work of the American Colonization Society.[14] Even during the Civil War the Episcopal Church was the only majority-White Christian denomination that did not split over slavery. Much of the Church at this time saw itself as ministering to White people, not Black Christians. The denomination intentionally took a conciliatory approach to the conflict and to slavery out of fear of alienating constituents.[15] As a northern slave state, New Jersey took the lead in this approach. Such conciliation toward slavery can be seen throughout the period of gradual abolition in New Jersey and no doubt was a cause of much Black alienation from the denomination. However, beyond the institutional attitude of conciliation

---

10. He was reprimanded for financial impropriety. Burr, *Anglican Church in New Jersey*, 462–65; WPA, *Inventory of the Church Archives of New Jersey*, 55–56.

11. This translates into an approximate proportion of Episcopalian communicants of 0.83 percent within the general population of a state of 672,025 inhabitants; it represents a dramatic rate of growth during Doane's tenure, while still accounting for only a small proportion of the overall population.

12. Burr, *Anglican Church in New Jersey*, 465–66, 480.

13. Burr, *Anglican Church in New Jersey*, 460–61.

14. Which, through racist logic, supported sending Black Americans back to Africa.

15. Drawing perhaps the wrong lesson from the Revolutionary War.

was an ongoing and active practice of participation in enslavement on the part of elite members of the denomination.

Two of the most influential priests in the formation of the diocese were Uzal Ogden and Abraham Beach. These two were among the few who attended the first diocesan convention and both ministered in the state for lengthy periods of time, shaping much of the future trajectory of the diocese. Ogden's family wealth was derived from the employment of enslaved labor at the Ringwood Iron Works[16] and he benefited from this accumulated power and wealth through an appointment as rector of Trinity Church, Newark, where he continued to affirm the institution.[17] Beach served as rector of Christ Church New Brunswick for decades, during which time he countenanced the practice of owning slaves among his parishioners.[18] He himself enslaved Black people on his estate and only freed them in his old age, when his retirement annuities from his church work fully covered his expenses.[19]

This practice among the clergy of building wealth through the enslavement of Black people and then freeing them only when most convenient was also practiced by Bishop Croes, the first bishop of the diocese. He is recorded as having practiced manumission immediately before he became legally liable for the care of those he had enslaved in their old age.[20] This kind of practice not only harmed those Black people manumitted under these conditions, but often required support of those manumitted through almshouses, due to the commonly destitute state of the newly manumitted.[21]

The spate of church growth under Bishop Doane was, in many instances, underwritten by wealth derived from enslaved labor. Doane himself was able to act with such energy, in part due to the wealth he held that had been produced through the transatlantic slave trade.[22] He was involved with the founding of many institutions, and courted southern donations,

---

16. Which also enabled his father to serve as a founding member of Trinity Church, Newark. He furnished the labor for its building. See Wheeler, *Ogden Family in America*, 64.

17. His sister married Peter Schuyler, another prominent Anglican whose wealth came from enslaved labor.

18. Fuentes and White, eds., *Scarlet and Black*, 1:181n33.

19. Burr, *Anglican Church in New Jersey*, 583–85.

20. Bayker, Blakley, and Boyd, "His Name Was Will," 80.

21. Hodges (*Black New Jersey*, 59) describes an example of this phenomenon in the 1820s in Cape May County.

22. This wealth came from his wife. Eliza Greene Callahan Perkins had first been married to James Perkins, who was a wealthy slaveowner and slave trader. See "Harvard & the Legacy of Slavery," 22.

Part I: An Outline of Anglican and Episcopal Slavery in New Jersey

in part, by affirming the practice of slavery.[23] Among other schools, he was significantly involved with the board of trustees at General Seminary in New York, which became notorious for its support of the American Colonization Society at this time.

This willingness to work with and benefit from slavery at the highest levels of leadership in the diocese also translated into lay comfort with the institution. One example comes from one of the prominent founders of Trinity Church, Princeton, Robert Stockton,[24] who gave a large percentage of the funds used to build the church. Stockton's own comfort with slavery went beyond his own in-state holdings. At his Georgia estate he enslaved hundreds of Black Americans.[25]

The wealth he derived from this practice allowed him to gain both significant political power, and power beyond government institutions, including in the Church. His geographically dispersed enslavement practices show that the ways the Church in New Jersey became established depended not only on the support of slavery in New Jersey, but on its protected exercise in other regions as well, including the South.[26] Stockton's significant involvement in the American Colonization Society, including his role in the conquering of the African territory that became Liberia, indicates the degree to which he was willing to control the fates of Black people in order to impose his preferred (and highly racist) priorities.

Perhaps the most egregiously abusive actions on the part of a New Jersey Episcopalian during this time period came from Middlesex County judge Jacob Van Wickle.[27] Under the slavery codes of the time, no sales out-of-state of enslaved persons were allowed without the express consent of the person being sold. This was particularly important during the period of gradual abolition. Many Black people then enslaved in New Jersey would

---

23. Such as at Trinity College, Hartford. See "George Washington Doane."

24. Later also a US senator from New Jersey, he was a founding parishioner who served on the first vestry at Trinity Church, Princeton. See Stockton and Thomson, "Subscription Book of 1827 to Build a Protestant Episcopal Church in the Borough of Princeton." See also Rector, Wardens and Vestrymen of Trinity Church in the Borough of Princeton, "Certificate of Incorporation."

25. United States Bureau of Census, *Fifth Census,* 264. According to this data there were at least 108 Black people held as slaves on his plantation in Brunswick, Georgia at the time. See also Brockmann, *Commodore Robert F. Stockton,* 72–73.

26. Not unlike the pattern evidenced in his father-in-law John Potter's holdings. See the entry on Trinity Church, Princeton in chapter 11 for more information.

27. Also spelled "Van Winkle."

The Development of the Episcopal Church and Its Relation to Slavery

ultimately be freed after their legal term of service in New Jersey. However, if they were sold into slavery in a state that allowed permanent enslavement, they would lose this legally enshrined promise of future freedom.

Van Wickle sought to benefit from the arbitrage opportunity presented by higher valuations for the enslaved in the Deep South than were common in New Jersey.[28] He and his son ran a slave-trading ring encouraging New Jersey owners to sell to his brother-in-law for prices higher than New Jersey market rates but significantly below valuations common in the Deep South. Van Wickle forged papers of acquiescence for at least seventy-five enslaved Black people, who were smuggled out of state. Eventually he was stopped, partly by concerned Quakers,[29] and partly by other slave-holding Episcopalians,[30] but he was never convicted of a crime even when it was clear that he had been breaking the law. Van Wickle is buried at St. Peter's Church, Spotswood[31] along with other family members.

"Portrait of Absalom Jones" by Raphaelle Peale (1774–1825). Held by the Delaware Art Museum (courtesy Wikimedia Commons).

28. Gigantino II, *Ragged Road to Abolition*, 157–60.

29. Hodges, *Black New Jersey*, 79.

30. Including James Parker Jr. of St. Peter's Church, Perth Amboy. See "James Parker Jr. (1776–1868)."

31. Macy Jr., "Van Wicklen/Van Wickle Family," 250–51.

Part I: An Outline of Anglican and Episcopal Slavery in New Jersey

Before the Revolutionary War a significant number of enslaved Black Americans were exposed to Anglican worship and teaching. However, after the war, for the most part, free Black Americans went elsewhere. Of course, this was not universally true, but the attraction of worshipping communities (Methodist, Baptist, the nascent AME) that would more readily affirm Black Americans' religious experience, abilities, and leadership was strong. Those denominations that insisted on traditional, expensive, elite education (mostly accessible only to White people) as the only acceptable avenue to the priesthood (e.g., the Episcopal Church), lost many faithful and gifted potential Black leaders who simply went where the exercise of their gifts was allowed or even welcomed. There were exceptions of course (e.g., Rev. Absalom Jones[32] in Philadelphia) but this was the general pattern of the time, and the road for those who persisted was beset with racist obstacles.[33]

Many prominent Black Christian leaders and writers in this period, such as George White and Jon Jea, narrated a separation from an Anglican Church expression or background.[34] Black aspirants to the priesthood from around the country were routinely rejected at General Theological Seminary, where the bishop of New Jersey served on the board of trustees.[35] The first Black American born in New Jersey to be ordained to the priesthood was Rev. Peter Williams Jr.,[36] though he became Episcopalian after leaving the state. The first Black Episcopal Church in New Jersey, St. Philip's, was formed in 1856 in Newark,[37] however governance from the diocese was highly paternalistic. Some Black Episcopalians managed to persist in the faith in spite of overwhelming obstacles in the diocese at this time. However, it is not hard to see why many Black Americans sought alternate institutional religious expressions when the prevailing attitudes and practices of elite White Episcopalians in New Jersey were so inhumane even toward Black people who were fellow Christians.[38]

32. See "Reverend Absalom Jones."

33. See Gigantino II, *Ragged Road to Abolition*, 201–2.

34. See Hodges, *Black Itinerants of the Gospel*, 53, 130.

35. The rejection of Alexander Crummell for admission to General was actually fought by Bishop Doane (see Wilder, "Driven . . . from the School of the Prophets").

36. See "Reverend Peter Williams Jr."

37. Bennett, "Black Episcopalians," 238. St. Philip's gained formal parish status in 1856 but the community was founded in 1848.

38. Writing the history of the treatment of Black Americans in the Diocese of New Jersey during the period of gradual abolition is a massive undertaking and this text is only meant to serve as an initial, introductory treatment. Further research and

The Development of the Episcopal Church and Its Relation to Slavery

"Rev. Peter Williams." From Woodson, *The History of the Negro Church*, 94–95 (courtesy Wikimedia Commons).

Summary: The establishment of the Diocese of New Jersey was accomplished with resources derived through the enslavement of Black Americans. The earliest influential priests gained their wealth from enslaved labor and directly held Black people in slavery, as did the early bishops. The building of churches during this period used funds derived from the enslavement of Black people, and elite lay Episcopalians were among some of the worst abusers of the institution. In spite of missionary attention to enslaved Black people during the colonial period, Black Christians in New Jersey generally did not widely embrace the Episcopal Church during the gradual abolition period, seeking instead religious institutions that better affirmed their leadership and initiative.

---

documentation are required and ongoing.

PART II

Historical Documents

A NUMBER OF CRITICAL historical documents that establish the facts relating to slavery and racism in the Anglican Church in New Jersey during the colonial era and in the Episcopal Church in New Jersey during the early Republic continue to be difficult to access. This Part presents several of these documents, with accompanying interpretive commentary, in order to provide a fuller view of the realities of slavery in the Church in New Jersey at that time. As mentioned in the introduction, at times it has been necessary to preserve some of the archaic racialized language from early sources that is now considered offensive. This has only been done when necessary to give an accurate sense of these early sources and is not in any way an affirmation of the use of such language in modern parlance.

7

George Keith's Anti-Slavery Sermon of 1693

GEORGE KEITH WAS AN influential Quaker in the early days of the colonies of East and West Jersey, when he served as the chief surveyor of East Jersey. After several years in the Jerseys he converted to the Church of England, became a missionary priest under the auspices of the Society for the Propagation of the Gospel (SPG), and ministered to a number of nascent congregations in the region (including at Perth Amboy, Elizabeth, Piscataway, Woodbridge, Shrewsbury, Burlington, Colestown, and Freehold) before finally settling in England.

Before he converted to Anglicanism, however, he penned in 1693 what was perhaps the earliest North American anti-slavery tract, entitled "An Exhortation & Caution to Friends Concerning Buying or Keeping of Negroes." At the time, the permissibility of slavery was not nearly as decided an issue among Quakers as it became over the following century. It was however, a very decided issue in the Anglican Church, but decidedly in favor of the institution. This fact did not prevent Keith from becoming Anglican not long after writing. Neither did the funding of the SPG, and by extension his salary, through slavery profits from the Codrington Plantation in Barbados. Neither did whatever remained of his anti-slavery convictions prevent his friendship with prolific enslavers who supported

Part II: Historical Documents

and endowed his churches, such as, for instance, Thomas Boels of St. Peter's Church in Freehold.[1]

Thus the sentiments expressed in Keith's tract, though appearing salutary to modern eyes, seem to have had a limited effect on Keith's relationships. Perhaps he did not view disagreement over the issue of slavery to require the kind of response he seems to intimate in his tract (e.g. to "Come out" of those relationships). He himself was disavowed in Quaker fellowships soon after publishing the tract and this rejection may have affected his willingness to press the issue in the Anglican circles he came to inhabit. At the very least, the tract indicates that the often-repeated argument that enslavers of the time didn't or couldn't have known any better is preposterous.

Detail from "Portrait of George Keith (c. 1638–1716)." From Hills, *History of the Church in Burlington*, 18–19 (courtesy Wikimedia Commons).

1. See Burr, *Anglican Church in New Jersey*, 498. Among the records showing this is the "Inventory of the personal estate" accompanying his will, which included multiple "nigrose" [sic]. See "Boell," in *Documents*.

"An Exhortation & Caution to Friends Concerning Buying or Keeping of Negroes."[2] By George Keith

[Seeing] our Lord Jesus Christ has tasted Death for every Man, and given himself a Ransom for all, to be testified in due time, and that his Gospel of Peace, Liberty and Redemption from Sin, Bondage and all Oppression, is freely to be preached unto all, without Exception, and that Negroes, Blacks and Taunies are a real part of Mankind, for whom Christ has shed his precious Blood, and are capable of Salvation, as well as White Men; and Christ the Light of the World has (in measure) enlightened them, and every Man that comes into the World; and that all such who are sincere Christians and true Believers in Christ Jesus, and Followers of him, bear his Image, and are made conformable unto him in Love, Mercy, Goodness and Compassion, who came not to destroy men's Lives, but to save them, nor to bring any part of Mankind into outward Bondage, Slavery or Misery, nor yet to detain them, or hold them therein, but to ease and deliver the Oppressed and Distressed, and bring into Liberty both inward and outward.

Therefore we judge it necessary that all faithful Friends should discover themselves to be true Christians by having the Fruits of the Spirit of Christ, which are Love, Mercy, Goodness, and Compassion towards all in Misery, and that suffer Oppression and severe Usage, so far as in them is possible to ease and relieve them, and set them free of their hard Bondage, whereby it may be hoped, that many of them will be gained by their beholding these good Works of sincere Christians, and prepared thereby, through the Preaching the Gospel of Christ, to [embrace] the true Faith of Christ. And for this cause it is, as we judge, that in some places in Europe Negroes cannot be bought and sold for Money, or detained to be Slaves, because it suits not with the Mercy, Love & Clemency that is essential to Christianity, nor to the Doctrine of Christ, nor to the Liberty the Gospel calls all men unto, to whom it is preached. And to buy Souls and Bodies of men for Money, to enslave them and their Posterity to the end of the World, we judge is a great hinderance to the spreading of the Gospel, and is occasion of much War,

---

2. Edited by Jolyon G. R. Pruszinski. The transcription of the tract has been edited for clarity according to modern language conventions. Spelling alterations to the original text made for the sake of clarity appear as [plain text in brackets]. Punctuation changes, expansions of abbreviations, and updated archaisms (e.g., substitutions of "you" for "thee" or "thou") are not noted. Text is based on the Text Creation Partnership edition hosted by the University of Michigan Library System with reference to the edition printed in *The Pennsylvania Magazine of History and Biography*.

Violence, Cruelty and Oppression, and Theft & [Robbery] of the highest Nature; for commonly the Negroes that are sold to white Men, are either [stolen] away or robbed from their Kindred, and to buy such is the way to continue these evil Practices of Man-stealing, and transgresses that Golden Rule and Law, "To do to others what we would have others do to us."

Therefore, in true Christian Love, we earnestly recommend it to all our Friends and Brethren, Not to buy any Negroes, unless it were on purpose to set them free, and that such who have bought any, and have them at present, after some reasonable time of moderate Service they have had of them, or may have of them, that may reasonably answer to the Charge of what they have laid out, especially in keeping Negroes' Children born in their House, or taken into their House, when under Age, that after a reasonable time of service to answer that Charge, they may set them at Liberty, and during the time they have them, to teach them to read, and give them a Christian Education.

Some Reasons and Causes of our being against keeping of Negroes for Term of Life

First, Because it is contrary to the Principles and Practice of the Christian Quakers to buy Prize or [stolen] Goods, which we bore a faithful Testimony against in our Native Country; and therefore it is our Duty to come forth in a Testimony against [stolen] Slaves, it being accounted a far greater Crime under Moses' Law than the stealing of Goods: for such were only to restore four fold, "but he that steals a Man and sells him, if he is found in his hand, he shall surely be put to Death," (Exod. 21:16). Therefore as we are not to buy [stolen] Goods, (but if at unawares it should happen through Ignorance, we are to restore them to the Owners, and seek our Remedy of the Thief) no more are we to buy [stolen] Slaves; neither should any who have them keep them and their Posterity in perpetual Bondage and Slavery, as is usually done, to the great scandal of the Christian Profession.

Secondly, Because Christ commanded, saying, "All things whatsoever that you would have men do unto you, do also to them." Therefore as we and our Children would not be kept in perpetual Bondage and Slavery against our Consent, neither should we keep them in perpetual Bondage and Slavery against their Consent, it being such [intolerable] Punishment to their Bodies and Minds, that none but notorious Criminal [Offenders] deserve the same. But these have done us no [harm]; therefore how inhumane is it in us so grievously to oppress them and their Children from one Generation to another.

Thirdly, Because the Lord has commanded, saying, "You shall not deliver back to his Master the Servant that has escaped from his Master to you, he shall dwell with you, even amongst you in that place which he shall [choose] in one of your Gates, where he likes best; you shall not oppress him," (Deut. 23:15–16). By which it appears, that those who are at Liberty and freed from their Bondage, should not by us be delivered into Bondage again, neither by us should they be oppressed, but being escaped from his Master, should have the liberty to dwell amongst us, where he likes best. Therefore, if God extends such Mercy under the legal Ministration and Dispensation to poor Servants, he does and will extend much more of his Grace and Mercy to them under the clear Gospel Ministration; so that instead of punishing them and their Posterity with cruel Bondage and perpetual Slavery, he will cause the Everlasting Gospel to be preached effectually to all Nations, to them as well as others; "And the Lord will extend Peace to his People like a River, and the Glory of the Gentiles like a flowing Stream; And it shall come to pass, says the Lord, that I will gather all Nations and Tongues, and they shall come and see my Glory, and I will set a sign among them, and I will send those that escape from them to the Nations, to Tarshish, Pull and Lud that draw the Bow to Tuball and Javan, to the Isles far off that have not heard my Fame, nor have seen my Glory, and they shall declare my Glory among the Gentiles," (Isa. 66:12, 18).

Fourthly, Because the Lord has commanded, saying, "You shall not oppress [a] hired Servant that is poor and needy, whether he is of your Brethren, or of the Strangers that are in your Land within your Gates, [lest] he cry against you unto the Lord, and the sin be attributed to you; You shall neither vex a stranger nor oppress him, for you were strangers in the Land of [Egypt]," (Deut. 24:14–15. Exod. 12:21). But what greater Oppression can there be inflicted upon our Fellow Creatures, than is inflicted on the poor Negroes! They being brought from their own Country against their Wills, some of them being [stolen], others taken for payment of Debt owed by their Parents, and others taken Captive in War, and sold to Merchants, who bring them to the American Plantations, and sell them for Bond-Slaves to them that will give most for them; the Husband from the Wife, and the Children from the Parents; and many that buy them do exceedingly afflict them and oppress them, not only by continual hard [Labor], but by cruel Whippings; and other cruel Punishments, and by short allowance of Food, some Planters in [Barbados] and Jamaica, it is said, keeping one hundred of them, and some more, and some less, and giving them hardly [anything] more than they raise on a little piece of Ground appointed them, on which they work for themselves the seventh [days] of the Week in the [afternoon], and on the first days, to raise their own Provisions, that is, Corn and Potatoes, and other Roots, etc. the remainder of their time being spent in their Masters' service; which doubtless is far worse usage than is [practiced] by the Turks and Moors upon their Slaves. Which tends to the great Reproach of the Christian Profession; therefore it would be better for all who fall short of the Practice of those Infidels, to refuse the Name of a Christian, that those Heathen and Infidels may not be provoked to blaspheme against the blessed Name of Christ, by reason of the [unparalleled] Cruelty of these cruel and hard hearted pretended Christians: Surely the Lord does behold their Oppressions and Afflictions, and will further visit for the same by his righteous and just Judgments, except they break off their sins by Repentance, and their Iniquity by [showing] Mercy to these poor afflicted, tormented miserable Slaves!

Fifthly, Because Slaves and Souls of Men are some of the "[Merchandise] of Babylon" by which "the Merchants of the Earth are made Rich"; but those Riches which they have heaped together, through the cruel Oppression of these miserable Creatures, will be a means to draw God's Judgments upon them; therefore, Brethren, let us hearken to the Voice of the Lord, who says, "Come out of Babylon, my People, that you be not partakers of her Sins, and that you receive not her [Plagues]; for her Sins have reached to Heaven, and God has [remembered] her Iniquities; for he that leads into Captivity shall go into Captivity," (Rev. 18:4–5 & 13:10).

Given forth by our [Monthly] Meeting in Philadelphia, the 13th day of the 8th [Month], 1693, and recommended to all our Friends and Brethren, who are one with us in our Testimony for the Lord Jesus Christ, and to all others professing Christianity.

THE END.

8

Correspondence with the SPG
Letters from Sharpe (1712), Haliday (1717), and Holbrooke (1727)

Rev. John Sharpe's Account of the 1712 New York City Slave Revolt

THE REV. JOHN SHARPE served as an Anglican priest in New Jersey at the behest of the Society for the Propagation of the Gospel (SPG) at various points between 1704 and 1717 (to congregations including those at Perth Amboy, Burlington, Woodbridge, Maidenhead, and Hopewell), but in the latter portion of this time served primarily as the chaplain to the British forces in New York City.[1] In the summer of 1712[2] he wrote a letter[3] to the Secretary of the Society that dealt largely with a recent rebellion[4] by enslaved persons that had occurred in the city on April 6 of that year. The text[5] of the letter pertaining to the revolt follows.

   1. Burr, *Anglican Church in New Jersey*, 639–40.
   2. Dated from New York to June 23, 1712.
   3. Courtesy of the British Online Archives, SPG Correspondence Collection, A Series, Vol. 7: 214–17.
   4. A number of recent books have recounted some aspects of this event including Hodges, *Root and Branch*, 64–65; Glasson, *Mastering Christianity*, 82–85; Gerbner, *Christian Slavery*, 120–23; Fauquez, "'Bloody Conspiracy.'"
   5. Transcription edited for clarity according to modern language conventions. Alterations to the original text made for the sake of clarity appear in brackets. Of these

Part II: Historical Documents

By the Clergy's Address you will see what new Obstacles are in the way of converting the Heathen, and [though] it has given the greatest offence, I hope it may be at least for the advancement of the good work. Some Negro Slaves here of the Nations of Carmantee and Pappa plotted to destroy all the white[s] in order to obtain their freedom, and kept their Conspiracy Secret that there was not the least Suspicion of it (as formerly there had often been) till it come to the Execution. It was agreed to on New Year's day, the Conspirators tying themselves to Secrecy by Sucking the blood of each other's hand. And to make them invulnerable, as they believed, a free [negro] who pretends Sorcery gave them a powder to rub on their [Clothes] which made them so confident that on Sunday night *après* about 2 [o']clock, [*at*] about the going down of the moon, they Set fire to a house which, [alarming] the town, they stood in the Streets and Shot down and Stabbed as many as they could [until] a great Gun from the [fort] called up the Inhabitants in Arms who soon [scattered] them. They murdered about 8 and wounded about 12 more who are Since recovered. Some of them in their flight shot themselves. One shot first his wife and then himself and some who had hid themselves in Town, when they went to apprehend them, [cut] their own throats. Many were Convicted and about 18 have [suffered] death. This barbarous Conspiracy of the [Negroes] which was first thought to be general, [opened] the mouths of many against negroes being made Christians. Mr. Neau [*dared not*] hardly appear. His school was [blamed] as the main [occasion] of it, and a Petition [*was*] to have been presented if the Governor had not Stood to his Cause. Amongst all those that suffered Here none but two [*were*] of his School, one of which only was baptized and he was condemned on slender Evidence in the heat of the People's resentment. I saw him suffer and heard him declare his [innocence] with his dying breath and then but too late for him he was pitied and proclaimed innocent by the Generality of the People. The other of the [Catechumens] was Slave to an eminent merchant, one Hendrich Hooghlandt who was murdered. He had for two years solicited his master for leave to be baptized but could not obtain it. He was certainly in the Conspiracy, but was hanged in Chains for the murder of his Master. After his hanging three days I went to him and exhorted him to confession. He said he knew of the Conspiracy but was not guilty of any bloodshed in the tumult. The cry against [Catechizing] the negroes continued

---

alterations, spelling changes appear as plain text, while slightly altered or added language for the sake of clarity appear in italics. Punctuation changes, expansions of abbreviations, and updated archaisms (e.g., substitutions of "you" for "thee" or "thou") are not noted.

[until], upon conviction, they were found to be Such as never frequented Mr. Neau's School, and what is very observable, the Persons whose Negroes have been found guilty are such as are declared opposers of Christianizing Negroes.

The Spanish Indians were at first most Suspected as having most understanding to carry on a plot and being Christians. There was no Evidence against any but two, and that was presumptive, however they were condemned. I visited them in prison, and went with them to the gallows where after they were [tied] up they declared their [innocence] of what was laid to their charge and behaved themselves as became Christians. While I was at prayers with them, interest was made with the Governor for their reprieve: Upon the whole. . . the Christian Religion has been much Blasphemed, and the Society's Pious design has been much obstructed. By this bloody attempt of the Negroes, I am [hopeful] that both shall be promoted since it appear[s], on [trial], that those are Innocent who have been Seasoned with principles of Religion and those are but a small number that come to School in comparison of the many hundred that are in this place. I believe not above a tenth.

Sharpe's account of the revolt is revealing for a number of reasons. It indicates an awareness of the reality that punishments of Black people were often not the result of law-breaking on an individual level. White anxiety frequently led to unjust verdicts that included torture and capital punishment for innocent Black people. The letter describes some of the early stages of the White crackdown following the revolt, which in the ensuing years would expand in scope to the passing of even more draconian laws in New York and New Jersey in 1712 through 1714. Furthermore, Sharpe himself is involved in the cross-examination—under torture—of some of those who were accused, showing that priests participated hand-in-glove in the system of legal authority in the colonies that embraced slavery.

The letter also shows that attempts to Christianize the enslaved were controversial at the time, and certainly not exhaustive or widespread. Sharpe mentions that no more than one-tenth of the enslaved in the city had ever attended Mr. Neau's School, which was oriented to this purpose. It is possible that Sharpe is attempting to de-emphasize the danger posed by Christianizing enslaved persons, but various studies support the conclusion that outreach efforts to the enslaved were quite limited.

Perhaps most significantly, the interrogations yielded a particular conviction for Sharpe that he passed along as salutary: that Christian instruction made enslaved persons more obedient and less likely to revolt.

Part II: Historical Documents

Thus the letter shows a key moment in the concretization of this ecclesial policy toward slavery. The interpretive work done by Sharpe as a minister of the Church of England assumes the legitimacy of slavery, and highlights the value of the Christianization of the enslaved in the Church of England as a useful buttress of the institution of slavery. The SPG supported and broadly promulgated this conclusion.[6]

Rev. Thomas Haliday's "more comfortable subsistence"

One of the Anglican priests stationed in New Jersey by SPG in the early eighteenth century was the Rev. Thomas Haliday. He served several congregations including those at Perth Amboy, Woodbridge, Freehold, Elizabeth, and Piscataqua. Not unlike many of the other priests sent to New Jersey in the colonial era, He found his stipend inadequate to his needs. In response to this difficulty, in a letter[7] dated October 9, 1717, he proposed a scheme to the SPG to allow for a "more comfortable subsistence." Below is the text of his proposal.[8]

> There is [something], which I hinted [at] in my last [letter], that further consideration [*of which*] [confirms] me still in the Opinion. That is, that if the society would procure a donation of 200 acres of land from the Proprietors of the soil for the use of the Church in each place where they send a Missionary, and if the Society could spare for some time a dozen of good Negroes from [Barbados] who might clear the land, fence, dung, Plant, Orchard, Make Clover Pasture, burn brick Kilns, build Parsonage houses, and not only so, but with a [little expense] they might build Churches. This Plantation, so improved, would afford a Missionary a more creditable, [Plentiful] subsistence [than] the remittance of 70 or 100 £ Sterling from England. From this, with [Labor] by

6. Gerbner, *Christian Slavery*, 123.

7. Courtesy of the British Online Archives, SPG Correspondence Collection, A Series, Vol. 12: 301–7.

8. Transcription edited for clarity according to modern language conventions. Alterations to the original text (largely spelling) made for the sake of clarity appear in brackets. Of these alterations, spelling changes appear as plain text, while slightly altered or added language for the sake of clarity appear in italics. Very brief omissions from the original text for the sake of clarity appear as ellipses. Punctuation changes, expansions of abbreviations, and updated archaisms (e.g., substitutions of "you" for "thee" or "thou") are not noted.

his servants, he might be [supplied] with [*what*] is necessary for the Maintenance and [support] of a family. And such a Plantation would be a freehold in Property of the Church in the Presentation of the Society, or on [whomsoever] they should devolve it to, [*on*] which the Missionary should be legally instituted and Inducted, and this would remain to the Memory of the Pious [endeavors] of the Honored Society in all future Ages.

This would be a more sure, certain, and [Perpetual subsistence than] the remittance of fifty or sixty pounds from home. And it prevents the inconvenience of a Missionary's running before his allowance, and so, all mercy, to have his bills protested or otherwise imposed upon with the merchants [he] deal[s] with.

As it would be a surer and more comfortable subsistence to the Missionary, so it would be cheaper to the Society. It requires the Interest of 1000 £ sterling to the Maintenance of Every Missionary in this Province. But such a plantation, both as to the purchase and improvements needed, [would] not amount to much more [than] 200 £ sterling principal, and this, once done, all remittances from home might cease, for the plantation might be improved so as it might yield better [than] 100 £ yearly produce. If the Society were to make a purchase of the Land they could do it for less [than] 100 £, and if they sent over Negroes of their own the [Expenses] of improvements, and even building Churches and [Parsonages], would be inconsiderable. Some Masons and Joiners would be wanted, and several may be found in London who would come over and serve here for 4 [years], the society paying their passage. Whatever [others'] Opinion may be, I am sure I would sooner choose such a Plantation for life and family [than] the [remittance] I have [at] present. Lands increase [daily] in their value and the plantation would, still the longer, be the better.

As can be seen from the proposal, Haliday is aware that the SPG held many Black people enslaved in Barbados at that time. He is also aware that the most straightforward means to a comfortable living in New Jersey involved benefiting from the nascent plantation economy, which was very dependent on enslaved labor. He sees no problem with the enslavement of Black people and, on the contrary, views their enslavement as a useful means to beneficial ends. The letter is indicative of the general attitude of Anglican priests in the colony at the time. Though Haliday's proposed scheme was never universally implemented, many priests in New Jersey acted on the general principle of the proposal through their local parishes or their own private dealings.[9] A number of churches acquired glebes[10] that were rented out to plantation owners (enslavers) in order to support the clergy, or that the clergy managed directly for their own profit via their own enslaved labor. Several priests acquired plantation holdings and slaves through advantageous marriage, and in general, the best-established churches and most influential priests in colonial New Jersey managed to attain financial success and stability as a result of profits derived from enslaving Black people in the New Jersey plantation economy.

The Anglican plantation imaginary. "Slaves cutting the sugar cane" by William Clark (d. 1801). Held by British Library (courtesy Wikimedia Commons).

9. Among these priests were at least Abraham Beach, Robert Blackwell, Samuel Cooke, William Frazer, Alexander Innes, William Lindsay, Jonathan Odell, Uzal Ogden Jr., Samuel Seabury, William Skinner, John Talbot, Thomas Thompson, George Keith, and Edward Vaughan. Well over 50 percent of the years of service performed by colonial-era priests in New Jersey was supported directly by profit from the labor of enslaved Black people *in New Jersey* (to say nothing of the stipendiary support nearly all these priests received from the SPG, which was funded significantly through SPG enslavement of Black people on the Codrington Plantation in Barbados).

10. A technical term for church-owned agricultural land used for the support of the parish or parish clergy.

Rev. John Holbrooke's Salem County, New Jersey Anglican Slavery Audit of 1727

The Rev. John Holbrooke was a missionary priest assigned to Salem County, New Jersey in the late 1720s. In a letter[11] written to the secretary for the Society for the Propagation of the Gospel (SPG) updating the society on his work, Holbrooke describes the population of the region in some detail. In so doing, he produced what may be understood as perhaps the earliest precise Anglican slavery audit of a parish in New Jersey. The first relevant portion of the letter[12] (section 3) details the general population of Salem County:

> By a computation lately made by the Governor's order, it appears that there are about 4000 Inhabitants in this County, from which deducting 500 of the [Swedish Settlers], and 250 that up and down the County profess themselves members of the Church of England, the remainder are Dissenters of different Denominations, [*namely*], Quakers, Independents, Presbyterians, Anabaptists, Seventh Day men, etc. There is but one Baptist family in the County.[13]

The second pertinent section of the letter (section 6) describes the enslaved Black population of the county and the prevalence of slave ownership among Anglicans in the parish:

> The number of [Negro] and other Slaves in the County lately given in to the Sherriff was 150, of which twelve belong to six people of my Congregation. I have baptized one [Negro] Woman lately, as for the rest I have [endeavored] what I could to procure their Baptism, but what through the remissness of their masters and what through the stupid unconcernedness of the Negroes it is yet unaffected. The People in these Countries take little or no care to instruct either their children or Negroes. Such a Strong Spirit of [fanaticism] and Giddiness reigns here that I must confess I see but little hopes of gaining over many to a Sober Sense of Religion; and the practices of the People are generally as bad as their principles, among whom the [Hypocrisy], [*nepotism*], and oppression, not to

11. The letter is dated to November 17, 1727.

12. Courtesy of the British Online Archives, SPG Correspondence Collection, A Series, Vol. 20: 193–98.

13. Transcription edited for clarity according to modern language conventions. Alterations to the original text (spelling) made for the sake of clarity appear in brackets, while slightly altered or added language for the sake of clarity appear in italics. Punctuation changes, expansions of abbreviations, and updated archaisms (e.g., substitutions of "you" for "thee" or "thou") are not noted.

mention other vices, are Common. The men that act with great [Candor] and Integrity are, I think, those that join with us, but among those there are some I fear that are only nominal Brethren.

From this account we can determine many things, among them that Holbrooke did not have a high opinion of the Black people in his parish, but he seems not to have had a very high view of the inhabitants of his parish generally. He viewed the proper responsibility for religious influence upon the enslaved as lying with their enslavers, and further, viewed said responsibility as largely neglected. And whatever his efforts may have been toward potential Black parishioners, he did not view these efforts as terribly successful.

As to the demographic data presented, it appears that the enslaved (mostly Black people) made up approximately 3.75 percent of the population of the county (150/4,000). Anglicans made up 6.25 percent (250/4,000). Holbrooke states that his parishioners account for the enslavement of twelve of these, that is, 8 percent of those enslaved in the county. These twelve he claimed were owned by only six Anglicans. The six mentioned here are probably not individuals but households, so we cannot take this data to mean that the rate of slave ownership among Anglicans in the county was only 2.4 percent (6/250) but probably much higher, as households, especially of the wealthy who owned slaves were typically much larger. The figure of 2.4 percent should be understood as an unlikely absolute minimum. The actual rate would appear to have been several times higher (perhaps 7–12 percent), a reality shown by the fact that though Anglicans made up only 6.25 percent of the population, they accounted for 8 percent of the total enslaved Black people in the county. Not only so, but official figures for slaveholding were often lower than the reality since enslavers had an incentive for tax purposes to undercount.[14] In later letters Holbrooke suggests that eventually his congregation at St. John's Church, Salem began to grow modestly in part as the result of what he called "imported servants" but this is likely a euphemism for enslaved Black people.[15]

These data suggest that while ownership of slaves was mostly a phenomenon prevalent among the wealthy, Holbrooke's descriptions of his parishioners as "poor" does not preclude the prevalence of slavery among the

14. See, for instance, the confirmed undercount at Lewis Morris's plantation reflected in his will at the time of his death, shown to be inaccurate by the private census conducted by his inheriting nephew Lewis Morris, later governor of New Jersey. The younger Morris found twice as many enslaved persons as the official documentation indicated (Geffken, *Stories of Slavery in New Jersey*, 47).

15. Burr, *Anglican Church in New Jersey*, 146.

Anglicans to whom he ministered. While it is unclear whether Holbrooke himself enslaved any Black people at this time, after 1732 he left Salem to take a parish in Virginia that would enable a more lucrative income, including income from participation in the plantation economy. By the time he passed away in Virginia in 1747 he had accumulated a large plantation estate and enslaved at least thirteen Black people.[16]

---

16. See "John Holbrook, Will, Northampton County, Virginia—1746," in Tallant, *Migration of Holbrooks*, 3.

9

Rev. Thomas Thompson's "The African Trade" Tract in Defense of Slavery (1772)

STATIONED BY THE SOCIETY for the Propagation of the Gospel in Monmouth County, New Jersey from 1745 to 1751, the Rev. Thomas Thompson served several Anglican congregations, including those at Shrewsbury, Middletown, Freehold, and Allentown. He was a celebrated figure in the Church and has continued to be spoken of in glowing terms, even by twentieth-century Episcopal Church historians.[1]

Immediately following his tenure in New Jersey he was assigned, at his request, to serve as a missionary (ostensibly the first Anglican) to the African Guinea coast. He did not serve very long in this capacity, apparently for health reasons, but while active, largely served as the chaplain for the slave trading company operating out of Cape Castle. While there, he recommended a few Africans for English education, including the boy who would become the Rev. Philip Quaque. Quaque went on to become the first ordained African in the Church of England and, after his ordination, returned to the Cape Coast, specifically the Cape Castle British slave-trade headquarters, as a missionary and chaplain like Thompson had been.[2]

1. See, for example, Burr, *Anglican Church in New Jersey*, 644–45.
2. For a more detailed treatment of Philip Quaque's life see Johnson, *African American*

Rev. Thomas Thompson's "The African Trade" Tract

Detail of "Cape Coast Castle." From Brown, *The Story of Africa and Its Explorers*, 40 (courtesy Wikimedia Commons).

After leaving the Cape Coast, Thompson wrote a very influential treatise defending the slave trade, which he dedicated to the Company of Merchants Trading to Africa, the primary British company operating the trade. He does not in the tract argue that the trade is useful for the project of Christianization, and, somewhat incredibly, he acknowledges that there would appear to be many reasons for qualms regarding the slave trade, including its obvious horrors. He goes on, however, to dismiss these qualms with a few scriptural prooftexts, an insistence that the trade is necessary for England's success, remarks that the trade accords with the laws of the African nations involved, and a few other cursory comments including some regarding the nature of trade itself. He does not conclude, however, without admitting that if his proof fails, the trade must be considered a gross "national sin."

In spite of how unconvincing the arguments may appear to modern readers, the text was influential upon its publishing, including in New Jersey, even as Thompson had not been resident in the colony for over twenty years. This can be seen by the fact that published rebuttals of Thompson's

---

Religions, 1500–2000, 35–55. Though Quaque worked in the same colonial African context Thompson had, his personal correspondence appears to suggest less comfort with the legitimacy of the slave trade.

tract appeared quickly among colonial Quakers.[3] The arguments Thompson made continued to be used by Anglicans and Episcopalians in the United States for more than one hundred years. Slavery would be outlawed in Scotland only six years after Thompson's tract was published, indicating that the qualms he was dismissing were widespread even then, but it would be thirty-five years before the British Parliament abolished the Atlantic slave trade, and ninety-three years before ratification of the Thirteenth Amendment to the United States' Constitution imposed the end of slavery upon the state of New Jersey. The text[4] of Thompson's tract follows.

The African Trade for Negro Slaves, [Shown] to be Consistent with Principles of Humanity, and with the Laws of Revealed Religion. **By Tho. Thompson, M.A., Sometime Fellow of C.C.C.**

To the Worshipful Committee of the Company of Merchants Trading to Africa: In Particular, to his much-esteemed friend, William Devaines, Esq; One of the Committee; This Treatise is Addressed by Their Obedient Humble Servant, Tho. Thompson.

As the happy, free constitution of this kingdom may, in some degree, account for the bravery of its people who are a terror to their enemies in every time of war, so its excellent religion, as distinguished from the merciless system of the church of Rome, has that influence upon the temper which does [honor] to the subjects of the British crown.

Hence, it is that the trade for negro slaves, which took its rise from a necessity of supplying our West [Indian] and American colonies with the fittest hands for plantation-work, is generally considered with feelings of tenderness, and but seldom spoken of without great humanity.

Though use inures men to certain businesses which are never practiced, for some time at first, without strong emotions of natural aversion, in

---

3. Among those responses that were reprinted in Philadelphia was that of Granville Sharp, *Just limitation of slavery in the laws of God*.

4. Originally published in 1772 in "Canterbury: Printed and Sold by Simmons and Kirkby." This edition edited by Jolyon G. R. Pruszinski, with reference to that included in *Sabin Americana*. The transcription of the tract has been edited for clarity according to modern language conventions with spelling alterations appearing as plain text in brackets. Punctuation changes, expansions of abbreviations, and updated archaisms (e.g., substitutions of "you" for "thee" or "thou") are not noted.

the slave trade it is otherwise; and several of our countrymen I have known abroad, who, after a long seasoning to it, have ingenuously owned, they could never well reconcile themselves to it.

It must be said there is something very affecting and disagreeable in the appearance and notion of human creatures, even the lowest of such, being treated like mere beasts or cattle.

For the negroes so to misuse one another—this passes in detail without any special remark made upon it. And though more of that [*may*] be said by a great deal than is true, yet, considering them as pagans, and of as dark a mind as complexion, one does not much [*wonder*] at the monstrous things which are reported of them. But that Christians maintain a commerce with those people for the numberless poor wretches which they enslave and drive down from the country to the factories and landing-places on the coast to be sold like bullocks at a fair—this is a fact that seems hardly capable of a [defense], notwithstanding the impossibility that our plantations can be cultivated without them.

Mr. Sandys, in his travels,[5] speaks of some charitable Turks that buy birds out of their cages to let them fly again. But how would the spirit of our benevolent religion shine forth in the nobler purchase of poor negroes, were it to ransom them to their lost liberty, and not to transport them to a slavery more oppressive and rigorous than what they have suffered in their own country! Fair as this seems in theory, it would exhaust the treasure of any kingdom to reduce it into practice. We must endeavor then to make the best of what we have: and it may be sufficient, if a lawful trade can be proved, where we cannot [show] a boasted virtue.

This subject will grow more serious upon our hands, when we consider the buying and selling negroes, not as a clandestine or piratical business, but as an open, public trade, encouraged and promoted by acts of parliament. For so, if being contrary to religion, it must be deemed a national sin; and as such may have a consequence, that would be always to be dreaded. But as ill a face as it seems to carry and as strong as the objections may be thought to be, which are commonly made against it, it is really as vindicable as any species of trade whatever.

The Jewish institution permitted the use of bond-servants. In Leviticus 25:39, etc.:

> If your brother that dwells near you [*becomes*] poor, and is sold to you; you shall not compel him to serve as a bond-servant: but

---

5. Lib. 1, p. 57.

> as [a] hired servant, and as a sojourner, he shall be with this and shall serve you unto the year of jubilee. And then shall he depart from you, both he and his children with him, and shall return to his family, and to the possession of his fathers shall he return. For they are my servants, which I brought out of the land of Egypt; they shall not be sold as bond-men. You shall not rule over him with [rigor], but shall fear your God. Both your bond-men and your bondmaids which you shall have, shall be of the heathen that are round about you; of them shall you buy bond-men and bond-maids. Moreover, of the children of strangers that do sojourn among you, of them shall you buy, and of their families that are with you, which they begat in your land, and they shall be your possession: and you shall take them as an inheritance for your children after you to inherit them for a possession: they shall be your bond-men [forever].

The latter part of this statute affords us these three observables:

1. An Allowance, or permission, granted to the Jews to have and to use slaves for any such work as they might have occasion to employ them in.
2. That these were to be such as they might buy from the nations which bordered upon their land, or of the heathen, called strangers, that dwelt among them.
3. That the same should be [part] of their goods and chattels, to [pass] to their heirs, and thus to be a succession of bond-servants to their families [forever]. And we further observe that there is no precept for the release of bond-servants in case of their turning and becoming proselytes to the law.

From these premises this conclusion may be drawn: that the buying and selling of slaves is not contrary to the law of nature. For the Jewish constitutions were strictly therewith consistent in all points. And these are, in certain cases, the rule by which is determined by learned lawyers and casuists what is, or is not, contrary to nature.

That there were bond-servants or slaves in Christian families, even in the apostolic age, appears clearly from St. Paul's first epistle to the Corinthians 7:20, etc. "Let every man," says he:

> abide in the same calling, wherein he was called. Are you called, being a servant? Care not for it. But if you may be made free, [*take the opportunity*]. For he that is called of the Lord, being a servant, is the Lord's freeman: likewise also he that is called, being free, is

Christ's servant. You are bought with a price, do not be the servants of men.

The sense of the words is this: whoever is called by divine grace to the possession of the gospel, if being a bond-servant let him content himself to remain in that state, his new and sacred relation by no means releasing him from it. For you, though being in bond-service, [are] nevertheless capable of the blessings and the interests of Christianity, which puts no difference [between] bond and free.[6] Therefore urge not to have your freedom, much less insist on or make a demand of, nor even so much as wish for it; but accept it as a [favor], if perchance an offer of it should be made you.

The words of the apostle, now cited, afford an argument à fortiori to the lawfulness of purchasing and using heathen slaves, they being evidently addressed to bond-servants, which had been brought into the Christian religion. For if those might be lawfully retained in servitude after their conversion, then were they lawfully slaves before.

The epistle of Paul to Philemon gives yet further light into this matter, which is a letter of intercession and request on behalf of one Onesimus, a bond-man, who had fled away from his master. Whom Paul, happening to meet with and having converted, sends . . . back with this epistle. The purport of which is not to assert this man's freedom, now become a Christian, but is only to entreat Philemon to pardon his fault, and that taking him in his former capacity, he would use him kindly.

With respect to the subject now before us, here are three particulars to be considered:

1. What is the case of slavery, abstracted from circumstances, and as it is simply itself.

2. What the general nature of trade is. And

3. Whether slaves are proper subjects of trade.

First, Slavery, as it differs from free service, is the subjection of one person to another as a servant for life. Justinian defines it, a constitution of the law of nations, by which, contrary to nature (or the natural freedom of mankind) one person is subject to the dominion of another.[7] And slaves were called *Servi* he says for the reason that generals of armies did use to

---

6. Colossians 3:11.

7. Servitus est constitution juris gentium, qua quis dominio alieno contra naturam subjicitur. *Institut.* i. 1, tit. 3.

sell those whom they took captive, and thus saved them from being put to the sword.[8]

The word "Slave" some derive from *Sclavus*, the name of a people in Scythia. Skinner gives its etymology from the nation or country *Sclava, Sclavona, Sclavonica*, a vast number of which people formerly were taken captives in war, partly by the Germans, partly by the Venetians, and sold away for servants.[9] But it seems rather that the word is a corruption of *Salvus*, from which comes "Salvage," a term signifying the [recompense] allowed by the statute and civil law, to such persons as have assisted in saving merchandizes, ships, etc. perishing in wrecks, or by pirates, or enemies.[10]

Slavery then had its origin from a principle of humanity, and averseness to shedding blood. Conquerors, rather than flay those whom they took in war, chose to dispose of them in a milder way, and sold them into servitude.

The condition of a slave, and that of a free servant, differ chiefly in these respects: the latter has a power to [choose] whom he will serve, which the other has not. And a free servant has wages; a slave, none. But the serving without wages is not serving for nothing, for there is his keeping, and all necessaries found him.

The state of servitude, simply considered, is nothing shocking, though circumstances too often make it so. The stress of [labor] that is endured by many, the mean diet, and scantiness of their provisions, the severity inflicted on them for their faults and offences, and other hard usage with which they are often treated, these miseries arise not from the nature of their case, considered merely as slaves, but from the injustice and cruelty of their owners. The proper work of slaves is nothing above their strength, and every real hardship that is imposed on them is an abuse of power.

By the law of nature, all persons are free. But absolute freedom is incompatible with civil establishments. Every man's liberty is restricted by national laws, and natural [privilege] does rightly yield to legal constitutions, which are designed and enacted for the public weal.

The Africans are generally held to be a savage people, committing all kinds of violence upon one another. And it is not uncommonly thought that most of the negroes which are brought from the [Guinea] coast have been forced into slavery by their stronger [neighbors], or betrayed by them into

---

8. Servi autem ex eo appellati fuat, quòd imperatores, captivos ventere, ac per hoc servara, nec occidere folent. *Id. ibid.*

9. Skinneri etymol. ling. Angl.

10. Chambers' cyclopaedia.

the merchant's hands; and they are said to sell their wives and children, and steal others where they can pick them up, to make merchandize of them. But though these practices are not without example, yet frequent they are not and cannot be, for every negro nation has its form of government. And by their public customs, which are statutory, the rights and properties of individuals are ascertained and those outrages in a great measure prevented which people living in a state of anarchy would commit. The customs of the blacks are many of them good rules of policy such as would not disgrace a more regular constitution.

The grand source whence the marts are supplied with negroes at all the trading places of the coast is war, which is carried on and waged by the contending nations with as little slaughter as possible, it being the business of the field not to kill, but make captives. Slavery therefore does not accrue by might overcoming right, but by the fortune of war, and partly from national customs of equal authority with laws as the selling of criminals, and insolvent debtors.

Secondly, What the general nature of trade is, this is next to be said, and that both with reference to the subject or thing dealt for and the manner of dealing.

[Anything] being made a subject of trade, which to sell is not contrary to godliness, to moral virtue, to humanity, to legal right and justice, nor to the laws in being, is lawful trade; and what is not consistent with these is unlawful.

Offences against godliness, in the way of commerce are, when things sacred are prostituted to sale.

Against moral virtue, are all bargains that subserve to vitious purposes of turpitude and naughtiness.

Against humanity, is the selling off any goods whereby distress is caused to persons, which have a family-right to them; as where a man puts off the most necessary of his [household] goods, or sells the [clothes] that would cover his children or wife, and this only to raise money to serve his own extravagancy.

Against right and justice, is the making sale of another's property without his knowledge or consent.

Against the laws in being, is all that is called illicit trade.

In these several kinds, nothing can qualify the transgression of the parties so as to render it lawful where neither side is ignorant of the unfitness of the subject that is [negotiated], it being evident that nothing is lawfully sold or bought which ought not to be sold at all.

Next, of the manner of dealing: what, as to the subject of commerce, is lawful trade may, in respect to the conduct, not be fair trade. But this is clear, and needs no explaining.

Thirdly, Whether slaves be proper subjects of trade. In denial hereof it is [alleged], that the setting to sale [of] human creatures is violating the natural distinction of the species, and levelling men with beasts. But to this it may be answered, that every person is treated as a human being, who is treated according to his lawful state and condition. The buying of a slave is taking him as what he is, and the sale does but signify that his owner is willing to part with, and another has a mind to have him. Here then is no violation of humanity, and the property in such individual is transferable like all other property.

Another argument is that whatever is sold, all that is natural to and [inseparable] from it, is included in the purchase. Consequently, the life of a slave is sold and bought. But to this the answer is that nothing can be deemed as sold which was not intended to be bought, and the matter of the purchase is nothing more than the [labor] and service of the slave.

The seizing and carrying off of negroes from the coast, which is called *panyaring*, is what the masters of ships in the African trade are sometimes obliged to, and is done by way of reprisal for theft or damage committed by the natives. If this method were not taken, there could be no trading with them. Every long-boat that goes with goods [ashore] would be in danger of being cut off. But the practice is established use among the natives themselves, so that they are only dealt with in this according to their own laws.

Our traders have been represented as spiriting up the blacks to war, which if true, and that any means are used to set those nations one against another in order to make a trading advantage by it, were a thing to be detested. But as the trade is conducted upon true mercantile principles, it is no more chargeable with this consequence than trade in general is, with the vices and luxury which are fed by the wealth and affluence it produces.

FINIS.

10

Bishops Addressing the Afterlives of Slavery

Bishop Doane's 1854 Reparations Mandate

IN HIS STATE CONVENTION address of 1854, Bishop of the Diocese of New Jersey, the Rt. Rev. George Washington Doane had the following to say about the fledgling Black congregation of St. Philip's Episcopal Church in Newark (the first Black church in the diocese):

> On Wednesday, 26 April, I laid the corner stone of St. Philip's (African) Church, in the City Newark, and made an Address. There were present the Rev. Messrs. Joshua Smith, the Rector elect, Rosé, Lowell, Hoffman, Doane, Leach, (of the Diocese Missouri,) and Berry, (of the Cape Palmas Mission.) It was with peculiar pleasure, that I laid this corner stone. These poor, and simple-hearted, people have clung, for years, through great discouragements, to their pious purpose, of building a House, where they may worship God, together. I trust, they will now be able to accomplish it. I have great confidence in the prudent zeal of their Minister, that they will. I commend them to the good will of their more favoured brethren. I claim for them, as a debt, the generous consideration of those, by whose forefathers, their fathers were brought to this country, without their own consent, and greatly to their hindrance.[1]

1. Doane, *Diocese of New Jersey: The Episcopal Address, to the Seventy-First Annual Convention*, 14.

Part II: Historical Documents

"G.W. Doane, Bishop of New Jersey" by William G. Jackman. Held at New York Public Library (courtesy Wikimedia Commons).

Mingled with a paternalistic sentiment of concern toward the "simple-hearted" members of this Black congregation, Doane acknowledges White privilege, referring to the White Christians of the Diocese as the "more favoured brethren." What is more, he clearly states what should be done about this privilege and the gulf between it and the poverty of his Black brethren. He calls for reparations: "I claim for them," that is, the Black parishioners of St. Philip's, "as a debt," which is to say, something owed, this "consideration," i.e., reparations, due to the state of poverty of these Black Christians resulting from the enslavement of their forebears. The reparations are due not because of the actions of the present generation of White Christians, but because of those of their "forefathers." Doane claims this debt for the *descendants* of those whose "fathers were brought to this country, without their own consent, and greatly to their hindrance." It is from the current generation of White Christians that the debt is claimed and to the current generation of Black people that the debt is owed.

Bishops Addressing the Afterlives of Slavery

The original St. Philip's Episcopal Church, Newark. Artist's rendering by Kyra N. Pruszinski, based on archival photography courtesy of the Diocese of Newark.

Doane's convention address shows an awareness of 1) White privilege, and 2) the need for reparations for slavery to repair the presently felt negative effects of the sins of previous generations. As such, it is clear that these concerns are not modern inventions. The Episcopal Bishop of New Jersey recognized these issues over 170 years ago and insisted that their ongoing presence required remediation. In subsequent convention addresses he implored his White Episcopalian brethren to support St. Philip's financially.[2]

2. See Doane, *Diocese of New Jersey: The Episcopal Address, The Twenty-Third, to the Seventy Second Annual Convention*, 26; Doane, *Diocese of New Jersey: The Episcopal Address, The Twenty-Fourth, to the Seventy Third Annual Convention*, 17–18; Diocese of New Jersey, *Journal of Proceedings of the Seventy-Fifth Annual Convention*, 22.

Part II: Historical Documents

Modern acknowledgments of White privilege and the need for reparations, though at times deploying different language, align closely in structure and content with Bishop Doane's statement. The dramatic discrepancies in household wealth between White and Black households that persist to this day[3] suggest that the conditions that once drew Doane's pastoral concern have not yet been repaired, and still require redress.

Bishop Scarborough's Convention Address of 1890: An Admission of Diocesan Racism and Neglect

In his diocesan convention address of 1890, Bishop John Scarborough openly discussed the place of African Americans in the ministry of the diocese. This was the first such public statement at a convention of the Diocese of New Jersey. Bishop Doane had at times mentioned St. Philip's, Newark when it had been part of the diocese, and had spoken of the debt owed to that congregation by the rest of the diocese.[4] He had also invited support for the Episcopal mission to Liberia.[5] However, no bishop had previously mused in such a setting on the general state of ministry to Black people in the diocese, nor had any articulated a mandate or strategy for their incorporation into Episcopal life generally. This development constituted a significant step for an almost entirely White diocese, and the details of Scarborough's statement indicate both the difficulties confronting Black Episcopal life in the diocese at that time, and the approach that would be taken in subsequent decades. He wrote:

> Hitherto there has been little effort made on the part of our Church in this Diocese to reach the colored population, resident in and near its large cities. Formerly there was a feeble mission at Macedonia, near Eatontown, but it gradually died out, and the chapel is now used as a school-house. For some time past the Rev. Mr. Townsend, of St. John's, Camden, has had a most prosperous mission in that city, where the colored people are very numerous. It is named after the great Bishop of Hippo, St. Augustine, and

---

3. In 2019 the average White household in the US was approximately 700 percent wealthier ($983,400) than the average Black household ($142,500). See Bhutta et al., "Disparities in Wealth by Race and Ethnicity in the 2019 Survey of Consumer Finances."

4. Doane, *Diocese of New Jersey: The Episcopal Address, to the Seventy-First Annual Convention*, 14.

5. Doane, *Episcopal Address Delivered at the Convention of the Protestant Episcopal Church, in the State of New-Jersey; May 28, 1834*, 33.

its rapid growth has been both a revelation and a surprise to me. During the past year I confirmed forty-two in that modest chapel, and I venture to say the service was as reverent and hearty as any in the Diocese. If the work continues to grow and prosper, as it bids fair to do, I can see new responsibilities in it for the city and the Diocese. Why should we leave the colored people to the care of other Christian bodies? Liturgic worship and a well-ordered ritual are just suited to their temperament. And why should we send our money to the South to build churches and chapels when we have the same work at our own doors, and are leaving it undone? Clearly this work will soon outgrow the ability of a struggling parish to carry it on, and the question will force itself upon us: What are we going to do with that long list of communicants who have cast in their lot with us? We dare not leave them unshepherded, and we will not drive them into schism by cold neglect! We can solve the race problem very glibly for South Carolina and Georgia. Can we solve it for New Jersey? It may be said that in the Church of Christ there should be no distinction of race or color; that all should meet together and be one in the assembly of God's people, as well as one in hope and doctrine. But those most competent to judge are agreed that a separate place of worship is best for all interests. The colored folk will not attend where they are, perhaps, not made welcome, or feel themselves to be intruders. They prefer to worship by themselves, separate and apart from their white brethren. It may be that God is opening up for us here a new field for our missionary energy, to quicken and excite our enthusiasm. I dare say other cities might follow the example of Camden and organize missions for this neglected class—neglected certainly in our ministrations. They will be quick to respond to any effort, and will gladly take the hand out-stretched.[6]

From his statement we can learn a number of things about the state of affairs regarding Black ministry in the diocese at that time.

Perhaps most obviously, he admits to the presence of racism in the diocese, suggesting that White Episcopalians do not welcome Black Christians into their churches. He states that this has resulted in broad "neglect" of African Americans in the efforts of the churches of the diocese, and that Black Christians have been "left" to the care of other denominations. He even highlights the common preference among White Episcopalians for giving what limited attention and resources can be mustered for solving

6. The Protestant Episcopal Church in the Diocese of New Jersey, *Journal of the Proceedings of the One Hundred and Eighteenth Convention*, 168–69.

race-related issues to addressing such problems elsewhere (e.g., the American South)[7] rather than in their own communities.

Scarborough mentions some of the small attempts at ministry to African Americans in the diocese, though the "feeble"[8] ministry to the inhabitants of the Black settlement at Macedonia (in Tinton Falls) and the atypical outreach by Rev. Townsend to African Americans in Camden serve to prove the case of overall neglect rather than contradict it. These efforts also show the pattern of ministry to African Americans that was developing in the diocese: rather than produce integrated congregations, the predominant model (which had already begun to develop while slavery was fully legal) was one of segregated ministry.[9]

Though acknowledging ingrained White racism in his churches, Bishop Scarborough did not openly denounce it, and his blanket assumptions about all African Americans appear to indicate that he too may have held certain prejudicial views.[10] Nevertheless, he insisted that the Episcopal Church in New Jersey no longer neglect ministry to Black Christians, and he articulated what he saw to be a feasible path forward in spite of the obstacles presented by racist White congregations: increased diocesan support for dedicated Black missions, churches, and ministries. This model of segregated Black congregations would become the dominant mode of growth among Black congregants through the subsequent decades.[11] Dioc-

---

7. Priests at this time are thinking, in particular, of the debates in South Carolina and Georgia dioceses over whether to admit Black congregations with full rights. See Reimers, "Negro Bishops and Diocesan Segregation in the Protestant Episcopal Church," 232.

8. Then shuttered. Scarborough downplays the significance of the Macedonia ministry, but it was there that the first Black man approved as a candidate for Holy Orders in the Diocese of New Jersey, John N. Still, served faithfully during the period of over eight years (1857–1864), during which time his candidacy was never advanced. The ministry and associated school had over one hundred participants for well over a decade. See Pruszinski, "Episcopal Mission at the Free Black Settlement of Macedonia."

9. This was the default model throughout much of the Episcopal Church through at least 1955. See Lewis, "Racial Concerns in the Episcopal Church Since 1973," 468.

10. As perhaps indicated by his universal statements about Black people's "temperament" or that they are "quick to respond to any effort." This latter comment expresses a particularly untethered sentiment given the generally acknowledged aversion many Black Americans have had to the Episcopal Church in light of its "failure to take any definitive action" during the Civil War or Reconstruction, which "spelt disaster for its already unenthusiastic mission among Black Americans." On this issue see, for example, Bennett, "Black Episcopalians," 238–39.

11. At the time of its publication in 1922, George F. Bragg's *History of the African-American Group of the Episcopal Church* (here, 215), listed seven Black congregations in

esan support for segregated Black Episcopal churches also opened the door to the affirmation of ordained Black clergy in the diocese, begun in the ordination of the Rev. Eugene L. Henderson at St. Paul's Episcopal Church, Camden, in 1897,[12] and begun in earnest through the invitation in 1903 by Bishop Scarborough to the Rev. August Jensen to minister in the segregated mission at St. Augustine's, Asbury Park, but continued by many others thereafter.[13]

---

the Diocese of New Jersey, ministering to 768 communicants.

12. Rev. Henderson served only briefly in the diocese at St. Augustine's, Camden.

13. Pruszinski, "Rev. Eugene L. Henderson."

PART III

Vignettes and Afterlives

11

Congregational Histories

A FEW CONGREGATIONS IN the Episcopal Diocese of New Jersey have begun to research their history with respect to slavery and racism. One of the early public actions of the Reparations Commission was to bring together a few of these congregations to publicize this history in a Lenten service of repentance. The first Stations of Reparations Service,[1] held at St. Peter's Episcopal Church in Freehold, New Jersey in March of 2023, followed a structure derived from a traditional "Stations of the Cross" service, but rather than a story from the passion of Jesus, each station involved the testimony of a congregation. Summaries of the contributions from four of the churches are included here, with robust historical annotations.[2] The service has since been replicated in other settings with different participants and contributors.[3] In addition to the brief histories based on those shared at the

1. See St. Peter's Church, Freehold, "Stations of Reparations—History in Story, Song, and Prayer."

2. Christ Church Shrewsbury's contribution is not included here, as it was not a narrative, but rather a reading of the parish register records of baptisms of the enslaved. They have committed more resources over a longer period of time, and done more to publish the findings of their research, than any other congregation. See Kelley, "Slavery Evidenced in the Parish Register."

3. It formed the basis for the Province II Lenten service of repentance for slavery from February 2024 (see Episcopal Diocese of New Jersey, "Province II Slave Trade Lament and Repentance") and a Stations of Reparations service at St. Augustine's Episcopal Church, Asbury Park in March 2024 (see Rodriguez, "Stations of Reparations Service at St. Augustine's Episcopal Church, Asbury Park on 3/16/2024").

2023 Stations service, this chapter includes one further history, one which scholars consider perhaps the most appalling episode from the period of gradual abolition in New Jersey: the operation from 1817 to 1818 of the Van Wickle slave ring. These vignettes are neither exhaustive treatments of the history of these congregations, nor do they directly treat the vast majority of congregations in New Jersey at this time. However, they do present a representation of slavery in the Anglican and Episcopal Churches of New Jersey before the Civil War.

St. Peter's Church, Freehold[4]

When the Rev. Dirk Reinken first came to St. Peter's Church, he met a parishioner who was a person of color whose last name was the same as one of the local streets. He asked her if the street was named for her family. She was standing with a friend, and, with a wry smile her friend looked at him and said, "Well . . . their people owned our people." It was in this way that Rev. Reinken learned that there were many stories in the history of his church that the White Episcopalians there either did not know about or, at least, had not been telling.

When he arrived he had been pleased to find that the parish's founding priest, the Rev. George Keith, before he had become an Anglican, wrote that Christians should not be owners of slaves.[5] However, Keith, especially as an Anglican, remained very close to many people who did in fact practice slavery.[6] St. Peter's itself received both its land in Topanemus, the original location of the church, and its first building from Thomas Boels,[7] a wealthy local landowner, slave owner,[8] and close friend of the Rev. Mr.

---

4. What follows is a summary of the transcript of the address delivered by Rev. Dirk Reinken, March 25, 2023 at the first Stations of Reparations Service, St. Peter's Church, Freehold. For the annotated transcript see Reinken and Pruszinski, "A History of Slavery at St. Peter's Church, Freehold."

5. See Keith, *An exhortation & caution to Friends, concerning buying or keeping of Negroes*.

6. For instance, his relationships with Thomas Boels, Alexander Innes, and John Talbot.

7. See Burr, *Anglican Church in New Jersey*, 498.

8. Among the records showing this is the "Inventory of the personal estate" accompanying his will (recorded as "Boell, Thomas, of Freehold, Monmouth Co."), which included multiple "nigrose" [sic], as reproduced in "Documents Relating to the Colonial History of the State of New Jersey."

Keith. The church still owns the Topanemus property to this day, and there are many further stories of its early history remaining to be told.

In a history[9] of the congregation, written by a beloved rector from the 1960s, there are stories recounted of the Rev. Thomas Thompson, who had served at St. Peter's and the surrounding churches from 1745–1750. That history describes in glowing terms how hard Thompson worked to catechize and convert the enslaved. However, it appears that the book simply reproduced Thompson's own viewpoint on his work from his biographical accounts of his missionary voyages,[10] without questioning his retelling. This is hardly unbiased history.

After his time in New Jersey, Thompson was one of the first Anglican missionaries to Africa, and was funded, as was the Rev. Keith, by the practice of slavery.[11] Rev. Thompson, during his time in modern-day Ghana, actually served as the chaplain to the English company that ran the slave-trading enterprise. He wrote a tract defending the practice of slavery as necessary for British prosperity.[12] For him, it appears, Africans were a commodity to be used. And lest we believe that he couldn't have known better, we know for certain that other Christian writers of his time criticized Thompson's position.[13] Even as there were those like Thompson who defended slavery for economic reasons, there were also some who opposed it as inconsistent with the gospel.

---

9. Garlick, *History of St. Peter's Church, Freehold*.

10. Thompson, *Account of Two Missionary Voyages*.

11. Their sending agency, the SPG, was funded through profits derived, not only from private donations of slavery-derived wealth, but from directly owning and operating the Codrington Plantation in Barbados, on which hundreds of Africans were enslaved.

12. Reproduced in full in chapter 9, it is entitled "The African Trade for Negro Slaves, Shewn to be Consistent with Principles of Humanity, and with the Law of Revealed Religion." He dedicated the work "to the worshipful committee of the company of merchants trading to Africa: in particular, to his much esteemed friend, William Devaines, Esq.; one of the committee," from "their obedient humble servant, Tho[mas] Thompson." Among other assertions, he states regarding: "Whether slaves be proper subjects of trade. In denial hereof it is [alleged], that the setting to sale human creatures is violating the natural distinction of the species, and levelling men with beasts. But to this it may be answered, that every person is treated as a human being, who is treated according to his lawful state and condition. The buying a slave is taking him as what he is; and the sale does but signify, that his owner is willing to part with, and another has a mind to have him. Here then is no violation of humanity; and the property in such individual is transferable, like all other property."

13. Such as Sharp, *Just limitation of slavery in the laws of God*.

Part III: Vignettes and Afterlives

Other early priests associated with St. Peter's were the Rev. Samuel Cooke, and the Rev. Mr. Alexander Innes, both of whom practiced slavery. It is likely that St. Peter's property at its current location was donated by enslavers. Moreover, what can be seen from many early New Jersey wills is that a great many landowners in Freehold owned slaves, and many of these landowners were part of the St. Peter's community. At least two of the petitioners for St. Peter's royal charter in 1736 were enslavers: the Throckmortons, who are memorialized in a stained glass window in the church, enslaved no fewer that seven individuals,[14] and William Nichols, the sheriff of Monmouth county, regularly apprehended individuals he believed to be escaped slaves, and published accounts[15] of their arrest and imprisonment in the attempt to return them to their enslavers.

As we know, New Jersey was the last state in the north to end the practice of slavery, and we have no reason to assume that St. Peter's, Freehold was in any way different from the prevailing culture of the day, or its fellow Anglican and Episcopal Churches.

> But what we can take great hope from is that we are not the people who came before us and that we are living into a future that God is seeking to build. We have begun a journey, but we are still at its beginning and there are still many stories left to uncover. As for me I take to heart the words attributed to our patron St. Peter: "be living stones built on the foundation of Jesus Christ." And we pledge to be those living stones for the future that God is building.[16]

Christ Church, New Brunswick[17]

There have been several prominent and influential leaders at Christ Church, New Brunswick who have enslaved Black people. Among them are Philip French, the layman who gave the church its first property (a

---

14. Specifically here, the will of Job Throckmorton (1714–1748), recorded in "Book E of Wills, p. 307, Trenton, N. J. Will of Job Throckmorton (Colts Neck), made 23 April, 1748."

15. Such as one published in *The Pennsylvania Gazette* on July 4, 1729 (republished in Marrin, ed., *Runaways of Colonial New Jersey*, 268).

16. This final quotation presents the exact words of Rev. Reinken.

17. Based on the transcript of the reading delivered by Jonathan Gloster, vestry member of Christ Church, New Brunswick on March 25, 2023 at the "Stations of Reparations" service at St. Peter's Church, Freehold, New Jersey. See Pruszinski, "History of Slavery at Christ Church, New Brunswick."

two-thousand-year lease at the rent of "one peppercorn [per year] only if demanded")[18] on which the first building was erected (in 1742) and the current nave still stands.[19] He published a runaway notice in the local newspaper seeking the return of "Claus" in 1741,[20] and on at least one occasion brought one of the Black people he enslaved (in 1767, "Toney") to the Rev. Beach for baptism.[21]

The Rev. Samuel Seabury, who served from 1754 to 1757, and was later the first bishop of the Episcopal church, became an active enslaver during his time as the priest of Christ Church.[22] Seabury continued to accumulate more enslaved persons through his career. The Rev. McKean[23] and the Rev. Leonard Cutting[24] both enslaved or facilitated the enslavement of Black people. The Rev. Abraham Beach served as rector of Christ Church New Brunswick from 1767–1784, during which time he countenanced the practice of owning slaves among his parishioners. He himself enslaved Black people on his estate and only freed them in his old age when his retirement annuities from his church work fully covered his expenses.

This practice among the clergy of building wealth through the enslavement of Black people and then freeing them only when most convenient was also practiced by Bishop Croes, the first bishop of the diocese. He served as the rector of Christ Church, New Brunswick starting in 1801 and served through his episcopate, until 1832. He is recorded as having practiced manumission immediately before he became legally liable for the care of his enslaved Black people in their old age.[25] This kind of practice not only harmed those Black people manumitted under these conditions, but

---

18. Burr, *Anglican Church in New Jersey*, 546.

19. Burr, *Anglican Church in New Jersey*, 546.

20. "Run Away on the 23rd of August Past from Philip French," *American Weekly Mercury* (Philadelphia), August 27, 1741, reprinted in Hodges and Brown, eds., "*Pretends to Be Free*," 17. See also Fuentes and White, eds., *Scarlet and Black*, 1:181n32.

21. McKean and Beach, "Some Early Records for Christ Church, New Brunswick," 8. See also Fuentes and White, eds., *Scarlet and Black*, 1:181n33.

22. This occurred through a dowry gift upon his marriage to Mary Hicks in 1756, though Seabury's father had also been an enslaver.

23. McKean served Christ Church from 1757 to 1763, married the granddaughter of Gov. Lewis Morris (who accumulated vast wealth through slavery), and as such came into ownership of a plantation on the Raritan.

24. Early in his career, Cutting ran plantations for wealthy enslavers. He later served Christ Church from 1764 to 1766.

25. Bayker, Blakley, and Boyd, "His Name Was Will," 80.

Part III: Vignettes and Afterlives

often required support of those manumitted through almshouses due to the commonly destitute state of the newly manumitted.[26]

The oldest person now interred in the Christ Church graveyard is

> "Dinah" (there is no surname, just Dinah). The records indicate that she was born sometime around 1760, and was the property of James Dore. He came to New Brunswick via Novia Scotia and has family members buried here. Dinah died in 1866, in service in the Boggs household, whose family members are also buried in the graveyard of Christ Church. This makes her 106 years old at the time of her death . . . Her life spanned [from before] the Revolution to the Emancipation Proclamation. Born enslaved, died free.[27]

> The legacy of colonial times continued for Black [people] at Christ Church well into the twentieth century. Black [Christians] were members of the church but they were not seated with Whites. In the 19th and 20th century Black [people] were seated in the gallery, along with those who could not afford pew rents. When pew rents were abolished in the early 1920s the decision was made to relocate the organ from the chancel to the gallery displacing the Black members of the church. Taking that as an indication that they were not particularly welcome, the displaced African-American members formed their own parish, St. Alban's Episcopal Church in New Brunswick, a prominently Afro-Anglican mission parish. Today Christ Church is a multi-cultural, multi-racial congregation with a significant African-American membership, with many immigrants from Africa and the Caribbean. In 2013 the parish called its first African American priest, the Rev. Joanna Hollis.[28]

Hollis remarked:

> And so here I am, the rector of a parish with a long history of slavery. Every Sunday I stand in the chancel and look down at the cross that marks that Bishop Croes is buried underneath my feet. I walk back to the church and read the list of rectors knowing the history of those whose names are written above mine. When I look at the pictures and the sketches of all the former rectors, I notice

---

26. Hodges (*Black New Jersey*, 59) describes an example of this phenomenon in the 1820s in Cape May County.

27. Text furnished by Rev. Joanna Hollis of Christ Church, New Brunswick, from the planned virtual graveyard tour of Christ Church graveyard.

28. Quotation of Jonathan Gloster from the 2023 Stations of Reparations Service, quoted from Pruszinski, "History of Slavery at Christ Church, New Brunswick."

that while I am not the first woman rector of Christ Church, one thing is not like the other. I do not take lightly the significance of my presence as the first Black rector of Christ Church. And I know that for some of our little ones, I am who they are growing up with as their priest. I am their normal. And yet I link the far past to the present by virtue of my own enslaved ancestors and pray that I am doing them proud. And I pray that I am doing right by Dinah and by the many enslaved people who were connected with Christ church. I quite literally am their wildest dream. Yet there is still so much more work to do; so much to atone for. And with God's help we can do what needs to be done.[29]

Trinity Church, Princeton[30]

During the colonial era, the Princeton preaching station,[31] which laid some of the groundwork for the later founding of Trinity Church, Princeton, included such devoted loyalist Anglicans as Absalom Bainbridge and Richard Cochran, both of whom kept several Black people enslaved on their nearby plantations.[32] During the Revolution, a Black man enslaved by Bainbridge named "Prime" was confiscated by the revolutionary government and forced to serve in the continental army. He did not escape threats to his legal freedom until, finally, the New Jersey legislature intervened through a postwar legislative act to clarify his legal status.[33]

Trinity was later established in 1833 in large part through the initiative and donations of the Stockton and Potter families, who remained the parish's most influential members through the Civil War.[34] Both families enslaved people on their family estates in the Princeton area, as well as

---

29. Concluding remarks by the Rev. Joanna Hollis, Rector, Christ Church, New Brunswick from the 2023 Stations of Reparations Service, quoted from Pruszinski, "History of Slavery at Christ Church, New Brunswick."

30. Text for this entry by Kyra N. Pruszinski. First delivered at March 25, 2023, Stations of Reparations Service, St. Peter's Church, Freehold; based on her research at Trinity Church, Princeton in cooperation with Abigail Edwards and Jolyon G. R. Pruszinski.

31. It was visited and supported by priests assigned to St. Michael's Church in Trenton.

32. Gigantino II, *Ragged Road to Abolition*, 31–33, 60.

33. Gigantino II, *Ragged Road to Abolition*, 32.

34. See Stockton and Thomson, "Subscription Book of 1827 to Build a Protestant Episcopal Church in the Borough of Princeton," August 16, 1827. See also, The Rector, Wardens and Vestrymen of Trinity Church in the Borough of Princeton, "Certificate of Incorporation," May 17, 1833.

on their plantations in the state of Georgia. Senator Robert Field Stockton continued his family's practice of enslaving people at their Morven estate in New Jersey until at least 1829, and possibly until 1839. He also owned a sugar plantation in Brunswick, Georgia on which at least 108 Black people were enslaved in 1830. His father-in-law, John Potter, and Potter's sons James and Thomas Fuller, owned and managed the Coleraine Tweedside plantation in Georgia, where at least 423 people were enslaved.[35] The Stockton and Potter families profited directly from the exploitation of enslaved Black people, and donated large sums of that money to sustain Trinity Church. They controlled the affairs of the church, including the hiring of priests, through the end of the Civil War.[36] Potter was extremely influential in the diocese as well. A personal friend of Bishop Doane, he served on various diocesan committees and regularly represented the diocese as a lay delegate at the (national) general convention of the Episcopal Church throughout the 1830s and 1840s.

In addition to enslaving people, both Robert Stockton and John Potter supported the work of the American Colonization Society. The society was an ostensibly anti-slavery organization, but promoted principles of White supremacy, race essentialism, and segregation, seeking to send freed Black people to Africa. Stockton and Potter spearheaded the establishment of the New Jersey chapter of the society in 1824,[37] and Robert Stockton led the American military campaign to subdue native Africans and conquer African lands for the ACS colonial project that would become the nation of Liberia.

Trinity's first five priests, handpicked by the Stocktons and Potters, were also implicated in the institution of slavery. The first rector, Reverend George Emlen Hare,[38] inherited money from slavery[39] and kept Black ser-

---

35. These facts are represented in the US Census data. See the compilation in Edwards, "Trinity's Founding Fathers."

36. "If ever there was a 'family church,' it was Trinity during the more than three decades of active Stockton-Potter dominance from 1833 into the 1860s." Burt, "First Rectors," 12.

37. Society of the American Colonization Society in New Jersey, "Proceedings of a Meeting Held at Princeton, New Jersey, July 14, 1824 to Form a Society in the State of New Jersey to Cooperate with the American Colonization Society."

38. He served from 1834–1843.

39. He was a scion of some of the oldest Philadelphia families, including the Willings and the Emlens, who derived significant wealth from slavery. See, for example, regarding Thomas Willing's participation in the slave trade, Wax, "Africans on the Delaware"; see also Laskowski, "Updated."

vants.[40] His successor, Rev. Andrew Bell Paterson,[41] was from an influential family of enslavers[42] and oversaw the founding of a segregated school for Black children at Trinity.[43] This school was created to ensure Black children would have White teachers and to keep Black students out of the Princeton public school run by Betsey Stockton, a free Black woman formerly enslaved by the Stockton family.[44]

The third rector, Rev. Joshua Peterkin,[45] enslaved Black people himself[46] and continued oversight of the segregated Trinity school.

The fourth rector, Rev. William Hanson,[47] was Peterkin's brother-in-law, and did not appear to disrupt these patterns of relations at the church.[48] Trinity's fifth rector, Rev. William Armstrong Dod, who served through the end of the Civil War,[49] was Robert Stockton's son-in-law and brother to the high-profile enslaver and slavery apologist Albert Baldwin Dod.[50] Records suggest that Rev. Dod did not publicly disagree with his brother's beliefs until the 1870s,[51] that is, well after his brother's, and Stockton's, deaths, after he had retired, and after slavery had already been made illegal throughout the United States except as punishment for a crime.

Trinity and St. Philips Cathedral, Newark[52]

In 1733, following a lengthy period of heavy rain, the wealthy Col. Josiah Ogden, then a member of First Presbyterian Church of Newark, harvested his

40. As US Census records of Princeton during his tenure (1840) indicate. See US Bureau of the Census, *Population Schedules of the Sixth Census*, 35.

41. He served from 1844–1851.

42. The city of Paterson is named for his grandfather, one of New Jersey's first US senators who, though ostensibly opposed to slavery, enslaved multiple Black people during his lifetime, including while participating in the constitutional convention.

43. Burt, "First Rectors," 15.

44. See, among other accounts, Escher, *She Calls Herself Betsey Stockton*.

45. He served from 1852–1855.

46. See Klein, "From the Archives."

47. He served from 1855–1859.

48. Accounts of his rectorship call him "unobtrusive." See Burt, "First Rectors," 18.

49. He served from 1859–1866.

50. See Mack, "Albert Dod."

51. See Dod, *Paul of Tarsus*, 194 and following.

52. Based, in part, on material from the address delivered by Anne Calloway, historian, Diocese of Newark Racial History Committee, at the Stations of Reparations Service,

wheat on a Sunday in order to prevent its spoilage. He was met with censure for sabbath-breaking and left his church as a result, insisting, so the story goes, "I'll have a church to attend if I have to build one myself."[53] He provided the founding impetus and funds for Trinity Episcopal Church, Newark.

Ogden's wealth came from the operation of mines, including one in Boonton and another at Ringwood, which he jointly owned with various family members and business partners. He was certainly neither doing the mining nor harvesting his crops himself. On both his mines and his plantation he used slave labor. He also provided the laborers for the construction of Trinity, Newark, which almost certainly included enslaved labor.

One kind of evidence for how integral slavery was to the life of Trinity Church parishioners comes from its architectural plan. The balcony that was built on the second floor of Trinity Church, now known as Trinity and St. Philip's Cathedral,[54]

> was not built to house extra communicants, but was built for the slaves of the owners who owned the pews . . . they bought pews . . . they took care of those pews. And, of course, they had to buy the box that the slaves [sat in too] . . . So if you ever come to our church and look up at our balcony, you will see that it's like boxes in the theater. And each slave owner owned one of those boxes where his slaves sat. So the church welcomed the slaves and their families . . . But they condoned slavery.[55]

March 25, 2023, St. Peter's Church, Freehold. For an edited and annotated transcript see Calloway and Pruszinski, "History of Trinity and St. Philip's Cathedral."

53. Geisheimer, "Trinity Episcopal Church."

54. Now the Episcopal seat of the Diocese of Newark.

55. Anne Calloway, 2023 Stations of Reparations Service, quoted from Calloway and Pruszinski, "History of Trinity and St. Philip's Cathedral."

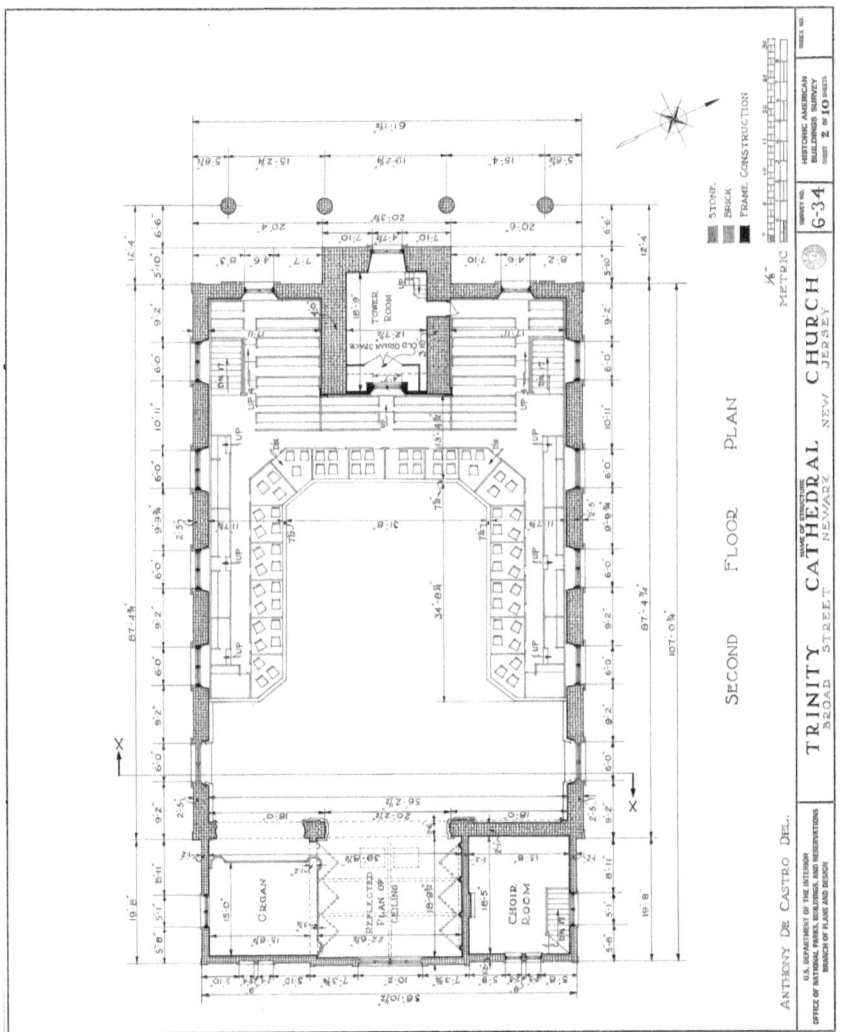

Slave galleries of Trinity Cathedral, Newark. Courtesy of the Historic American Buildings Survey.

This was a typical practice at the time in the Anglican and Episcopal churches of New Jersey. Slave ownership was common among wealthy Anglicans, priests were among those who owned slaves, and the enslaved were allowed in worship in many instances, but seating was segregated.

Part III: Vignettes and Afterlives

Trinity's key founder, Josiah Ogden, passed away prior to the Revolution and was buried in the "Old Burying-Ground,"[56] but this burial ground was not just used for White members of the church. The enslaved were buried there as well,[57] specifically, the Africans and African Americans enslaved by its parishioners. The burial practices on display in the graveyard provide further evidence of how inextricably intertwined Trinity Church's history has been with slavery. This deep linkage is further shown through Trinity's long relation to St. Philip's Church in Newark. Today they make one single congregation: Trinity and St. Philip's Cathedral, but in its early life St. Philip's was birthed out of Trinity.

> There were several slaves who were communicants of Trinity Church [Newark] . . . The names of the founders of St. Philip's Church, [the historically Black church formed by former congregants at Trinity, Newark] confirmed the British origin [of their former enslavers. Among the founders of St. Philip's were] Nicholas Duffin, Samuel Thompkins, John and Peter O'Fake, Elias Ray, and George Mitchell . . . [St. Philip's . . . became a mission in 1847, and] Trinity Church made the difference for St. Philip's. Trinity Church . . . was a very rich church . . . [that] supported any missions that they opened, and quite a few of the missions, [which became] churches in the Diocese of Newark, were founded through Trinity Church . . . And so, when St. Philip's became a parish, of course, Trinity said, "you're on your own now. Move it, we've somebody else we've got to help." And so that is how Trinity [both] became . . .[58]

---

56. Geisheimer, "Trinity Episcopal Church."

57. Anne Calloway stated that it was located "behind 24 Rector Street, which was [where] the Cathedral house . . . was built, and it was covered over and became the parking lot. So once we sold the building to the New Jersey Performing Arts Center we had to go and exhume all the bodies. And Jim Churchman—maybe some of you . . . know the Churchman family who [were] the first Black undertaker family . . . in the city of Newark—[Jim Churchman] took it upon himself to get all the paperwork that was necessary . . . [to] dig up all of those graves, all of those bodies. Some are in columbaria behind the Cathedral and some are buried in Fairmont Cemetery in Newark, and that is where Josiah Ogden is now, in Newark in the Fairmont Cemetery." See also Geisheimer, "Trinity Episcopal Church."

58. Anne Calloway, 2023 Stations of Reparations Service, quoted from Calloway and Pruszinski, "History of Trinity and St. Philip's Cathedral." That Trinity did not do as much for St. Philip's as it could have as often as it could have can be seen from the financial plea from Bishop Doane in his convention address of 1854 (see chapter 10 of this book).

critical for the formation of St. Philip's, but at the same time, did not perhaps provide quite as much support as it might have.

The first priest officiating regularly at St. Philip's was the Reverend James H. Tyng, who was at that time also the headmaster of Newark Academy. And, according to historian Anne Calloway, the local St. Philip's church tradition holds that Mr. Tyng was a Black man,[59] though diocesan records indicate that he was a White priest who was part of the early paternalistic diocesan oversight of St. Philip's.

Trinity's first royal charter was granted in 1746, though the first building had already been finished in 1743. This first church burned down in 1804, and was rebuilt in 1810 on a parcel of land on Broad Street. It became part of the Diocese of Newark when New Jersey was split into two dioceses in 1874, and it was made the cathedral in 1942. Then in 1966, due in part to its dwindling financial base as a result of White flight, and in a turn of some historical irony, it merged with St. Philip's, creating the congregation known since 1992 as "Trinity and St. Philip's Cathedral."[60]

> There is so much history . . . I find it with the New Jersey Historical Society . . . I have gone into other churches and found Trinity's history. It is very sweet. I call her God's house because it was built by the hands of his people. Because it has been destroyed and it's still coming back up. It has been empty and it still lives.[61]

---

59. Unfortunately Rev. Tyng was not in fact a Black man. There is no record of Rev. James H. Tyng in the scholarship on early Black Episcopal clergy, and he served as the founding rector for several White congregations both in New Jersey and elsewhere at a time when a Black man holding that position was effectively unheard of. He was in fact the brother of the comparatively better-known Dr. Stephen H. Tyng. For a portrait of Dr. Stephen H. Tyng, see Barratt, *Outline of the History of Old St. Paul's Church Philadelphia, Pennsylvania*, 135. The Rev. James Tyng was part of the early paternalistic oversight of St. Philip's, Newark from the Diocese of New Jersey. Bishop Doane's convention address of 1848 refers to his "disinterested zeal" in gathering the congregation, likely a reference to his ministry there being to those not of his own race. See Doane, *Diocese of New Jersey: The Episcopal Address to the Sixty-Fifth Annual Convention*, 10.

60. Geisheimer, "Trinity Episcopal Church."

61. Anne Calloway, 2023 Stations of Reparations Service, quoted from Calloway and Pruszinski, "History of Trinity and St. Philip's Cathedral."

Part III: Vignettes and Afterlives

Judge Jacob Van Wickle, His "Slave Ring," and St. Peter's, Spotswood

James Gigantino, in his recent book[62] about the gradual abolition era in New Jersey,[63] describes one enslaver's actions as especially heinous: Middlesex County Judge Jacob Van Wickle, who used his standing as a judge to facilitate an illegal kidnapping and slave-trading ring for his own family's profit.[64] A number of scholars[65] and public history projects[66] have lately documented many aspects of his actions.

One largely neglected part of this story, however, is that Van Wickle acted as he did while serving as a committed and influential leader at St. Peter's Episcopal Church in Spotswood, New Jersey. Neither he, nor his immediate church community, saw anything wrong with what he was doing from the standpoint of Episcopal faith practice at the time. He was never removed from church leadership and there is no record of any church censure for his actions. In fact, other leaders from his church helped to cover up his actions. What he did is not only appalling in retrospect, but the public outcry at the time shows that many, at least outside of his church, considered it a sensational transgression even then.

62. Gigantino II, *Ragged Road to Abolition*.

63. That is, the period in New Jersey after the passing of the 1804 bill which "gradually" abolished slavery (children born into slavery after the passing of the bill had to serve as a slave twenty-one years if female or twenty-five years if male before the law required that they be freed) and 1865 when the ratification by the states of the Thirteenth Amendment made slavery illegal except as punishment for a crime throughout the United States. See chapter 5 of this book.

64. Also known as "Van Wicklen," "Van Winkle," "Van Sickle," etc.

65. Some excellent documentation of primary sources related to Van Wickle and the slave ring are available through the Rutgers University Scarlet and Black Research Center, which hosts New Jersey slavery records. See the New Jersey Slavery Records entry hosted by Rutgers University: "Jacob Van Wickle (1770–854)." See also Pingeon, "An Abominable Business"; Gigantino II, "Trading in Jersey Souls"; Schermerhorn, *Business of Slavery and the Rise of American Capitalism*, 69–80; Hodges, *Black New Jersey*, 79; and Gigantino II, *Ragged Road to Abolition*, 157–60.

66. See the presentation from the Lost Souls Memorial Project, Langford, "Inside the Van Wickle's Slave Ring," the material published by the East Brunswick Historical Society, "Van Wickle and Morgan Slave Ring Leaders East Brunswick, NJ (1818)," "The 1619 Project" article by Bailey, "They Sold Human Beings Here," the Rutgers University Scarlet and Black Research Center article "Removal to Louisiana: The Van Wickle Slave Ring," Fitzpatrick, "New Jersey State Archives Van Wickle Slave Ring Free Digital Collection," and the State of New Jersey, "Documents at the New Jersey State Archives relating to the Van Wickle Slave Ring."

In 1795 Van Wickle married Sarah Morgan and thereafter became inextricably connected with Morgan family financial concerns related to plantation ownership in Pointe Coupee Parish, Louisiana. His professional life of many decades was spent as a judge in Middlesex County, New Jersey.

During this time, the New Jersey legislature passed its gradual abolition legislation in 1804, limiting the number of years enslaved persons born after that date could remain enslaved to at most twenty-one years for women and twenty-five years for men.[67] Soon after, in 1808, federal law ended the legal importation of enslaved persons to the United States.[68] One effect of this change was to increase the volume of domestic (interstate) slave trading, since no additional enslaved persons could be brought into the US. This limitation on supply, combined with the increase in interstate slave trading, created a problem for enslaved persons in New Jersey. They were now in the very great danger of being sold or moved to states that had no gradual abolition law and where their promise of ultimate emancipation would not be upheld. The New Jersey legislature responded to this issue by passing further legislation in 1812 preventing the sale of out-of-state of enslaved persons without their express consent.[69] This legislation, combined with the gradual abolition law, depressed the sale value of the enslaved in New Jersey markets since their enslavement was legally temporary and they were not easily transferable to other markets. Meanwhile, the federal ban on importation had dramatically increased the value of already enslaved persons in the South. Van Wickle and his family saw this valuation discrepancy between the local slave markets as an opportunity for massive profit through arbitrage.

---

67. "Act for the Gradual Abolition of Slavery," February 15, 1804, Acts 28th G.A. 2nd sitting.

68. See "Act to prohibit the importation of Slaves into any port or place within the jurisdiction of the United States, from and after the first day of January, in the year of our Lord one thousand eight hundred and eight," passed March 2, 1807.

69. "Act supplemental to the act entitled 'An act respecting slaves.'"

Part III: Vignettes and Afterlives

Jacob Van Wickle. Artist's rendering by Kyra N. Pruszinski based on "Jacob Van Wickle" by George H. Durrie (1841) reproduced in Bruns, *Louisiana Portraits*, 292.

The consent required by law in New Jersey to transfer an enslaved person out-of-state had to be verified by a judge of the county Court of Common Pleas. In Middlesex County, that was Van Wickle. His family members and co-conspirators canvassed their contacts, including many politically connected individuals in the state, soliciting the sale of enslaved Black people. When they wanted to acquire more, they engaged their henchmen in kidnapping, deceitful recruiting through promises of paid labor, and by the purchase of imprisoned free Black people being held by local jails for being apprehended without papers. They kept the entrapped at the Van Wickle compound in South River, which was described by one visitor as "like a garrison."[70] Then Van Wickle would use the authority of his office to forge papers of acquiescence to allow the export of these enslaved Black people, under color of law, to the Morgan family plantations in Louisiana. He even claimed that the cries of infants constituted consent.[71]

70. As reported in the *Philadelphia Franklin Gazette*, May 22, 1818.
71. Gigantino II, *Ragged Road to Abolition*, 158.

Van Wickle was never indicted, even though some of his indicted co-conspirators were found guilty after public outcry came to a head in 1818.[72] However, the sentences these co-conspirators received were exceedingly mild. Citizen petitions and legislative action[73] put an end to the operation of the ring, but not before at least 137 enslaved and free Black residents of New Jersey had been removed from the state against their will and pressed into a lifetime of slavery by Van Wickle and his cronies.[74]

Van Wickle's notoriety among slavery researchers is one thing. Less well known is the fact that he was a devoted and celebrated Episcopalian and an integral member of St. Peter's Episcopal Church in Spotswood, New Jersey for well over half a century, including the entire period of the operation of the "ring."

Van Wickle was baptized as an infant,[75] but it seems unlikely that this was a *pro forma* baptism since as a very young adult[76] he was already serving on the vestry of St. Peter's. This began coincident with his older brother Evert's service as church clerk in 1787.[77] Spotswood was very clearly their family church. Jacob's wife and children were later baptized at St. Peter's, and he and his family are listed first on the parish list of communicants in 1823.[78] Such pride of place on the list indicates that he was held in high regard in the church, even in the immediate aftermath of the slavery ring controversy. He served on the vestry periodically during his time at St. Peter's, but most

---

72. It is possible that this was due to his practice of attributing ownership of the enslaved Black people held on his property to his family members rather than to himself. It is also possible that he was not indicted simply because he was a sitting judge and such an indictment would have tarnished the reputation of the justice system generally. But he also turned on his fellow conspirators and testified against Charles Morgan and others in the ring in the trial, all the while publicly claiming that nothing illegal had been done. See Gigantino II, *Ragged Road to Abolition*, 160. Van Wickle's public letter to this effect was published in the New Brunswick *Freedonian* on August 13, 1818.

73. "Act to prohibit the exportation of slaves or people of color out of this State," November 4, 1818.

74. According to the documentation of The Lost Souls Memorial Project.

75. Beyond of course the record of his infant baptism on June 24, 1770 (less than two months after birth); see Reichner, "Nicasius de Sille Bible," 128.

76. Today he would be considered a minor (sixteen or seventeen) at the age when he began to serve on the vestry of St. Peter's. Grace, *History of St. Peter's*, 78.

77. He was the first clerk listed in the vestry minutes according to Grace, *History of St. Peter's*, 12. At the close of the eighteenth century, the church had also purchased a home from Evert to be used as the rectory; Grace, *History of St. Peter's*, 14.

78. According to Macy's notes on the parish register in Macy Jr., "Van Wicklen/Van Wickle Family."

consistently held the office of church warden, starting in 1810. He continued in this role without interruption to the time of his death in 1854.[79] In summary, he was a very central member of the church lay leadership well before the slave ring affair, during it, and long after it. Just before his death he gave a very large sum of money for the building of the second church building,[80] which is the building in use by St. Peter's today.

He, his wife, and many of his children are buried in the graveyard,[81] an exclusive honor typically allowed only to those who were highly regarded in the church and involved heavily in its financial support. The funeral entry made in the parish register at the time of his death, likely by the rector, reads: *per multos annos sacrorum ustor dem in aedem sacram*,[82] or "for the sake of many years of sacrifice I, the cremator, commit [van Wickle] to a holy tomb." This note may explain the rationale for interring his remains in the particularly honored burial place of the church graveyard.

The honor in which he was held, and the leadership he was allowed to exercise, were not a result of Van Wickle's actions in the ring being unknown to his church community. The court case was very high profile, being both initiated by printed newspaper allegations and covered extensively thereafter.[83] Moreover, Van Wickle's fellow church leaders actually helped him cover up his crimes. A former St. Peter's vestryman, Cornelius Johnson,[84] testified before a justice of the peace that he was "well acquainted with the house of Jacob Van Wickle" and the condition of the "colored people" there, claiming that he "never saw anything like a garrison or a guard, or cruel treatment, but the reverse, they all appeared to have their liberty and to

---

79. Grace, *History of St. Peter's*, 73.

80. Grace, *History of St. Peter's*, 20.

81. Macy Jr., "Van Wicklen/Van Wickle Family," 241–51.

82. According to the flawed transcription reported in Van Wicklin's "Family of Jacob Charles Van Wickle," the parish register entry reads *per nultos annos sacrorum oustordem in aedem sacram* but this cannot be entirely correct. It is unlikely that the priest knew enough Latin to make the note but mistakenly wrote "*nultos*" for what should clearly be "*multos*." The text "*oustordem*" may be a correct transcription but should probably be understood as *ustor dem* and could indicate a variant spelling used by the priest. *Aedem sacram* could also refer to the church columbarium, which would likely have been a temporary location for the holding of ashes before interring them in the graveyard.

83. Including in *The True American* (Trenton, NJ), the *Trenton Federalist* (Trenton, NJ), *The Fredonian* (New Brunswick, NJ), and *The Times and New-Brunswick General Advertiser* (New Brunswick, NJ).

84. Grace, *History of St. Peter's*, 75.

be well-satisfied."[85] His testimony, and that of five other men, was taken by Oliver Johnston,[86] who was a then- and long-serving vestryman at St. Peter's Episcopal Church.[87] Johnston submitted this testimony to the New Brunswick *Fredonian* for printing alongside Van Wickle's aforementioned public statement disavowing any illegal activity.

It is clear from the complicity of fellow church leaders in the cover-up, from his seamless participation in St. Peter's leadership before, during, and after the affair, and his election to the Standing Committee of the Diocese from 1822–1824[88] that Jacob Van Wickle's horrific actions against free and enslaved African Americans in New Jersey for the sake of his own family's profit were not widely considered untoward or unchristian in the Episcopal Church in New Jersey at the time.

---

85. *The Fredonian*, New Brunswick, NJ, August 13, 1818.
86. That is, the aforementioned Justice of the Peace.
87. Grace, *History of St. Peter's*, 76.
88. See *Journal of the Proceedings of the Thirty-Ninth Annual Convention of the Protestant Episcopal Church in the State of New Jersey, Held in Christ-Church, Shewsbury, on the 21st and 22nd Days of August, 1822*, 23; *Journal of the Proceedings of the Fortieth Annual Convention of the Protestant Episcopal Church in the State of New Jersey, Held in St. John's Church, Elizabethtown, on the 20th and 21st Days of August, 1823*, 16; *Journal of the Proceedings of the Forty-First Annual Convention of the Protestant Episcopal Church in the State of New Jersey, Held in St. Michael's Church, City of Trenton, on the 18th and 19th Days of August, 1824*, 22.

12

Black Believers in and out of the Episcopal Church in Antebellum New Jersey

As has been mentioned several times, Black Christians experienced what can only be described as, at best, a partial and halting welcome in the Anglican Church before the Revolutionary War, and in the Episcopal Church following the war. Their leadership was limited, their engagement was circumscribed, they were subject to abuse when enslaved, and often treated as a threat when free. This chapter portrays some aspects of these patterns in greater detail.

Sourland Region African Americans Who Left the Episcopal Church

In the aftermath of the American Revolution, many African Americans who had been involved to some degree with the Anglican (or after the war, Episcopal) Church moved away from the denomination in New Jersey, and elsewhere. There were many reasons for this, including ongoing Episcopal support for slavery, continued horrific treatment by White enslavers, segregation of even emancipated Black Christians in the church, and limited opportunities for Black leadership. These factors often were more important than the ostensible, but at best paternalistic, welcome and educational attention offered by the Episcopal Churches. Other denominations, such as Baptists and Methodists, often permitted greater freedoms of participation, and the various Black churches that were founded during the early Republic, such as the African Methodist Episcopal (AME) Church, afforded complete affirmation of Black religious leadership.

One documented example of free Black Christians choosing to leave the Episcopal Church comes from the Sourland Mountain region of New Jersey, as described by Elaine Buck and Beverly Mills, founders of the Stoutsburg Sourland African American Museum, in their recent *If These Stones Could Talk: African American Presence in the Hopewell Valley, Sourland Mountain, and Surrounding Regions of New Jersey*. They describe details of the religious affiliations of some of the earliest free Black landowners in the region, William Stives and Catherine Vanois.

Stives settled in the region as a free Black man following his decorated service in the Revolutionary War. Soon after, he married Catherine, who was likely previously enslaved by the Vanois family (also spelled Vannoy), who locally owned a great deal of agricultural land. The two were married November 15, 1789 by the Rev. William Frazer at St. Andrew's Episcopal Church in Ringoes, New Jersey.[1] Ten years later, William Stiver (another name Stives sometimes went by) was listed as a member of the Old School Baptist Church of Hopewell, New Jersey. He remained a faithful member there until his death in 1839,[2] but there is no record of the reason for his change in congregations. It is possible that Stives left St. Andrew's because of the death of Frazer in 1795, after which the congregation never again had a regular minister in that location.[3]

However, it is also possible that Stives's affiliation with the Old School Baptist Church predates his listing in the rolls and may have occurred for other reasons. The Rev. Joseph Vannoy was born in Hopewell in 1716 and went on to become a Baptist minister, indicating the Baptist leanings of the Vannoy family. Such family affiliation may have led William also to affiliate with the local Baptist church due to his wife's likely connections there.

---

1. Buck and Mills, *If These Stones Could Talk*, 58–60. See also Race and Frazer, "Rev. William Frazer's Three Parishes," 212–32. The church was sometimes known as St. Andrew's Church, Amwell, and has since moved to Lambertville, New Jersey.

2. See Buck and Mills, *If These Stones Could Talk*, 125–26. See also Gedney, ed., *Town Records of Hopewell, New Jersey*.

3. Burr, *Anglican Church in New Jersey*, 526–29.

Another possibility is that Stives chose to be married by the Rev. Frazer at St. Andrew's in order to ensure that his marriage to Catherine was fully and legally recognized by the courts, and by powerful White people in the area. Frazer served simultaneously at St. Michael's Episcopal Church in Trenton, and was politically connected in the state capital. Free Black people in the region at times used this kind of strategy as a way of protecting their often highly contingent legal rights.[4]

Whatever the reason, Stives left the Episcopal Church and remained a Baptist thereafter. The limited historical records of his church life provide an example of a very common change in religious affiliation at the time for African Americans in New Jersey, even if our suppositions about the reasons for the change can only be conjectural. For those seeking additional information, Elaine Buck and Beverly Mills's book is an excellent resource.

Emancipated African Americans Leaving the Episcopal Church: A Case Study from Middletown, New Jersey

Various historians have noted the attentions paid to enslaved Africans by the Anglican Church in colonial New Jersey.[5] In many ways the Anglican Church did more than most denominations in the colonial period to evangelize, baptize, and worship with enslaved Africans. However, this attention did not translate into widespread Black participation in the Episcopal Church once freedom had been gained. Key early Black Christian leaders in the region, like George White and John Jea, had exposure to Anglican worship and teaching, but chose to affiliate elsewhere.[6] The Methodist split resulted in many Black Christians with some Anglican background affiliating with the Methodists,

---

4. This kind of tactic may have been used by another local free Black man, Samson Adams, as seen in his will, preserved in the "Samson Adams Papers." In his will, which is dated to the same period and which implicates the same clergyman (as Frazer also served St. Michael's in Trenton), he left a modest amount of money to St. Michael's Episcopal Church in Trenton, while leaving the majority of his estate to his sister. It is likely the gift to St. Michael's would ensure that the politically connected White people at St. Michael's Church would insist on the legal legitimacy of the document in order to claim their church's portion of the estate, and by extension protect Adams's sister's right to the bulk of the estate.

5. See Burr (*Anglican Church in New Jersey*, 224–28) for an explanation that puts a very positive face on it. See Hood ("From a Headstart to a Deadstart") for a more realistic accounting.

6. See Hodges, ed., *Black Itinerants of the Gospel*.

and then subsequently with the African Methodist Episcopal Church once it was founded. Various independent Baptist churches also afforded a greater degree of freedom of worship for free Black Americans seeking religious self-governance and leadership opportunities.

While it is generally agreed among scholars that the majority of African Americans who had been exposed to Christianity through the Anglican, and later Episcopal, Church while enslaved did not go on to worship with the Episcopal Church after gaining their freedom,[7] there is limited documentary evidence available to establish many of the details of this phenomenon in New Jersey. Accurate accountings of such dynamics were not made reliably at the time and, in general, it is not the kind of phenomenon that received robust written documentation. However, an emblematic example for which we do have some documentary evidence is the experience of Charles and Hannah Reeves.

In his recently published *Stories of Slavery in New Jersey*, Rick Geffken describes the story of a Middletown, New Jersey couple, Charles and Hannah Reeves.[8] Charles had been enslaved by David Williamson, a Middletown farmer. Reeves was freed at the age of twenty-five in 1848 under the New Jersey gradual abolition law. He married Hannah Van Cleif in 1850 at Holmdel Baptist Church. While Geffken suggests that it is not definitively known who Hannah's enslavers were, the "Taylor family of Middletown had at least two slaves named Van Cleaf at their Kings Highway property."[9] Geffken notes that "speculations about Hannah's origins might be validated if a Williamson/Taylor nexus could be proved."[10] That nexus is likely the mid-nineteenth-century lay leadership of the Christ Churches of Shrewsbury and Middletown.[11]

---

7. See Hood, "From a Headstart to a Deadstart."

8. Geffken, *Stories of Slavery in New Jersey*, 82–98. Research into their lives was compiled by their great-granddaughter, Amanda Mae Edwards. Geffken's book relates many of the elements of Edwards's research.

9. Geffken (*Stories of Slavery in New Jersey*, 88) notes that there were various spellings of this same last name including Van Cleif, Van Cleaf, and Van Cleve.

10. Geffken, *Stories of Slavery in New Jersey*, 88.

11. The parishes were governed by a joint vestry and served jointly by a single priest for many decades until 1854.

Part III: Vignettes and Afterlives

As the archives of the Christ Church, Shrewsbury parish attest, David Williamson[12] and Joseph Taylor[13] both served in the lay leadership of Christ Church during this time, Williamson as a warden and Taylor on the vestry.[14] Though Hannah's great-great-granddaughter, Mae Edwards, was never able to determine how the couple met, the Christ Church connection allows ample opportunity for Charles and Hannah to have become acquainted.[15] Moreover, the parish register of Christ Church, Shrewsbury paints a very disturbing picture of the treatment of enslaved Black people while slavery was legal in New Jersey. The presence of myriad baptismal entries for enslaved "bastard" and "mullato" "servants"[16] shows that it was a common practice for the members in good standing at the church to rape their enslaved female domestics, and then enslave and baptize their progeny. This practice is widely attested in similar period documents, and as Geffken states, it was an "all too common occurrence at the time."[17]

These and other facts suggest a particularly difficult experience during Hannah Van Cleif's enslavement prior to her marriage. Geffken notes that her first child was born five years before her marriage to Charles Reeves, and that in the Reeves family Bible, this son, Isaiah, has no listed father, though all ten of Hannah's subsequent children are stated to be children of Hannah and Charles. Hannah was likely enslaved when Isaiah was born; she was likely enslaved by Joseph Taylor; and during that enslavement she was likely raped.[18]

---

12. See also Steen, *History of Christ Church, Shrewsbury*. David Williamson is celebrated yearly by Christ Church, Shrewsbury at their memorial observance. See Schjonberg, "Historic New Jersey Church Honors Deceased Veterans."

13. After the Shrewsbury and Middletown churches ceased to have shared leadership in 1854, Taylor continued to serve in Middletown (see, for example, the Diocese of New Jersey Convention minutes of 1855 and 1857, which show him to be a lay deputy from Christ Church, Middletown).

14. Also Williamson was married to Phebe Hendrickson, with whose family Taylor was friends. See Hammond, "Orchard Home," 20.

15. The Williamson-Taylor connection makes it exceedingly likely that Hannah Van Clief's mother was Elizabeth, a woman enslaved by the Taylors whose own mother was also named Hannah.

16. Parish Register of Christ Church, Shrewsbury. See also Kelley, "Slavery Evidenced in the Parish Register."

17. Geffken, *Stories of Slavery in New Jersey*, 89.

18. This theory accords with the educated guess of descendant John Smack that "most likely the slave owner . . . fathered Isaiah." Geffken, *Stories of Slavery in New Jersey*, 90.

Though Charles and Hannah Reeves were certainly exposed to Episcopal worship during their enslavement since the men who enslaved them were prominent members of the well-endowed Christ Church Shrewsbury/Middletown, upon gaining their freedom they did not worship in the Episcopal Church. There are any number of reasons this may have been the case,[19] and indeed there were likely many reasons—among them the likelihood of Hannah being raped by her well-regarded Episcopal enslaver—but lack of piety was not one of them. All indications from the historical record suggest that Charles and Hannah were very pious.[20] Yet, when they were free to, they did not worship in the Episcopal Church, but in Baptist churches. They were married in Holmdel Baptist Church and later were founding members of Pilgrim Baptist Church in Red Bank.

While the story of Charles and Hannah Reeves is somewhat conjectural, the explanation described here is the most plausible option. Moreover, the experience of the Reeves couple is indicative of the patterns experience of many Black Americans at the time. Many were exposed to Episcopal worship and teaching, but they were also exposed to Episcopal hypocrisy, mistreatment, and paternalism, and as such, comparatively few, when free to, chose to participate in Episcopal worship.

Rev. James C. Ward (1777–1834), the first African American Clergyman in the Diocese of New Jersey

In his invaluable *History of the African-American Group of the Episcopal Church*, George F. Bragg lists James C. Ward as the fourth ordained African American clergyperson in the Episcopal Church, one of only seventeen ordained before the end of the Civil War.[21] Bragg's brief biographical precis states: "*James C. Ward*, deacon in 1824. By Bishop White. Mr. Ward was a school teacher, and it does not appear that he was ever in pastoral work. He only lived a few years."[22] Ward had formerly been ordained as a Presby-

---

19. See Pruszinski, "Revolutionary Period and Early Black Estrangement from the Episcopal Church" and chapter 4 of this book.

20. See, for example, the comments of John Smack, related in Geffken, *Stories of Slavery in New Jersey*, 90.

21. Bragg, *History of the African-American Group*, 15.

22. Bragg, *History of the African-American Group*, 185. Italics original. Bishop White was the bishop of Pennsylvania.

terian. He left the Presbyterian Church for the Episcopal Church and was ordained a deacon by the bishop of Pennsylvania in 1824.[23]

The Rev. Ward was a schoolteacher in Philadelphia while canonically resident in Pennsylvania. His ordination was not an entirely traditional ordination, though. He was ordained to the diaconate on the condition that he would not have voting rights in convention proceedings,[24] and even when in attendance he was not considered among the clergy composing the convention.[25] During his time in Pennsylvania he was under consideration for an appointment with the Church Missionary Society (CMS) as a teacher in Sierra Leone, but the appointment was never finalized.[26]

However, in his state convention address of 1830, the bishop of the Diocese of New Jersey, the Rt. Rev. John Croes, notes among the clergy changes that year the following: "The Rev, James C. Ward, a coloured man, lately a Deacon of the Diocese of Pennsylvania, has, by a letter dimissory from the Right Rev. Dr. White, Bishop of that Diocese, been admitted into this."[27] In the state convention journal of that year the Rev. Ward is included in the list of clergy, but is listed last, after the priests, and after the other deacon ministering in the diocese.[28]

It is unclear where Ward taught when in New Jersey, or if he taught at all. In the 1830 convention journal nearly all other clergy have their church assignment listed,[29] but Rev. Ward does not. Marion M. Thompson Wright, in her magisterial treatment of Black education in New Jersey, does not mention him, though she reviewed the diocesan records that refer to him.[30] It appears that she concluded that he did not end up teaching in New Jersey, or at least, not very much. Due to the ambiguity of the records, it is difficult to determine where Rev. Ward may have taught in the diocese during his tenure.

---

23. Bragg, *History of the African-American Group*, 185. See also the General Convention record for 1826. For records of some kind of proceedings against him in the Presbyterian Church, see "Records of the Presbytery of New Castle, 1814–1834," 95. Holmes ("Making of the Bishop of Pennsylvania," 260) reports his ordination as having occurred in 1825. This date accords with most Episcopal Church records.

24. Burgess, *List of Persons Admitted*, 13.

25. Holmes, "Making of the Bishop of Pennsylvania," 260.

26. Dunn, *History of the Episcopal Church in Liberia*, 37.

27. Croes, "Address," 12.

28. Croes, "Address," 29.

29. All save Ward and one other.

30. Wright, *Education of Negroes in New Jersey*.

Black Believers in and out of the Episcopal Church

In 1830 nine churches in the diocese mention formalized regular Sunday schools in their convention reports,[31] including Christ Church, New Brunswick, St. Mark's Church, Orange, St. Peter's Church, Morristown, St. John's Church, Elizabethtown, Christ Church, Newton, St. James Church, Piscataway, St. Mary's Church, Burlington, St. Peter's Church, Berkeley, and St. John's Church, Salem. By 1831 the Sunday School Society had reorganized its constitution and worked to formalize instruction and membership. According to their reports there were five churches running Sunday schools that met the society guidelines, including 483 students, though most still-unaffiliated churches had some kind of Sunday school program.[32] There is no list of diocesan clergy in the 1831 convention journal, and no mention of Rev. James C. Ward. One wonders if this aberrant lack of a list (which is out of character for the journals of the time) is evidence of an attempt to avoid listing Ward among the clergy.

By 1832 there were seven churches in the diocese that had affiliated Sunday schools and among all of those schools and hundreds of students there were a total of only twenty-three "coloured" children listed as students.[33] At this time the education of African Americans in Episcopal churches was, almost without exception, segregated. As such, it is possible that the Rev. Ward did not have adequate pupils among the Sunday schools, and by extension, did not have adequate teaching opportunities (or pay) in the diocese at that time to warrant continued residence. There is no record of a diocese-associated school for those of African descent at this time, either on Sunday or otherwise, unlike those in Pennsylvania and New York. New Jersey was one of the few colonies where such a school had never

---

31. And they would have every incentive to do so.

32. The Protestant Episcopal Church in the State of New Jersey, *Journal of the Proceedings of the Forty-Eighth Annual Convention*, 34. Churches affiliated with the Society included Christ-Church, New Brunswick, St. John's Church, Salem, St. Peter's Church, Spotswood, Christ Church, Newton, and St. Mark's Church, Orange.

33. The Protestant Episcopal Church in the State of New Jersey, *Journal of the Proceedings of the Forty-Ninth Annual Convention*, 33. Most of the churches had Sunday schools of some kind, but not all had yet affiliated with the Sunday School Society. Churches with some kind of Sunday school included Christ Church, New Brunswick, St. Paul's Church at Paterson, Trinity Church, Newark, St. John's Church, Elizabethtown, St. James Church, Knowlton, St. Peter's Church, Perth Amboy, St. Peter's Church, Spotswood, St. Mary's Church, Burlington, St. Andrew's Church, Mount Holly, St. Peter's Church, Berkeley, St. John's Church, Salem, St. George's Church, Penns Neck, St. Mark's Church, Orange, Christ Church, Newton, and St. Luke's Church, Hope.

Part III: Vignettes and Afterlives

been founded by the SPG during the colonial era,[34] and by the time of Rev. Ward's residency no such school appears to have yet been founded.[35]

According to the state convention journal of 1834, Trinity Church, Newark had just then started a segregated school for Black children.[36] It is possible that Rev. Ward taught there briefly, but it is unlikely and no evidence of this has been discovered. It is possible, though also unlikely, that Rev. Ward continued to work as a schoolteacher in Philadelphia while living in New Jersey during this period. However, it seems most likely that Rev. Ward had been invited, perhaps aspirationally, to the Diocese of New Jersey to teach African American students at one or more of the churches with a significant segregated Sunday school, or to found an "African school" affiliated with one of the churches, but that the arrangement did not work out. It is also possible that he simply moved to New Jersey and was listed, but never had an assignment.

Bishop Croes's letter to the convention of 1832 provides another terse update: the Rev. Ward had left the diocese. "The Rev. James C. Ward (a coloured man) a Deacon in the Diocese, having made application to me for a letter dismissory to the Rt. Rev. Dr. Stone, Bishop of the Diocese of Maryland, it was granted to him and of course he no longer belongs to this Diocese."[37]

It appears that this move was already in the works as early as the previous summer. Bishop Croes had written a favorable letter of reference for Rev. Ward on July 16, 1831, which he sent to Ward in Annapolis, Maryland.[38]

---

34. New Jersey is conspicuously missing from the accounts in Pennington, "Thomas Bray's Associates and Their Work Among the Negroes." In his correspondence with the SPG, Rowland Ellis expressed an intention to teach a night school for those of African descent in Burlington in the winter of 1715–16 but it is unclear if he ever actually followed through, and certainly the intended "school" was never formalized. See "Rowland Ellis to SPG, October 8, 1715," British Online Archives, SPG Correspondence Collection, A Series, Vol. 11: 118.

35. Wright mentions no school of this kind in *Education of Negroes in New Jersey*.

36. Protestant Episcopal Church in the State of New Jersey, *Journal of the Proceedings of the Fifty First Annual Convention*, 10.

37. Protestant Episcopal Church in the State of New Jersey, *Journal of the Proceedings of the Fifty First Annual Convention*, 8.

38. John Croes to Revd. James C. Ward, July 16, 1831; Record ID 108178, Accession number MA 365.121, The Morgan Library and Museum. It is essentially a form letter: "The Rev.' James C. Ward (a coloured man,) a Deacon of this Diocese, having made application to me for a letter dimissory to the Rt. Rev.' the Bishop of the Diocese of Maryland, I hereby cheerfully grant his request, and do certify, that he has not, so far as I know, been liable to evil report for error in religion or viciousness of life, during the the [sic] three years last past."

Apparently Ward had either already moved, or was in the process of setting up what would be his next teaching job in Maryland. This would mean that Ward was functionally a resident in New Jersey for as little as a year, though Croes's letter suggests that it was a bit more. Unfortunately Ward did not teach long in Maryland, passing away soon after his move in 1834.

Whatever the circumstances that led to Rev. Ward's extremely brief tenure in the Diocese of New Jersey, we can at least conclude a few things. Firstly, Rev. Ward's experience shows that Bishop Croes, who was an enslaver for much of his life, was willing to acknowledge and possibly even work with Black clergy, at least to some degree. He affirmed Ward's ordination and welcomed him to the diocese. Secondly, however much support Rev. Ward received from the bishop, it did not translate into a stable teaching position in the diocese. There was likely not yet widespread support for Black clergy in any particular White churches in the diocese. Further, Ward would likely have needed a church affiliation to start a school of his own creation, and churches in the diocese, in addition to having limited established programs for Black pupils at the time, showed in the subsequent period a significant interest in hiring only White instructors for segregated parish schools.[39] All this is to say, Ward did not find the Diocese of New Jersey to be as hospitable a location for his teaching as Pennsylvania (Philadelphia) had been, or Maryland would be, and as a result, his tenure in New Jersey was fleeting. He remains, however, the first Black man to be counted among the clergy of the Diocese of New Jersey.

The Earliest (Formal) Black Church Leadership in the Diocese of New Jersey

Before the Civil War there were few outlets for formally recognized Black leadership in the Diocese of New Jersey. As just described, James C. Ward, an ordained deacon and schoolteacher who temporarily transferred his canonical residency from Pennsylvania to New Jersey, and, as such, was the first ordained Black man in the diocese in 1830, quickly moved to Maryland as he found a more hospitable teaching appointment there.[40] It was not for decades after the Civil War before another Black man was approved for

---

39. See, for instance, the example of Trinity Church, Princeton described in Pruszinski and Pruszinski, eds., "Trinity Church, Princeton and Slavery," and chapter 11 of this book.

40. Pruszinski, "Rev. James C. Ward (1777–1834)."

Part III: Vignettes and Afterlives

ordained ministry in the diocese.[41] There were at times, however, modest, but formally recognized outlets for Black men to exercise church leadership.

One occasion for this diocesan affirmation of Black leadership came after the founding of St. Philip's Episcopal Church in Newark, an "African" parish formed mostly by former attendees of Trinity Church, Newark.[42] Though the first several priests of the congregation were White, and the diocesan treatment of the parish was paternalistic,[43] the lay leadership was, of course, Black, and the first leader to be formally licensed as a "reader" for the congregation was Elias Ray.[44] He was a frequent diocesan convention representative of St. Philip's, starting as early as 1858,[45] and was licensed as a lay reader on September 10, 1864.[46] A "lay reader" leads the liturgy in the absence of a priest, though he or she does not consecrate the eucharist. This was viewed as an important role at the diocesan level, to the point that the diocesan convention journals of the time list licensed lay readers alongside active priests and deacons, but not wardens or vestry members. Jacob Rhodes was also licensed to serve at St. Philip's under Rev. Dr. Rees on July 22, 1867, and served in that capacity for a couple of years.[47] Various other Black men and women have led St. Philip's as wardens, vestrymen, and diocesan convention representatives (among other capacities) from the earliest time of its formation[48] in 1848 to the present day.

---

41. It is true that Bishop Doane (of New Jersey) worked to support the seminary admission and ordination of Alexander Crummell, but that process took place largely outside of New Jersey and involved Doane due to his role on the board of trustees of General Seminary in New York City. See Wilder, "Driven . . . from the School of the Prophets."

42. Calloway and Pruszinski, "History of Trinity and St. Philip's Cathedral." See also chapter 11.

43. See, e.g., Doane, *Diocese of New Jersey: The Episcopal Address, to the Seventy-Third Annual Convention*, 17: "It was [a] matter of great joy to me to meet these simple-minded, earnest, people . . . [they] have my warmest sympathies."

44. Listed in some records as "Elias Kay."

45. Diocese of New Jersey, *Journal of Proceedings of the Seventy-Fifth Annual Convention*, 11.

46. Diocese of New Jersey, *Journal of the Proceedings of the Eighty-Second Annual Convention*, 154.

47. Diocese of New Jersey, *Journal of the Eighty-Fifth Annual Convention*, 171.

48. Among these early lay leaders were Elias Ray, Nicholas Duffin, Samuel Thompkins, John and Peter O'Fake, Elias and George Mitchell, and Jacob Rhodes. See Calloway and Pruszinski, "History of Trinity and St. Philip's Cathedral." See also chapter 11 of this book, and Diocese of New Jersey Convention Journals from 1848 to 1874.

Black Believers in and out of the Episcopal Church

Another Black leader in the diocese at this time was Daniel B. Landin. He was actually the first licensed lay reader in the diocese, being licensed for service (slightly before Elias Ray, in April 19, 1863) in the mission at the African American settlement known as "Macedonia" (in Tinton Falls), which was sponsored by Christ Church, Shrewsbury.[49] He was the teacher for the "colored" school, also sponsored by Christ Church, that counted many pupils among the residents of "Macedonia."[50] Landin had been preceded as lay reader at Macedonia by the Black abolitionist John N. Still. There is no record of Still having been formally licensed, but he had been formally accepted as a candidate for ordination in the diocese in 1856, making him the first Black man to be accepted into the process in the Diocese of New Jersey. He was the most important early leader in the ministry at Macedonia, but he was never ordained. His candidacy languished at the diocesan level for more than eight years before it was abandoned.[51]

The last time Daniel Landin and Elias Ray are listed, it is as "lay leaders" in the diocesan records is 1874. By the time of the diocesan convention of 1875 (post-split), Landin was apparently no longer holding this office, and Elias Ray, along with St. Philip's, was now part of the Diocese of Newark. It seems likely there was some significant shake-up at the Macedonia mission when the diocese split. There was a new rector at Christ Church, and soon after the responsibility for the Macedonia mission was passed to St. James Memorial Church, Eatontown. The mission seems to have shrunk after Daniel Landin stopped serving as lay reader (and teacher). By 1883 the mission had only four families involved (though one had a son studying out-of-state for the priesthood),[52] and soon after that, folded.[53]

St. Philips would not have a Black clergyman for decades yet, and no Black man would be allowed to serve in a sustained ordained ministry in the Diocese of New Jersey until August Jensen was invited by Bishop Scarborough beginning in 1903 at Asbury Park.[54]

---

49. Diocese of New Jersey, *Journal of the Proceedings of the Eighty-First Annual Convention*, 73.

50. Diocese of New Jersey, *Journal of the Proceedings of the Eighty-First Annual Convention*, 133.

51. See Pruszinski, "Episcopal Mission at the Free Black Settlement of Macedonia."

52. Diocese of New Jersey, *Journal of the Proceedings of the One Hundred and Eleventh Convention*, 131.

53. That's how Bishop Scarborough describes its state (defunct) in 1890: Scarborough, "Episcopal Address to the One Hundred and Sixth Annual Convention," 168.

54. At least, as far as our research has yet found. Bragg, *History of the African-American Group of the Episcopal Church*, 177.

13

White Episcopalian Rejection of Black Participation

Support for the American Colonization Society (ACS) in the Diocese of New Jersey

FOUNDED IN 1816 AT the impetus of New Jersey native Rev. Robert Finley and friends, the American Colonization Society (ACS) had the stated goal of ridding the United States of free Black people. At times over the history of the organization their rhetoric appeared benevolent, and they worked very hard to present themselves as a charitable organization. But this charitable rhetoric cloaked a conviction that free Black Americans could not and should not live alongside White people. In some members of the society this conviction resulted from a belief in the inherent inferiority of Black people. For others the conviction resulted from a fear of violence or economic competition from free Black people. And for still others, the conviction that free Black Americans should not live alongside White people derived from a strong desire to maintain a smoothly functioning slave society, which the advocacy of free Black people hampered.[1] Suffice to say, the organization

---

1. These various motives have been documented by a number of scholars including Yarsiah, *Episcopal Church—Early Missionaries in Liberia*, 33–34. Rev. Dr. Yarsiah is currently a priest in the Diocese of New Jersey.

White Episcopalian Rejection of Black Participation

was based entirely on racist principles, even though at times (usually in the north) it presented itself as supportive of abolition.

That the organization was racist, in spite of its protestations that it only had the best interests of African Americans at heart, can be seen from the near universal rejection of its mission and aims by African Americans at the time, chronicled in Ousmane K. Power-Greene's *Against Wind and Tide: The African American Struggle against the Colonization Movement*. Various well-known African Americans resisted the efforts of the ACS, publishing constantly in abolitionist and African American newspapers and journals. Frederick Douglass pushed back against the ACS not only to assert the right of African Americans to live in the US, but because the ACS had advocated for forced deportation of free Black residents.[2] The Rev. Absalom Jones, the first Black priest ordained in the Episcopal Church, opposed the ACS early on.[3] Rev. Alexander Crummell, a nationally known Black Episcopal priest and intellectual,[4] also rejected the organization for decades, traveling extensively to combat ACS fundraising efforts.[5]

In spite of these African American efforts, including those by Black Episcopalians, White New Jersey Episcopalians heavily supported the ACS. New Jersey was important to the founding and support of the organization, and New Jersey Episcopalians particularly. Christian leaders generally were the founders and leaders of the organization. Robert Finley, the first president, was a Presbyterian minister in New Jersey, but from the outset the ACS involved ecumenical collaboration. Key early members from New Jersey included Commodore (and later Senator) Robert F. Stockton and John Potter. Stockton was instrumental in forcibly obtaining the land that would become Liberia for the ACS.[6] Stockton was also the first president of the New Jersey Chapter (1824), while Potter was one of the founding vice presidents.[7] As

---

2. Power-Greene, *Against Wind and Tide*, 115.

3. Dunn, *History of the Episcopal Church in Liberia*, 15.

4. Bishop Doane of New Jersey had supported his admission to General Seminary in spite of racist opposition (Wilder, "Driven . . . from the School of the Prophets").

5. After decades of fighting the ACS, Crummell only moved to Liberia after the plight of African Americans in the United States had become so dire (after the passage of the Fugitive Slave Act of 1850) that he had given up hope for any successful advocacy in the States.

6. Colonization Society of the City of Newark, *Sketch of the Colonization Enterprise*, 2–3.

7. Society of the American Colonization Society in New Jersey, *Proceedings of a Meeting Held at Princeton*, 39.

Part III: Vignettes and Afterlives

mentioned in chapter 11, they would jointly go on to found Trinity Church (Episcopal), Princeton in 1833,[8] to continue to own hundreds of slaves each,[9] and to remain lifelong boosters of the ACS.

Diocesan records of church giving in New Jersey show consistent congregational and institutional support for the ACS starting in 1834.[10] This interest coincides with the launch of "African Missions" to Liberia[11] supported by the national Episcopal Church in cooperation with the ACS.[12] Both Episcopal mission literature[13] and ACS documentation,[14] along with subsequent scholarship on the Episcopal African mission,[15] acknowledge the high degree of cooperation between the institutions. The local manifestation of this cooperation in New Jersey came particularly in the form of fundraising and prayer in the diocese and in local churches.

In his convention address of 1834, Bishop Doane, in mentioning services held across the diocese on July 4, acknowledged the fundraising for the ACS in his congregations, noted Episcopal collaboration with the ACS, and encouraged giving in support of the collaborative Episcopal mission to Liberia.

> One improvement [to the Independence Day worship service] has suggested itself to me as worthy of being incorporated with the plan. The day on which we acknowledge the goodness of God in establishing our own freedom, is a day on which we should do what we can towards letting "the oppressed go free." As a nation, we are held by peculiar obligations to promote the civil and

---

8. Stockton and Thomson, "Subscription Book of 1827 to Build a Protestant Episcopal Church in the Borough of Princeton," August 16, 1827. See also the Rector, Wardens and Vestrymen of Trinity Church in the Borough of Princeton, "Certificate of Incorporation," May 17, 1833.

9. See Pruszinski and Pruszinski, "Trinity Church, Princeton and Slavery," and chapter 11 of this book.

10. See Appendix 5 for the full record of congregational giving through 1865.

11. That is, the region that soon became Liberia.

12. The Episcopal periodical *Spirit of Missions* was begun in 1836 to support the new interest and initiatives in missions.

13. E.g., Protestant Episcopal Church, *Historical Sketch of the African Mission*, 6–7. This promotional document even goes so far as to claim that "the colonization scheme originated with us," which is to say, Episcopalians (here 59).

14. E.g., American Society for Colonizing the Free People of Color of the United States, *Twenty-First Annual Report of the American Society for Colonizing the Free People of Color of the United States*, 14.

15. E.g., Dunn, *History of the Episcopal Church in Liberia*, 31, 35, 83–84.

religious liberation of Africa. The duty has been very generally recognized among American Christians, by the practice of making collections, after the religious services of the day, for the benefit of the American Colonization Society. Of that institution, I design to express no opinion—none certainly of an unfavourable character. But the fact, that the Domestic and Foreign Missionary Society of our Church, has been . . . desirous of establishing a Mission there, with the recent resolution of the Board of Directors, instructing the Executive Committee to send two Missionaries to Africa with all convenient speed, has seemed to me, to call especially for our approbation and patronage. I propose, therefore, that the services of the day be partly *of a Missionary character*; and that a collection be recommended in all the Churches of the Diocese,—the proceeds of which, shall be transmitted to the Treasurer of the Society above named, in aid of *Missions to Africa*.[16]

Church giving to the ACS that year from St. Peter's Church, Perth Amboy surpassed its giving to the Episcopal Domestic and Foreign Missionary Society, and the ACS was the only non-Episcopal organization designated in its giving.[17] Giving to the ACS that year from Trinity Church, Newark was similarly significant, outpacing other categories of giving, and singling out the ACS as the only non-Episcopal organization receiving funds.[18]

Doane's address had a significant effect. Giving to both the ACS and the Episcopal African Mission increased dramatically during his tenure, with churches often designating gifts to both initiatives. Reports of congregational giving between 1834 and 1856[19] reveal donations to the ACS from Trinity Church (Newark), St. Peter's Church (Perth Amboy), Christ Church (New Brunswick), and St. John's Church (Somerville). However, congregational giving to the Episcopal "African Mission" to Liberia, which cooperated with the ACS, exploded following Doane's exhortation, with regular donations appearing during this same period from the following congregations:

---

16. Doane, *Episcopal Address Delivered at the Convention of the Protestant Episcopal Church, in the State of New-Jersey; May 28, 1834*, 33. Italics original.

17. *Journal of the Proceedings of the Fifty First Annual Convention*, 17.

18. *Journal of the Proceedings of the Fifty First Annual Convention*, 10.

19. As documented in the State Convention Proceedings Journals of the time. See Appendix 5.

Part III: Vignettes and Afterlives

St. Peter's Church, Perth Amboy

St. Andrew's Church, Mt. Holly

St. Mark's Church, Orange

St. James Church, Piscataway

Trinity Church, Woodbridge

St. James Church, Knowlton

St. Luke's Church, Hope

Christ Church, Shrewsbury

St. John's Church, Elizabethtown

St. Paul's Church, Hoboken

St. Peter's Church, Berkeley at Clarksboro

Christ Church, Middletown

Trinity Chapel, Red Bank

St. Stephen's, Mullica Hill

St. Peter's Church, Morristown

Church of the Redeemer, Morristown

Beyond the aforementioned Episcopal strategic cooperation with the ACS in Liberia, at the national level in the US, and even at the state diocesan level, there was significant Episcopal collaboration with the ACS at the local level in New Jersey as well, even beyond the founding of the state auxiliary. For instance, when the Newark, New Jersey auxiliary of the ACS was formed in 1838, the Rev. Matthew H. Henderson (rector) and Joel W. Condit, Jabez Hays, David Clarkson, and Silas Merchant (lay leaders) of Trinity Church (Episcopal), Newark were elected managers of the society, while Hanford Smith, another lay leader at Trinity, was elected vice president.[20] J. C. Garthwaite, a lay leader of Grace Church (Episcopal), Newark was also elected a manager, as was the Rev. Dr. George T. Chapman, then rector of Grace Church. Clearly, Episcopalians were disproportionately represented among the leadership of the local auxiliary compared to their overall presence in the city, indicating a very strong interest in and support for the initiative.[21]

20. All these men appear as frequent delegates representing their parishes to the diocesan conventions at the time.

21. For the roster of elected leaders see Colonization Society of the City of Newark, *Sketch of the Colonization Enterprise*, 13–14.

White Episcopalian Rejection of Black Participation

In the immediate aftermath of the passage of the federal Fugitive Slave Act in 1850, general interest in the ACS in the United States grew to an all-time high.[22] Alexander Crummell actually gave up on changing the United States for the better and emigrated to Liberia, so dismayed was he at the apparently deteriorating state of Black freedoms in America. However, the final mention of the ACS in the New Jersey diocesan convention proceedings journals occurs not long after this in 1856 (mention of a donation from St. John's, Somerville to the ACS).[23]

Why the loss of interest, or at least, direct financial support at this time when the ACS was at its zenith? By this time much of the direct giving in the diocese related to Africa had shifted to Episcopal-specific "African Mission." The Episcopal initiative in Liberia was still cooperative with the ACS and still shared much with it in the way of racist ideology and rhetoric,[24] but it was also big enough by this time that it was a viable and more pertinent charitable target for Episcopal giving, at least at the congregational and diocesan level, than the ACS. An example of the dynamics underlying this shift is in the particular connection felt in the Diocese of New Jersey at the time for the new (non-Liberian) African mission of the Rev. Hamble J. Leacock, a missionary who had formerly served as the rector at St. Peter's Church, Perth Amboy, and who remained on the New Jersey diocesan rolls while he sought to found a mission station at Rio Pongas (now in Gambia). Some congregational giving within the diocese went specifically to Leacock's work,[25] and some to the general "Africa Mission" fund that apportioned donations across various initiatives, but after this point, none to the ACS.

After the end of the Civil War, the goal of removing African Americans from the United States became even more obviously absurd.[26] And

22. Power-Greene, *Against Wind and Tide*, 118–20.

23. See Diocese of New Jersey, *Journal of the Proceedings of the Seventy Third Annual Convention*, 41.

24. As can be seen by the fact that White clergy dominated the mission throughout this period, and that the White American Bishop of Liberia (Bishop Payne) who for decades (1850–1874) insisted on tight control of the diocese, did not trust African or African American church leadership, worked to prevent power-sharing, and regularly acted paternalistically. See Dunn (*History of the Episcopal Church in Liberia*, 93) for a discussion of accusations of racism brought against Payne during his tenure.

25. Donations from St. Peter's Church, Morristown noted in the 1856 Convention Proceedings Journal are specifically designated to the "Leacock Fund, Africa." Diocese of New Jersey, *Journal of the Proceedings of the Seventy Third Annual Convention*, 34.

26. It had been rather prohibitively expensive before the war, but afterward it was largely mooted by the significant, if qualified, advance of African American rights and freedoms within the US.

Part III: Vignettes and Afterlives

while the ACS met with even less African American interest in emigration, efforts to revive it nevertheless continued to arise. T. Thomas Fortune, a well-known African American publisher and important figure in the racial uplift movement,[27] and later a parishioner at St. Thomas's (Episcopal) Church, Red Bank (New Jersey), continued to reject the ACS project and its rhetoric when attempts were made in the 1880s to revive the organization. He took up the arguments of earlier Black intellectuals who had insisted that at root the "colonization movement [was] an anti-Black program."[28]

"T. Thomas Fortune." From Washington et al., *The Negro Problem*, 211–12 (courtesy Wikimedia Commons).

---

27. He is actually responsible for popularizing the term "Afro-American."
28. Power-Greene, *Against Wind and Tide*, 197.

White Episcopalian Rejection of Black Participation

Carrie Smiley Fortune. Artist's rendering by N. T. Pruszinski of archival photography courtesy of the Sag Harbor Historical Society.

Neither the ACS nor its White New Jersey Episcopalian supporters had managed to rid the US of free Black Americans by the time of the Civil War, but they had both managed to produce long-standing suspicion among African Americans. They had also jointly managed to produce an American colony in Africa (Liberia) that in spite of its increasingly Black colonial political leadership, replicated many of their own prejudices toward Black Africans.[29] Ultimately the Episcopal Diocese of Liberia would come to be administered by a Black bishop and led by a predominantly

---

29. Rev. (and later Bishop) John Payne wrote in 1848 that "the time has not come yet, nor will it, for a long time when socially, natives can rank with colonists. The latter are destined by providence to be the teachers and governors of the former in this region." Payne to Latrobe, November 22, 1848 (as quoted in Dunn, *History of the Episcopal Church in Liberia*, 80). Early Black Episcopal missionary James Thomson also perpetuated this attitude, insisting not simply on teaching Christianity, but promoting Western culture and removing natives from their "unwholesome social environment" (Dunn, *History of the Episcopal Church in Liberia*, 47). Yarsiah (*Episcopal Church—Early Missionaries in Liberia*, 40) notes that this attitude produced particularly problematic approaches toward nation-building: "the settlers' government focused on increasing the national population through new immigrants rather than from the local ethnic groups whose potential for nation building was great but needed to be developed."

Black clergy, but by that time much damage had already been done, including a long-standing normalization of Western (and White) cultural chauvinism[30] in the teachings and organization of the Liberian Episcopal Church.[31]

Early African Mission Giving (Foreign) in the Diocese of New Jersey

The first instance in the Diocese of New Jersey of reported funds being specifically and separately designated for "African mission" was in 1835.[32] This followed the aforementioned exhortation by Bishop Doane in his 1834 diocesan convention address,[33] in which he encouraged churches within the diocese to support the fledgling Episcopal mission to the region of west Africa that would later become Liberia.[34] In 1835 six of the thirty-two churches in the diocese took up this call and among them collected a total of $18.15.[35]

At this time, dedicated ministry to African Americans within the diocese was very limited. According to diocesan records,[36] St. John's Church, Elizabethtown periodically ran a segregated Sunday school starting in 1818, initially said to have twenty students of color,[37] but it does not ap-

---

30. As noted by Yarsiah, *Episcopal Church—Early Missionaries in Liberia*, 39.

31. Which could be seen in the segregation that was established then in Liberian Episcopal Churches between native Africans and African American colonists. See Dunn, *History of the Episcopal Church in Liberia*, 81. See also Yarsiah, *Episcopal Church—Early Missionaries in Liberia*, 40–41: "Many features of the negative effects of the policies and practices of the Christian churches are evident in contemporary Liberia. Two examples were the black/mulatto social cleavage in Liberian society and the absence of indigenous involvement in the affairs of the Church and state."

32. The Protestant Episcopal Church in the State of New Jersey, *Journal of the Fifty Second Annual Convention*, 12–27.

33. Doane, *Episcopal Address Delivered at the Convention of the Protestant Episcopal Church, in the State of New-Jersey; May 28, 1834*, 33.

34. For more on the history of the mission see Dunn, *History of the Episcopal Church in Liberia*, and Yarsiah, *Episcopal Church—Early Missionaries in Liberia*. For a rather hagiographic promotional account see Protestant Episcopal Church, *Historical Sketch of the African Mission*.

35. Even in 1835 dollars this is not a lot of money, and six out of thirty-two churches is only 18.75 percent.

36. Gleaned from yearly convention journal reporting.

37. There is no discrete financial accounting reported for this school in diocesan

pear to have been in operation consistently. Baptisms of African American "domestics" are specifically mentioned in the diocesan reporting of St. Peter's Church, Spotswood, and we know that other churches performed similar baptisms at this time. In 1832 the diocesan Sunday School Society noted twenty-three "coloured children" participating in its schools,[38] but this modest number only accounts for 5 percent of total students. In 1834 Trinity Newark reported that it was running a segregated "coloured infant school," but no similar school for older children. All this is to say, only limited attention had been given to ministry specifically to African Americans in the diocese at the time.

Over the following decades, giving to the African mission continued, and generally increased (see Appendix 6),[39] however, in many ways this giving operated as an outlet for White Episcopal "philanthropy" ostensibly aimed at Black people, while never actually challenging either the status quo of their treatment within the diocese or White Episcopalian control.

The African mission of the Episcopal Church was born of much the same impetus that formed the American Colonization Society (ACS), an organization committed to removing freed Black people from the United States and using them to colonize Africa.[40] This idea was promoted as beneficial for Africans, who would receive the influence of Western culture and Christianity from African American settlers, for freed African Americans, who would have an opportunity to thrive independently from White people (assuming they could never do so in a majority-White society), and for White Americans who felt threatened by the presence of free Black people in the United States and believed that the presence of free Black Americans created a difficulty for the effective functioning of a slave society. Though the work was presented as "charitable," on each of the aforementioned counts the plan was clearly racist, and nearly all African Americans rejected the scheme and the ACS.[41] Nevertheless, the Episcopal Church actively co-

---

convention journal annual reports of the time.

38. Cost to educate is not broken out, nor are the number of the "coloured" scholars listed by participating church. See Protestant Episcopal Church in the State of New Jersey, *Journal of the Proceedings of the Forty-Ninth Annual Convention*, 33.

39. Though the total number of churches giving in any particular year (through the end of the civil war) never exceeded the initial six in 1835. See Appendix 6 for the record of giving.

40. Bishop Doane's elision of these ideas in his aforementioned address in 1834 is indicative.

41. See all of Power-Greene, *Against Wind and Tide*.

operated with the ACS in the colonial-missionary enterprise, particularly at its founding, and, as previously mentioned, churches within the Diocese of New Jersey continued to support the ACS (see Appendix 5) in parallel to their support for the Episcopal African Mission (though donations to the Episcopal African Mission giving eventually well outpaced ACS giving in the diocese).

Essentially, the African Mission was viewed by White Episcopalians as a way of "giving back" to formerly enslaved Black people, while also removing them from the US, and simultaneously Christianizing Africa (a win-win-win in the racist imagination). This giving and attention paid to the African Mission also enabled churches in the diocese to ignore the needs of their free and enslaved African American neighbors, and as shown in chapter ten, little designated giving or program for domestic African American ministries in the diocese developed until after the Civil War.

Further, the governance structure of the African Mission for decades privileged the leadership and authority of White Americans (including the long-governing first bishop of Liberia, John Payne). Thus the effect of African Mission giving in the diocese during this period was to siphon money and concern away from potential use in domestic African American ministry and toward a largely White-controlled foreign mission significantly aligned with the goal of the removal of African Americans from the US and the promotion of western cultural hegemony in Africa.

During this period African Americans in the Diocese of New Jersey, almost without exception, continued to be consigned to marginal status, excluded from leadership, relegated to balconies and segregated seating, and, in general, treated as second-class citizens even when free (their baptisms and confirmations are often reported as if they were unusual events). The only significant Black ministries begun during this time (of otherwise absolutely exponential growth in the diocese)[42] were St. Philip's (African) Church, Newark (admitted to the diocese in 1848),[43] the outreach ministry of Christ Church, Shrewsbury in the "African" settlement of Macedonia in Tinton Falls,[44] and a small handful of segregated parish schools including

42. Doane's tenure from 1832 to 1859 saw the number of churches in the diocese increase from thirty-two to eighty-five, clergy from eighteen to ninety-eight, and communicants from approximately 800 to 5,000. See Burr, *Anglican Church in New Jersey*, 478.

43. The long financial hardship of which is indicated, in part, by pleas from Doane for support. See, for example, Doane, *Diocese of New Jersey: The Episcopal Address, to the Seventy-First Annual Convention*, 14.

44. First mentioned in parochial annual reports to the diocese in 1854.

White Episcopalian Rejection of Black Participation

those at St. Peter's Church, Perth Amboy,[45] St. Michael's Church, Trenton,[46] Trinity Church, Princeton,[47] and Christ Church, Shrewsbury.[48] These schools were typically, though not always,[49] taught by White teachers, and oriented toward keeping Black students "in their place."

In sum, the funding for these domestic Black ministries constituted a vanishingly small percentage of church and diocesan budgets, certainly in no way approaching an amount commensurate with the proportional representation of African Americans in the general population at the time. African Mission giving among the White churches diverted (already meager) funds and concern away from domestic Black ministries and was part of a culture in the diocese at the time that prioritized maintenance of a status quo oriented around Black marginalization.

---

45. First mentioned in parochial annual reports to the diocese in 1856.

46. First mentioned in parochial annual reports to the diocese in 1860.

47. A segregated school was run out of the church and supported by its leadership: Diocese of New Jersey, *Journal of Proceedings of the Sixty-Seventh Annual Convention*, 27–28. It seems it was intended to provide a school for Black children taught by White teachers as an alternative to the other segregated school in town run by local African American leader Betsey Stockton. See Pruszinski and Pruszinski, "Trinity Church, Princeton and Slavery."

48. First mentioned in parochial annual reports to the diocese in 1854.

49. The annual parochial report to the diocese in 1857 suggests that Christ Church, Shrewsbury had hired John N. Still, a "colored" teacher for their segregated "African" school of 112 students.

PART IV

Conclusions and Next Steps

14

Conclusion

WE'VE COVERED A LOT of ground in working to provide an initial accounting for how the Anglican Church in colonial New Jersey, and the Episcopal Church in early-republic New Jersey, helped establish slavery, benefited financially from slavery, and participated in and contributed to widespread and pervasive racism toward Black Africans and African Americans, so a reminder of some of the key points is merited.[1]

Key Observations on Slavery and Racism in the Pre-Civil War Diocese of New Jersey

As we noted at the outset, there was little Anglican presence in what later became New Jersey when the British took it from the Dutch in 1664, but slavery was already well established. The British continued to employ slavery in both East and West Jersey as part of their goal to establish a plantation economy in the colonies. During this time the Crown operated a monopoly on the transatlantic slave trade with the colonies (through the Royal African Company). And in the Caribbean colonies Anglicans helped create the legal and linguistic conventions of associating "White" with

---

1. The text of this chapter is based on a presentation made on behalf of the Reparations Commission to the 240th convention of the Episcopal Diocese of New Jersey on March 9, 2024.

Part IV: Conclusions and Next Steps

"free" and "Christian" and "Black" with "slave" and "pagan." These conventions were imported into the Jerseys, especially East Jersey, by Barbadian transplants who brought enslaved Africans with them as part of an early speculative land grab. White settlers were compensated with as much as 150 acres of land for each enslaved person they brought with them. In 1704 many of these influential Anglican colonists worked to establish the legal approaches to slavery developed in the Caribbean across the whole, now unified, colony of New Jersey. Manumissions were severely discouraged, and in support of formation of these slavery codes, the staff of the Archbishop of Canterbury sent draft legislation to New Jersey legislators seeking to ensure that baptism of an enslaved Black person would not be allowed as grounds for manumission. This provision, through the efforts of influential Anglicans, was incorporated into the legislation and became colonial law.

During this time the Anglican Church was looking to become better established in the colony, which was then peopled mostly with dissenters who were not very interested in the Church of England. The Society for the Propagation of the Gospel (SPG), a voluntary Anglican missionary organization, was formed in 1702 to support the development of the church in the colonies and it began sending priests. These priests worked in concert with local elite Anglicans to establish congregations and by the end of the colonial period there were approximately twenty-four churches established in the colony and a similar number of preaching stations. The Anglican Church never became the official church of the colony, so financial support was provided by local congregations and the SPG. Local congregations were expected to pay for building and upkeep and to provide some support for a priest, and the SPG provided the bulk of the base salary to the priests, though the Crown also furnished an initial bounty for the sending of many priests. Because the Crown was directly profiting from the slave trade and because the SPG derived significant income from its plantation in Codrington, Barbados (which enslaved hundreds of Africans) we should understand the financial backing for priests in New Jersey at this time to be the product of enslaved labor.

But even more directly, the financial backing for building and establishing Anglican *churches* in colonial New Jersey came from using enslaved labor. Most of the wealthiest Anglicans in the colony at this time were participating fully in the plantation economy and enslaved Black Africans. Col. (and later governor) Lewis Morris, for instance, owned a mine at Tinton Falls in the early 1700s on which he enslaved at least sixty-five Africans.

Conclusion

He was involved in the establishment of the SPG and in the founding of a few different congregations (including Christ Church, Shrewsbury, and St. Michael's, Trenton). He was probably the most prolific enslaver at that time in all of the American colonies. Col. Peter Schuyler, from the well-known Schuyler family, was heavily involved in the establishment of a few different New Jersey churches as well (including Trinity, Newark). His wealth came from his plantation and from the inheritance of his father's copper mine in what is now North Arlington. His father was *the* wealthiest British colonist in the Americas at the time, and operated his mine for decades with enslaved labor. Perhaps a bit better known is Governor William Franklin, son of Ben Franklin, who gave generous gifts to help establish a few different New Jersey churches (including St. Mary's, Burlington). His wealth was, in part, a product of slavery.

And it was not just the laity that were involved in enslaving Africans and African Americans. Many priests came to the colony, not merely to establish the church, but to participate in and benefit from the plantation economy. Several of the longest-serving and best established and influential priests who served in colonial New Jersey (such as Alexander Innes, Edward Vaughan, and Samuel Cooke) owned plantations, enslaved Black people, and fostered a culture of support for the institution of slavery in their congregations. For example, Rev. Thomas Thompson, who served five years in New Jersey (including at Shrewsbury, Middletown, Freehold, and Allentown), and went on to become the first Anglican missionary to Africa, wrote a very influential treatise supporting the institution of slavery and praising its utility for converting African slaves.

Thompson's work shows that the Anglican missionary attentions devoted toward enslaved Black people during this period were not really benevolent. These attentions were in almost every way, self-serving for White Anglicans, particularly in New Jersey where free White people were, in general, not interested in the Anglican Church. As such, the potential to develop loyalty among enslaved Africans was viewed as politically and economically useful. This fact became crystal clear when the British offered them freedom in the rebelling American colonies during the Revolutionary War. The British had been happy to enslave Africans when that benefited the Crown economically, and were ready to free them when that appeared likely to give them an advantage in different circumstances. Thousands of the enslaved escaped their bondage during this time as a result of these

Part IV: Conclusions and Next Steps

offers of freedom, and the population of the enslaved in New Jersey did drop markedly as a result of the war.

After the war the Anglican Church in the state was in disarray as many of the priests had fled and worship at almost every Anglican Church in the state had been very interrupted. The state of New Jersey kept slavery intact after the war and the nascent Episcopal Church continued to use it for its benefit. It was not until 1804 that New Jersey voted to enact gradual abolition, the last northern state to formalize legislation of this kind. And while the legislation promised freedom after twenty-one to twenty-five years of service to African Americans born into slavery after 1804, the immediate effect of the law was to shore up the institution.

In the meantime, the most influential priests in the founding of the diocese during this post-revolutionary period, the Revs. Abraham Beach and Uzal Ogden, both personally enslaved Black people and derived significant income from industry and farming using enslaved labor. They fostered a culture of support for the institution in their churches and the diocese and many influential laity during this time continued to own slaves, even laity who identified as abolitionists such as James Parker Jr. of St. Peter's, Perth Amboy. However, most of the laity who enslaved Black people were not abolitionists, such as Senator Robert Stockton of Trinity, Princeton, who was influential in the racist American Colonization Society, used force to seize what became Liberia to support the colonization project, himself enslaved Black people in New Jersey, and kept a sizable plantation in Georgia where he kept more than one hundred Black people enslaved at any given time.

However, perhaps the most notorious Episcopal enslaver during Gradual Abolition was the corrupt Middlesex County Judge Jacob van Wickle. During this time the enslaved had to consent to sale out of state, as such a sale could result in the alteration of their status from "slaves for a term" to permanently enslaved. Van Wickle sought to profit from such interstate sales and so forged dozens upon dozens of papers of acquiescence, even going so far as to claim that the cries of infants constituted consent. His ring also kidnapped free Black residents in order to sell them south. He and his family were closely associated with St. Peter's Spotswood, where he is buried.

It is perhaps unsurprising that such actions were normative among the elite Episcopal laity of the time because slavery was left unchallenged by the early bishops. The first consecrated bishop of the diocese, John Croes, actually enslaved Black people himself and would even manumit them

Conclusion

just prior to becoming legally liable for their financial support in old age. The second bishop, George Washington Doane, left the institution unchallenged and sought to curry favor with wealthy slave-owning southerners to garner financial support for his projects. The wealth that allowed him to serve as bishop, derived from his wife, was the product not merely of profiting from slave labor, but from the transatlantic slave trade itself.

While many Black New Jersey residents did not feel welcomed or humanely treated in the diocese at this time, some persisted in the denomination and sought to carve out a way of being Black and Episcopalian in spite of paternalistic treatment, segregation, and other horrific challenges. The first Black congregation in the diocese, St. Philip's, was founded in Newark in 1848. After New Jersey was forced by the Thirteenth Amendment to end slavery and the diocese was split into the Diocese of Newark and the Diocese of Southern New Jersey (now known as the Diocese of New Jersey), the difficulties Black Episcopalians suffered did not cease but transformed into a new set of challenges. The development of Jim Crow laws, the resurgence of the Ku Klux Klan, and the ongoing White efforts to disempower Black Episcopalians in the diocese are all subjects of our ongoing historical review.

In summary:

- Anglicans and the Anglican Church were fully involved in the enslavement of Black people in colonial and antebellum New Jersey.
- The church and its laity worked to create a legal establishment of slavery in the state.
- Many of the priests, bishops, and laity sought to (and did) benefit financially from slavery.
- Their churchly attentions to enslaved Black people were limited and largely for self-interested reasons, and few influential New Jersey Anglicans or Episcopalians fully opposed slavery.
- All colonial-era churches, and most if not all antebellum churches in the diocese, were established through the use of funds connected directly to slavery.

Our research is ongoing and we are examining more recent history going forward. In our current phase of research we are investigating the history of racism in the diocese from the Civil War to the present and the development of our historically Black churches, taking oral histories of Black parishioners, deacons, and priests, and looking into the ways that

Part IV: Conclusions and Next Steps

racism continues to be a problem in the diocese. Our research thus far suggests that as New Jersey developed in racist directions, in general, the diocese went along with it.

Initial Observations Concerning Racism in the Diocese of New Jersey after the Civil War

There were very limited Black ministries in the Episcopal Church in New Jersey in the period immediately following the Civil War. St. Philip's in Newark had recently been founded,[2] approximately five churches were running segregated schools, and there was an inadequately funded ministry sponsored first by Christ Church Shrewsbury to the residents of the Black settlement of Macedonia in Tinton Falls. In all these instances, the ministries were segregated. In some churches Black residents were allowed in worship, but they were consigned to segregated seating almost without exception.

During this time the diocese supported the National Episcopal Church Freedman's Commission, designed to aid those African Americans who had until recently been enslaved in the South. However, the support was never significant or adequate to the need, and the commission was not viewed as a success either in its own time or in retrospect. In order to escape the hostile environment of the failed Reconstruction of the South, millions of Black Americans migrated to northern states in the hopes of finding a less oppressive environment. Unfortunately their welcome from the Episcopal Church in New Jersey was generally cool.

As mentioned in chapter 10, as early as 1890 Bishop Scarborough publicly acknowledged both the widespread racism in the diocese, and the neglect with which Black New Jerseyans and recent migrants from the South had been treated by White Episcopalians.[3] But he did not want this racism to prevent Black Americans in the state from becoming Episcopalian. In order to accomplish his goal of improved outreach, he left the status quo of broad White refusal to worship with Black Episcopalians unchallenged, but initiated a program of increased support for the formation of Black churches. His episcopate was marked by the opening of many of the

---

2. The Diocese of New Jersey did not split into the Diocese of Newark and the Diocese of Southern New Jersey (now called the Diocese of New Jersey) until 1874.

3. Protestant Episcopal Church in the Diocese of New Jersey, *Journal of the Proceedings of the One Hundred and Eighteenth Convention*, 168–69.

Conclusion

historically Black churches that have continued faithfully to this day, and allowed for the calling of the first Black priests in the diocese, though for many years they were only allowed to minister in Black congregations.

Some of these churches, like St. Alban's, New Brunswick, were founded by Black Episcopalians fed up with racism in White churches.[4] Some, like St. Augustine's, Camden, were formed through segregated outreach from White congregations.[5] Many of these churches, like St. Thomas,' Redbank, used spaces rejected by White congregations,[6] and were long underfunded and under-resourced. Even when ordained Black clergy were allowed, the clergy were often not permitted to move from the diaconate to the priesthood, or were only allowed to serve the congregation for a short term.[7] Many of these churches, such as St. Augustine's Atlantic City, and St. Augustine's Asbury Park, were sustained, and even managed to grow dramatically, through the efforts of dedicated lay leadership working to insist on the rightful place of Black Christians in the Episcopal Church, even as the rest of the diocese was often openly hostile.

The early twentieth century saw the further development of Jim Crow laws enforcing additional forms of segregation. This legal development was paralleled by the resurgence of the Ku Klux Klan in many parts of the state. In many instances White Episcopalians collaborated with the Klan, such as in Long Branch and Asbury Park, while all the White congregations in Atlantic City[8] hosted Klan rallies. The diocese was home to openly Nazi-sympathetic priests as well, including the long-serving Rev. Dr. Ridgeway in Camden.[9] In the decades following World War II the cities of New Jersey experienced dramatic episodes of White flight, as, rather than live as

---

4. See chapter 11 and Pruszinski, "History of Slavery at Christ Church, New Brunswick."

5. Largely through the efforts of Rev. John H. Townsend of St. John's, Camden. See Bragg, *History of the Afro-American Group of the Episcopal Church*, 229.

6. St. Thomas' Church, Redbank, had to lobby the bishop heavily to let them use a defunct chapel.

7. Both diocesan records and the oral history interviews we have conducted indicate this reality. This accords with the general patterns observed in the Episcopal Church during this period, some of which are detailed in The Episcopal Church, "Racial Justice Audit of Episcopal Leadership."

8. See Hodges, *Black New Jersey*, 166, and the *Baltimore Afro-American, National Edition*, May 23, 1924. It would appear that this included St. James' Church, Church of the Ascension, All Saints' Church, and possibly the Good Shepherd Mission.

9. See the *Courier-Post* Newspaper on September 30, 1938. See also Fanjul, "St. Wilfrid's Church," especially page 97.

neighbors with Black Americans, White New Jerseyans sought to cordon themselves off in all-White suburban developments.[10] The White churches of the diocese were, almost without exception, no different. Again and again, in Elizabeth, in Camden, in Trenton, in Atlantic City, White congregations were abandoned or shuttered as White parishioners left increasingly African American neighborhoods rather than live alongside and worship with Black Christian sisters and brothers.

For example: When, in the 1950s, property developers built a massive, racially restricted Levittown in the Willingboro area, they donated land to the diocese for the building of an Episcopal church in the exclusively White development.[11] The diocese jumped at the chance. The donation of land was accepted. A successful, diocese-wide fundraising campaign ensued to build Christ the King.[12] It had support from the top down, and a significant part of the funding came from the forced liquidation of the property of St. Monica's in Trenton.[13] In order to accomplish this, St. Monica's Black congregation was dissolved by the diocese in the name of integration and parishioners ordered to attend other churches. The only Trenton church that extended a formal welcome was St. Michael's.[14] In time race restrictions in Willingboro were relaxed, and many White people (including Episcopalians) left the area. Over the years Christ the King, Willingboro too has dramatically changed, transforming from its beginnings as an exclusively White church to one that is now predominantly Black.

Final Thoughts

We want to state clearly at this time, that though what we have written and publicized regarding this history is often referred to as "findings," this way of talking about the history is not terribly accurate, as many Black scholars

---

10. For an account of this phenomenon in New Jersey see Greason, *Suburban Erasure*.

11. Correspondence and legal documents from the diocesan archives indicate this, including the deed conveying the land from Levitt & Sons to the diocese recorded October 22, 1958.

12. See *The Witness* 46.39 (December 10, 1959), 8.

13. See Standing Committee meeting minutes for 1957–1958. MSS held in diocesan archives, Trenton, NJ.

14. At least within Trenton proper, according to oral history interviews conducted by the Commission, including with diocesan historiographer and archivist Rev. Canon Richard Wrede. St. Luke's in Ewing welcomed many of the congregants as well.

Conclusion

of the Episcopal Church have stated.[15] The use of this kind of language actually indicates one of the results of segregation in our diocese: the segregation of awareness. It would be more appropriate to say not that these are new discoveries, or findings, but that the willing in every generation of White Episcopalians have had to *rediscover* what we would have already known simply from being fully in community with and listening to our Black sisters and brothers. This is a *rediscovery* of our *neighbor*.

But often when, in the past, these things have become more fully known, when they have at times intruded upon the conscience of White Episcopalians, many have simply ignored these realities, thinking them perhaps either too embarrassing to admit, or not important enough to act on. Perhaps that is why for over eighty years, ever since the buildings were purchased, there have been swastikas embedded in the very structure of our diocesan headquarters.[16] Never removed, just allowed to exist on display, haunting the meeting space, haunting the halls, allowed to comfort whom they would, and to threaten whom they would.

Thankfully (as of the spring of 2024), as a result of the research, educational efforts, and pressure from the Reparations Commission, the swastikas have begun to be removed. But the White Christian racial complacency (if not overt and intentional racism) that allowed them to survive as long as they did in the primary meeting space at the diocesan headquarters cannot be denied.

As we have said, our research is ongoing, but the work of justice and repair for the wrongs that have been done and the wrongs that continue to be done, cannot be accomplished without your help. We invite you to read the work we are publishing on an ongoing basis in the *Diocese of New Jersey Racial Justice Review*. We want to invite you to get involved in researching your parish history, as some parishes have already begun to do. But don't just learn about your history. Learn about your present. We invite you to participate in educational events and liturgical observances that address this material. We invite you to support reparations publicly and politically. We invite you to organize. Learn about who has been harmed and excluded, and who *is being* harmed and excluded *today*. Reach out beyond the walls that have so often been used to separate, including beyond the Episcopal Church.

---

15. Including Lewis, *Yet with a Steady Beat*, 1–14.

16. See Pruszinski, "White Supremacist Symbols at the Diocesan Headquarters (1943–Present)."

Part IV: Conclusions and Next Steps

Thank you for taking the time to read, and to take seriously this difficult history as we consider together how best to acknowledge, repent, and repair the harms that continue to shape our life as a Church to this day.

Jolyon Pruszinski
Reparations Commission Research Historian
Episcopal Diocese of New Jersey

Epilogue
How Can I Research My Congregation?

IF YOU BELONG TO a colonial or antebellum-era Episcopal church in the Diocese of New Jersey and want to begin to investigate your church's ties to slavery and racism, we want to help. There is so much work to be done to uncover and document this under-acknowledged history and the prospect of beginning the work can feel daunting. Where does one start? What should be considered? Here are a few thoughts and resources to get you started.

Limitations

It will help to begin by admitting that you are not going to find everything out. There is a lot that happened for which there is no documentary evidence. And even if there once was documentary evidence, a great deal of it has been lost or destroyed, and much that remains has yet to be catalogued (and as a result is very hard to find, or to even know that it exists). Research programs of this kind must admit their own limitations. Any researcher attempting to paint a picture of the past will paint, at best, a partial picture of what happened. That picture may be (and hopefully will be) representative, but it will not be exhaustive. The limitations of the research endeavor are important to acknowledge, and even as the limitations of the process may be disappointing to a beginning researcher, it is nevertheless important to discover and document what can be found as it is necessary for the process of repentance and repair.

    It is also important to understand the limits of your research for knowing how to speak responsibly about your work. Sweeping generalizations have a way of being inaccurate, while carefully caveated and contextualized reporting is inherently more defensible, and therefore, valuable. You are

Part IV: Conclusions and Next Steps

only making a beginning, but a responsible beginning is far better than, on the one hand, inaccurately claiming to give the final word, or, on the other, giving up entirely because you will not be able to give the final word.

Moreover, it is critical to understand the limitations of your context. The vast majority of churches in the Diocese of New Jersey are, and have been, overwhelmingly White. If this is your context you must understand that this is a limited context from which to research. Looking through your parish records, or looking into the actions of historic parish leaders will only get you so far.

One of the key dynamics at play in this New Jersey church history of slavery and racism is that White people have often produced institutions, communities, and spaces that have alienated Black people. That means that in the records of Episcopal churches in New Jersey there is often little overt mention of Black people, or the treatment of Black people. That doesn't mean that there were no Black people, or that nothing can be known of Black people, or that Black people were treated well. It simply means that Episcopal Church sources, generally, are underreporting the Black experience. Thus, as a source for the information on how Black people were treated, Episcopal Church records, while a necessary element of the research program, are very limited.

White churches are institutions generationally shaped by White ideas, assumptions, biases, and decisions. In order to work to overcome these structural limitations as much as possible, White researchers from White churches will need to look beyond their own experience and institutions. They will need to look for sources and stories from their broader local community, surrounding communities and their larger region, non-Episcopal churches, and secular historical sources. They will need to work to overcome the separation of their church community from the records they need. This separation is the result of generations of unjust actions that have alienated their church communities from the people they have hurt. Much of this story is housed outside the Episcopal Church, and if one is to uncover and attempt to tell this story, and to admit the Church's role in that hurt, a great deal of humility is required. It is not only your story. It is not even primarily your story. Tread lightly. Be sensitive. Be willing to learn. Be willing to apologize. Know that your own biases limit your understanding and add caveats to the products of your research accordingly.

Epilogue

Getting Oriented

At the outset it is important to familiarize yourself with the general and local history of the period you are researching. Read through the research that has already been done, both by the diocese and by other researchers. Be sure to read through the *Diocese of New Jersey Racial Justice Review*, especially those articles related to colonial-era history or your local area. There are several helpful books that have been published on the colonial and antebellum history of this region, slavery in this region, and Black history of New Jersey. Familiarize yourself with them. See Appendix 1 to get you started.

Colonial Era Considerations and Leads

The importance of research into colonial-era history for the churches founded during that period is clear, but many churches founded later should also be doing this work for a number of reasons. Firstly, because many churches founded later were birthed, or planted, with the support of a colonial-era parish.[1] Thus, the financial establishment of the founding parish and its relation to slavery is relevant for the financial establishment of the later parish. Not only so, but, as has been shown, the Church of England established as many preaching stations as churches in New Jersey during the colonial era.[2] Many of these preaching stations went on to develop into churches after the colonial era, but prior to becoming churches, the preaching stations were supported by colonial priests and established parishes, many of whom participated in New Jersey's plantation economy, to say nothing of those lay Anglicans who directly supported the preaching station ministry.[3] Moreover, a number of churches in our diocese today were formed from mergers with colonial or early republic-era parishes,[4]

---

1. For instance, the now defunct St. Mary's, Colestown (founded in 1703), at the time of its destruction by fire in 1899, was considered a "mother church" by many nearby Camden area churches (Burr, *Anglican Church in New Jersey*, 573).

2. Burr, *Anglican Church in New Jersey*, 114–15.

3. See, for example Pruszinski and Pruszinski, "Trinity Church, Princeton and Slavery" and chapter 11 of this book.

4. For instance, St. Elizabeth's Episcopal Church in Elizabeth, NJ was formed through serial mergers incorporating a number of historic congregations including Christ Church, Elizabeth (formed 1853) and Trinity Church, Elizabeth (formed in 1859).

Part IV: Conclusions and Next Steps

and certainly the diocese itself has received the proceeds on occasion from the liquidation of colonial-era church property.[5]

So, clearly, many parishes beyond those parishes founded in the colonial era should be engaged in colonial-era research in order to best understand not only their dependence in their founding upon funds from enslaved labor, but also the ideological and theological positions and presuppositions that shaped the diocese from its outset and which produced the culture and attitudes of its later churches. But what should be considered in such research? What should researchers be aware of?

As we described earlier,[6] slavery was not merely legal, but was encouraged both by the Crown and by many elite Anglicans and priests. The legal system was set up, in part by Anglicans, to enable both it, and the system of law enforcement in which Anglicans were often influential,[7] to work smoothly. Most agriculture in New Jersey's plantation economy was occurring at the subsistence level. That means that farming of any large property involved the use of either hired labor, or, more typically, enslaved labor. Many churches derived income from "glebes," a term for church-owned agricultural lands rented out for farming. Such large-scale agriculture on church lands also typically involved enslaved labor.

The Society for the Propagation of the Gospel (SPG), as described in chapter 2, was the Anglican organization sending priests to the colonies at this time. Its funding was partly derived from the operations of its large plantation in Barbados, which was run using the labor of hundreds of enslaved Africans at a time. Thus all income for those priests serving in New Jersey in the colonial era was derived, in part, from profits off enslaved labor.[8]

As can be seen from these general observations, the structures of oppression operating through the use of enslavement in the plantation economy of colonial New Jersey were clearly intertwined with many aspects of Church funding and life. Though many records from the colonial era have been lost, the overall picture of New Jersey society generally, and the Anglican Church specifically, allow many conclusions to be drawn about individual colonial era churches' complicity in slavery. However, the further

---

5. Such as from the liquidation of the property of Christ Church, Allentown around 1940 (founded in 1730).

6. In chapter 3 of this book.

7. Including through the system of jails and sheriffs.

8. The initial bounty paid to priests when they were first sent, known as the King's or Queen's Bounty, also came partly as a result of the Crown's monopoly profits from the Atlantic slave trade.

Epilogue

details on a church-by-church basis matter a great deal and it cannot be said that more than a start has been made in parish-level research. As such, many historical resources for tracing parish histories in this research area have yet to be analyzed.

Of course, the most critical information to gather at the outset is information about who the leaders and members of each congregation were. A few parishes still have parish registers from the colonial era and these should be digitized for the benefit of future researchers. Such registers sometimes contain information about baptisms of the enslaved. In some instances the diocese holds scans of early documents in its archives.[9] Regarding colonial-era New Jersey priests, the most exhaustive primary sources available are the SPG letter archives. Nelson Burr's *The Anglican Church in New Jersey*[10] is a helpful reference for finding leads as you are starting to work with this archive, but the archives themselves are directly available as digital scans through the British Archives Online.[11]

Various other sources of information are available for learning about parish leadership as well. The most widely accessible are early New Jersey legal documents, including Church-related legal documents such as charters and deeds. These have often been published and many are available online,[12] but also through local libraries, state archives, and research libraries. Such documents often list lay church leaders who were party to or witnesses of legal proceedings, but also furnish useful information about church property.[13]

---

9. Reach out to the diocesan archivist and historiographer, as of the date of publication, Rev. Cn. Richard Wrede, to see what he can find for you in the diocesan archives.

10. Although there are significant problems with how Burr deals with slavery and racism. See Appendix 3.

11. See British Archives Online, SPG Correspondence at https://microform.digital/boa/collections/11/america-in-records-from-colonial-missionaries-1635-1928.

12. https://www.google.com/books has many of these. A good start can be made with *Documents Relating to the Colonial History of New Jersey*, a multivolume series published from the archives of the State of New Jersey which is in the public domain. See also State of New Jersey, *Laws of the State of New Jersey*.

13. If you are having trouble knowing where to start, or have difficulty finding much about the early years of your colonial church, Nelson Burr's *The Anglican Church in New Jersey* focuses on the colonial era, and is held in many Episcopal church libraries in the state. While it is not a great guide to issues of slavery and racism, it does reference many useful primary documents, and if you can read between the lines and filter its rosy perspective, it can provide some helpful leads, at the very least providing some information on key early leaders in most churches. You can then research the ties these individuals had to slavery.

Part IV: Conclusions and Next Steps

Once it has been determined who was involved with a particular church, research can begin on the ways those specific individuals were involved with enslavement. There are a variety of possible avenues for investigation. Due to the increasing interest in New Jersey's history of slavery, many institutions have begun to work to collect and organize their records that help illuminate that history. Among these are local libraries, historical societies,[14] museums,[15] municipal and county governments,[16] colleges and universities,[17] and the State of New Jersey.[18] Local institutions may be able to point you to relevant resources on the colonial history of slavery in your area. Some of these records have been formally published, and some excellent resources have been made available online. Often at least a record of the existence of records can be found through many institutional websites, especially at universities and the state level. Evidence of engaging in enslavement can be found in escaped slave advertisements from newspapers,[19] in census documents, in wills,[20] and a variety of other colonial era legal documents. Many of these records are available through the Northeast Slavery Record Index (NESRI) or the New Jersey Slavery Records database.[21]

Don't forget that it is important to consider not merely direct engagement in enslavement in your research, but support for the institution. Many Anglicans helped to pass the legal codes that established slavery and benefited and protected enslavers. Others supported the institution through public advocacy in newspapers,[22] or enforced it as agents of the state. Many

---

14. E.g., the Monmouth County Historical Association.

15. E.g., the Morven Museum: https://www.morven.org/slavery-at-morven.

16. E.g., the "Gloucester County Slavery Records" at http://www.westjerseyhistory.org/docs/gloucesterrecs/slavery/.

17. E.g., Rutgers University (https://scarletandblack.rutgers.edu/), Monmouth University (https://guides.monmouth.edu/RaceRacismPolicing), Princeton University (https://slavery.princeton.edu), and Princeton Theological Seminary (https://slavery.ptsem.edu).

18. E.g., https://www.nj.gov/state/archives/catsuslaves.html.

19. Many of which have been published in Marrin, ed., *Runaways of Colonial New Jersey*, and Hodges and Brown, eds., *"Pretends to Be Free."*

20. See, for example, Weiss, *Personal Estates of Early Farmers and Tradesmen of Colonial New Jersey*.

21. For NESRI see https://nesri.com.sc.cuny.edu. The New Jersey Slavery Records database, produced by Rutgers researchers, is available at https://records.njslavery.org.

22. Many archival resources for period newspapers are available online, including the databases developed through the National Digital Newspaper Program at https://www.loc.gov/ndnp/. Various online resources for digitized archival newspapers can be

inherited wealth produced through enslavement. These relationships matter for understanding all the ways that Anglicans made slavery an integral part of life in the colony. And research should not be limited to New Jersey only. In many cases, wealthy Anglicans owned property in multiple colonies. New Jersey at the time was very closely linked both to New York City and to Philadelphia, and so consideration must be given to records from those regions as well.

Early Republic/Antebellum Era Considerations and Leads

Just as it is important for many churches founded after the colonial era to consider the histories of antecedent colonial parishes for understanding their own history, so is it necessary not merely for churches founded during the early Republic to research their histories of slavery, but for churches founded after the Civil War to consider the history of connected parishes founded during the early Republic. Many post-Civil War churches were birthed, or planted, with the support of an early Republic-era parish or mission, so the financial establishment of the founding parish and its relation to slavery is critical to appreciate. And, as previously mentioned, many churches operating today formed through mergers between older parishes, and the slavery-related entanglements of the parent churches bears directly on the generational responsibility born by daughter churches. See Appendix 4 for a list of all the congregations, preaching stations, and missions that operated before the end of the Civil War.

The good news about researching this era is that there are many more documents and resources that have been preserved. The difficulty is that there are so many, and they are so widely dispersed and poorly catalogued that it can be difficult to track them down, and even to survey them all adequately. But do not be daunted by these difficulties, as the work is important to attempt even if we are not always entirely equal to the task.

During this period following the Revolutionary War, New Jersey kept slavery intact even as increasing strictures were placed on the institution. Under pressure from abolitionists, New Jersey was the last northern state to enact a gradual abolition law (1804), though the law is generally seen as

---

accessed through most local libraries. Many sermons and other publications appear in the "Eighteenth Century Short Title Catalogue" and the "Nineteenth Century Short Title Catalogue," resources also accessible through many library systems.

Part IV: Conclusions and Next Steps

having served to buttress the institution rather than undermine it. It wasn't for another twenty-one years that any enslaved person in the state became free as a result of the legislation, and once formerly enslaved Black people became free, they still faced horrible prejudice and a legal (and extralegal) system of oppression that continued to conspire to limit their freedom. In spite of modest limitations to slavery that were enacted over time,[23] the institution persisted in the state, along with White sentiment in favor of it, while strong sentiments against the increasing prospect of living alongside freed Black Americans persisted as well.

Newspapers of the time are full of White fearmongering on the issue. Many churches in the Diocese of New Jersey eagerly participated in the American Colonization Society (ACS), which sought to remove freed Black slaves from the United States and send them to Africa, in order to "solve" the "problem" they saw resulting from the presence of the formerly enslaved.[24] A few churches developed segregated schools at this time, but often these were viewed as a means to continue to control both enslaved and free Black people.[25] Generally speaking, during this time, the diocese made little effort at ministry to and with Black people, and the funding that did go toward Black ministry was generally dedicated to the ACS and Episcopal mission to Liberia.[26]

A further difficulty researchers will encounter with material from this period is the prevalent use of euphemism and indirect language for slavery. This requires careful analysis and reading (often between the lines). In documents of this time, the enslaved are regularly referred to as "servants" or "domestics" rather than slaves. In fact, even New Jersey state legislation from 1846, which claimed to "end slavery" in the state, only renamed the enslaved as "apprentices for life" who could still be bought and sold and whose practical status had changed not at all.

Ultimately the population of enslaved Black Americans in the state did dwindle into the period of the Civil War,[27] but support for the institution remained strong. Slavery, except as legal punishment for a crime, was only

23. See chapter 5 of this book.
24. As discussed in chapter 13.
25. See chapter 12.
26. As discussed in chapter 13.
27. Numbers dropped from an official high of 12,422 in 1800 (Gigantino II, *Ragged Road to Abolition*, 280n3) to an official low of eighteen in the 1860 census, though "probably hundreds of slaves for a term and apprentices [for life were] not properly recorded in the census" (Gigantino II, *Ragged Road to Abolition*, 240).

Epilogue

ended in the state once the necessary number of other states had ratified the Thirteenth Amendment. The Democrat-controlled New Jersey legislature refused to ratify the amendment, and abolition through the Thirteenth Amendment became the law of the land in spite of New Jersey legislators.[28]

As with the colonial era, determining prominent members of each congregation is an important first step in the research process. There is comparatively more material to work with here, as many churches from this era have preserved their records, or local church histories were written that are still kept in parish or local libraries. As many of these histories are old enough to have entered the public domain, they should be scanned and made available online whenever possible. Diocesan records are rather helpful for this period as well, with the vast majority of diocesan convention journals, which typically in this period include parochial reports, available online.[29] Once you determine who many of the key priests and parishioners were, you can begin to look at whether they enslaved anyone, whether their wealth was derived from slavery, and whether they used their respective positions of authority (either secular or churchly) to support the institution.

Government records are more robust for this period as well, including at the municipal, county, and state level. Under gradual abolition local New Jersey governments were required to keep an account of births of the enslaved, as well as who their enslavers were. This is a trove of important information, in some instances published in book form (e.g., in the *Black Birth Book of Monmouth County* [1989]),[30] but otherwise held in local or county archives.[31] A great deal of US Census data is also available online and is searchable.[32] As previously mentioned, many newspaper archives have been scanned and can be accessed through university libraries, and even local libraries. Again, various institutions have begun to collate their material related to slavery and you will likely have some success connecting with local librarians, museums, and historical societies. Also, be sure to use both NESRI and the New Jersey Slavery Records database. Some journals to examine as you research this history of the members of your parish include:

28. A later Republican controlled legislature voted to ratify the amendment.

29. These have been scanned and can be viewed at https://www.google.com/books, at least through 1920.

30. Such as records held by the Middlesex County Clerk, e.g. "Middlesex County Book of Manumissions and Removals . . . 1800–1825."

31. Many resources of this kind are available at the Newark Public Library, including "Essex County Slave Records," and scans of other county and municipal "slave books."

32. See https://www.archives.gov/research/census/online-resources.

Part IV: Conclusions and Next Steps

New Jersey Studies

Proceedings of the New Jersey Historical Society

Genealogical Magazine of New Jersey

Pennsylvania History: A Journal of Mid-Atlantic Studies

Pennsylvania Magazine of History & Biography

New York History

The New York Genealogical and Biographical Record

Along with the need for careful discernment in interpreting euphemistic language, there is the need to be aware of the tendency of writers with a Christian bias (e.g., church historians, priests, or diocesan officials) to promote the good things that were done during this period and to downplay the problems. Church histories are full of glowing depictions of the faithful and forgetfulness of the people they have harmed.[33] And even when the faithful did indeed do good, such as in the case of prominent New Jersey Episcopalian Hon. James Parker[34] (who helped stop the Van Wickle slave ring), the way their actions are described in church documents can allow the facts to be misconstrued.

For example, the biographical notice[35] on Parker from 1889 states that he was "very prominent in advocacy of the abolition of Slavery within the State," even though the slavery laws were never meaningfully altered as a result of his advocacy. Rather it appears that the main thing he accomplished was raising awareness of the need to enforce the slavery laws already on the books in New Jersey[36] (which had not yet, at the time of the operation of the Van Wickle Ring, resulted in freeing even a single enslaved person).

All this is to say, the primary documents of the time require careful handling in order to ensure honest treatment of the history and avoid misinterpretation. And as with the colonial era, care is required to capture the full geographic scope of the practices of enslavement. Various elite Episcopalians owned large estates in the American South, on which they enslaved hundreds of Black Americans. Those holdings account for a great deal of

---

33. Burr's *Anglican Church in New Jersey* is a clear local example of this.

34. Neither the first nor last of that name.

35. Compiled by his descendant, also of that name: Parker, ed., *Historical Sketches of Parishes*, 87–88.

36. According to newspaper accounts of the time.

their wealth, even as they may be hard to track down due to geographic separation from New Jersey.

What About After the Civil War?

Racism did not cease with the passage of the Thirteenth Amendment to the Constitution, even as the ratification of the amendment (over the protestations of the New Jersey legislature) did make slavery illegal in New Jersey except as punishment for a crime (so slavery did not in fact cease entirely either). And just as slavery had dramatic negative effects on the lives and livelihoods of Black Americans, so has the ongoing operation of racism. There have been many ways that New Jersey residents and citizens of African descent have continued to be harmed through unjust laws, unjust enforcement of laws, and prejudicial treatment, not only through secular avenues, but also by the Episcopal Church. Research in this area at the diocesan level is ongoing, but there is much work to be done. Whenever possible, individual parishes should devote themselves to researching their part in the history as well.[37]

Can We Approach a Forensic Accounting for Wrong?

In short, no. The wrongs done are utterly massive and truly incalculable. There is a tendency to want to know exact dollar amounts of culpability, to understand the scope. The reality is that this is not possible. Yes, many White people in the American colonies and in the United States have benefited financially from slavery and racism. Their wealth is a result of theft. And, yes, the Anglican and Episcopal Churches have benefited financially from slavery and racism. But determining what percentage of the gifts given, or the endowments have links to slavery, and what percentage of those funds is encumbered by connection to slavery, involves a gross inaccuracy. It assumes that those who benefited from slavery and racism reaped the whole value of what was lost by those harmed, an assumption that is entirely inaccurate.

---

37. The essay "Consulting the Past Through the Archival Record: A Guide for Researching the Impact of Slavery on Church Life and African Americans," published by The Archives of the Episcopal Church, is a good summary resource of many key questions for all churches to consider.

Part IV: Conclusions and Next Steps

The accumulation of wealth through enslavement required the murder of millions to reap the labor value of many fewer. It required the loss of full freedom to create and produce and live and flourish for millions, the limitation of their skilled contribution to humanity, in order to reap the (comparatively lesser) and inhumane value of the (often) menial labor of those millions of souls. The dramatically smaller monetary value reaped by those who enslaved and who benefited from slavery required the decimation of peoples and the decimation those peoples' full ability to live and produce to the best of their ability and creativity.

Such stolen wealth is not encumbered at its face value. It is supersaturated with encumbrance. It represents a tiny fraction of the value of what was destroyed in order to steal it. Slavery was a massive wealth destruction event, even as it served to transfer a small portion of the wealth it destroyed to those who benefited from it. The wealth that remains is a tiny fraction of what was lost. Even that wealth derived from the operation of racist systems of oppression (but not slavery) has a similar supersaturated encumbrance due to the Black wealth destruction and preclusion that occurred in order to produce it.

This supersaturated encumbrance attached to wealth derived from slavery has a further dimension. The question regularly arises about whether philanthropy (such as to churches) from enslavers should not be considered only partially encumbered by problematic associations with slavery, because only part of their wealth was the result of the enslavement they engaged in. This is, again, based on a confused understanding. In general, slave labor was often used in situations where the farming or mining being conducted would have been at a subsistence level had it been conducted by free laborers. The profit gleaned from the endeavor was often the exclusive result of stolen labor value from enslaved peoples.

Because the enterprise was typically only profitable as a result of the use of enslaved labor, any ability of the enslaver to donate out of their wealth was only possible due to profit above the subsistence level through the use of slavery. That means that their charity, regardless of how great their wealth or how diversified their portfolio, was coming from that portion of their enterprise profit above the subsistence level: i.e., directly from their profit from slavery.[38] Not only does this mean that there would be

---

38. And, to be clear, only a small percentage of this wealth from enslavement was ever given to the church. It remained, and remains largely, to this day, in private hands. The history of parsimony toward the church on the part of the wealthy, including in New Jersey, is very well documented (see, for example, Chute, "When Perth Amboy Was a

no portion of their giving that was not encumbered, but the giving, due to its connection to slavery is, as previously mentioned, supersaturated with encumbrance.

Research and Moving Forward

The unfortunate conclusion to be drawn from the reality of supersaturated encumbrance of White (and White church) wealth is that the true scope of the debt can never really be repaid. However, that does not mean that important and necessary steps cannot be taken to address current race-based wealth inequities.[39] Nor does it mean that detailed research into the wrongs committed by Anglicans and Episcopalians against Black people is moot. In fact, such research is necessary to determine with detail the scope of the wrongs in order to enable repentance and to build awareness of the need for critical reparative action.

Every church has a responsibility to reckon with both its past and present in this regard. Likewise, every Christian is obliged, by their corporate participation in the systems that have perpetrated the harms of slavery and racism, to reckon with their own responsibility for repair. This responsibility starts with cultivating an awareness of both "the evils we have done, and the evil done on our behalf."[40] We have not always been aware of all the ways we and the institutions we participate in have established, perpetuated, or benefited from slavery and racism. But once we begin to know, we must acknowledge that as Christians we have an inexorable obligation to address this unfortunate history, to recognize its persistent influence in our present, and to do what we can to make it right.

As I stated in the preface, our proper response can only be to "Do justly, now. Love mercy, now. Walk humbly, now. You are not obligated to complete the work, but neither are you free to abandon it."[41]

Seaport Town," 35, 45, which documents a parsimonious portrayal of even the celebrated James Parker). The church and its officials did much of the moral justification for this private accumulation of wealth from slavery, even as its own benefit was comparatively rather small. Regarding the Church's moral authority in this regard, the phrase "sold for a pittance" comes to mind.

39. Such ongoing remediation will be necessary until there is no longer a racial wealth gap in the United States.

40. Church Pension Fund, "Confession," 19.

41. *Pirkei Avot* 2.16.

Appendix 1

Further Recommended Reading

IT CAN BE HARD to know where to start when looking to learn more about slavery as practiced by Anglicans and Episcopalians in New Jersey. There are, however, several excellent books and articles that deal with various aspects of this history. Some solid resources that deal with the history of slavery and the Black experience in New Jersey include the following.

- Rick Geffken, *Stories of Slavery in New Jersey* (Charleston, SC: The History Press, 2021).
- James Gigantino, *The Ragged Road to Abolition: Slavery and Freedom in New Jersey, 1775–1865* (Philadelphia: University of Pennsylvania Press, 2015).
- Walter D. Greason, *Suburban Erasure: How the Suburbs Ended the Civil Rights Movement in New Jersey* (Lanham, MD: Rowman and Littlefield, 2013).
- Graham Russell Hodges, *Black New Jersey: 1664 to the Present Day* (New Brunswick: Rutgers University Press, 2019).
- Graham Russell Hodges, *Slavery and Freedom in the Rural North: African Americans in Monmouth County, New Jersey, 1665–1865* (Madison, WI: Madison House, 1997).

Appendix 1

Gary J. Hunter, *Neighborhoods of Color: African American Communities in Southern New Jersey, 1638–2000* (Glassboro, NJ: Rowan University Press, 2015).

Christopher Matthews, "The Black Freedom Struggle in Northern New Jersey, 1613–1860: A Review of the Literature," https://www.montclair.edu/anthropology/research/slavery-in-nj/.

Geneva Smith, "Legislating Slavery in New Jersey," https://slavery.princeton.edu/stories/legislating-slavery-in-new-jersey.

The aforementioned resources do not, however, deal to any significant degree with Anglican and Episcopal history or distinctives regarding these issues. The following texts provide essential information pertaining to the general picture of the Anglican and Episcopalian establishment of, support for, and cooperation with slavery and racism.

Robert A. Bennett, "Black Episcopalians: A History from the Colonial Period to the Present," *HMPEC* 43.3 (1974) 231–45.

George F. Bragg, *History of the African-American Group of the Episcopal Church* (Baltimore: Church Advocate, 1922).

Travis Glasson, *Mastering Christianity: Missionary Anglicanism and Slavery in the Atlantic World* (Oxford: Oxford University Press, 2012).

Robert E. Hood, "From a Headstart to a Deadstart: The Historical Basis for Black Indifference toward the Episcopal Church 1800–1860," *HMPEC* 51.3 (1982) 269–96.

Harold T. Lewis, *Yet with a Steady Beat: The African American Struggle for Recognition in the Episcopal Church* (Valley Forge, PA: Trinity, 1996).

Jennifer C. Snow, *Mission, Race, and Empire: The Episcopal Church in Global Perspective* (Oxford: Oxford University Press, 2024).

Lauren Winner, *The Dangers of Christian Practice: On Wayward Gifts, Characteristic Damage, and Sin* (New Haven: Yale University Press, 2018).

Excellent resources dealing with the issue of reparations specifically are also available. These include the recent open access article "Normalizing Reparations," by Linda Bilmes and Cornell Brooks, which articulates, perhaps contrary to the readers' expectation, the various ways that reparations are already a very well-established and normal practice in American society, and the recent book *Reparations* by Peter Jarrett-Schell, which discusses

Further Recommended Reading

reparations in a specifically Episcopal context. The New Jersey Reparations Council report released on Juneteenth, 2025, provides a robust treatment of the issue of reparations in New Jersey specifically.

- Linda J. Bilmes and Cornell William Brooks, "Normalizing Reparations: U.S. Precedent, Norms, and Models for Compensating Harms and Implications for Reparations to Black Americans," *RSF* 10.2 (2024) 30–68; https://doi.org/10.7758/RSF.2024.10.2.02.
- New Jersey Reparations Council, "For Such a Time as This: The Nowness of Reparations for Black People in New Jersey," New Jersey Institute for Social Justice (June 19, 2025); https://www.njisj.org/print/njrcreport.pdf
- Peter Jarrett-Schell, *Reparations: A Plan for Churches* (New York: Church Publishing, 2023).

And if you are unfamiliar with the important theological work done by Black theologians of the last fifty years, please do familiarize yourself. The following works of James Cone and Kelly Brown Douglas are a good place to start.

- James H. Cone, *The Cross and the Lynching Tree* (Maryknoll, NY: Orbis, 2011).
- Kelly Brown Douglas, *The Black Christ* (Maryknoll, NY: Orbis, 1994).

There are, of course, many more important and useful resources that address the various further aspects of all of these matters that may be found in the Selected Bibliography and through the *Diocese of New Jersey Racial Justice Review*, which can be found at https://dionj-racialjusticereview.blogspot.com.

Appendix 2

Questions for Discussions

THE FOLLOWING QUESTIONS ARE not meant to be exhaustive, but rather are intended simply to serve as a prompt for thinking thoroughly about the issues raised by this book. They are not designed to go with any particular chapter, but any of these could be used to foster a conversation prompted by any of the chapters. No doubt more particular questions that are uniquely germane to your own community and context will arise from reading, but these are provided specifically to support the work of examining ourselves, our actions, our relationships, our traditions, and our preexisting assumptions in order to inspire more than superficial change.

- Who has our complicity with slavery and racism harmed?
- What parts of the Bible form us to accept relationships of domination, enslavement, and servitude (e.g., Lord/master and servant/slave)? What parts of the Bible form us to reject relationships of domination, enslavement, and servitude?
- What aspects of Episcopal liturgy form us to accept relationships of domination, enslavement, and servitude? What aspects of Episcopal liturgy form us to reject relationships of domination, enslavement, and servitude?
- How am I working to reject domination, enslavement, and servitude as relational models?

Questions for Discussions

How is my church working to reject domination, enslavement, and servitude as relational models? What alternative relational models do we have in the church apart from domination, enslavement, and servitude?

What does the Bible say about generational sin? About repentance? About reparation? Across generations?

What historical models can you think of for making restitution and repair for wrongs?

What systems and practices does our society already use today for making restitution and repair for wrongs? What might we learn from these systems?

Where might I need to go beyond my church to find out what repair needs to be made for slavery and racism? Who might I need to build relationships with?

How can I do the work of anti-racism myself rather than continuing to expect others, especially people of color, to do it for me?

Who have I left out of my consideration?

What changes might be necessary to approach a full repair for the wrongs of slavery and racism? In my own relationships? In the church? In my community? In our diocese? In our state? In my denomination? In our nation? In the Anglican Communion? In the Christian church universal?

Appendix 3

The Anglican Church in New Jersey by Nelson R. Burr (1954), a Review.

THE ANGLICAN CHURCH IN *New Jersey*. By Nelson R. Burr. Philadelphia: The Church Historical Society, 1954. pp. xvi–768. $10.00 (now out of print).[1]

    Nelson R. Burr, the celebrated church historian,[2] has written a history of the development of *The Anglican Church in New Jersey*. Burr's text is the best known and most widely distributed book dealing with its subject, and while it does faithfully represent many aspects of the colonial correspondence of Anglican priests stationed in New Jersey, in general it does so uncritically. The effect of this authorial approach is that Burr has produced a credulous, often hagiographic, and frequently racist history that privileges the perspective of the privileged at the expense of marginalized peoples. It is a verbose testament to the power of survivor bias in the telling of church history and, while standing on the shelves of Episcopal church libraries throughout the state of New Jersey, it also stands as a warning to modern historiographers.

    Burr's text does not purport to cover exhaustively the entire history of the Anglican (and later Episcopal) Church in New Jersey, but focuses most closely on the colonial era, prior to the formation of the Episcopal Church

---

    1. Available through Hathi Trust at https://catalog.hathitrust.org/Record/001640884.

    2. For whom the annual *Anglican and Episcopal History* journal prize for best article is named.

(hence the title).³ In choosing this focus Burr relies overwhelmingly on a particular corpus of documentary evidence, that is, on the records of correspondence between New Jersey priests and the Society for the Propagation of the Gospel (SPG), a voluntary Anglican association founded in 1701 to send priests to the colonies and, by extension, expand the reach and influence of the Church. Copies of this corpus are housed in the Library of Congress in Washington, DC and in the Bodleian Library at the University of Oxford, while digital scans of the bulk of the holdings are now available for viewing online.⁴ As a reference to the New Jersey-related portion of this catalog of correspondence, and as a starting point for investigating the primary documents themselves, Burr's book is invaluable. It oscillates between summary paraphrase and fine-grained detail, at times approaching the tenor of an annotated bibliography, both highlighting many of the key themes of the correspondence and providing careful and specific reference to particular letters. However, if one is reading for narratological style, the structure of the text leaves something to be desired. Though the chapters move somewhat chronologically, they are clearly a product of a thematic collation of notes on the primary texts, presented in thematically designated chapters. The unfortunate result is that paraphrases of information drawn from the SPG correspondence appear repeatedly across multiple chapters, almost without awareness of the fact that the author is repeating himself. Thus the book at times resembles a reference text more than a history, and seems structured based on the assumption that the reader will not be digesting the whole text cover-to-cover as printed.

The more significant problem with Burr's presentation of his source material is his apparent credulity regarding the institution of the Church as an agent of exclusive good. His narration maintains throughout a cadence of inevitability (and facile solidarity with the figures of the past), suggesting that pious Anglicans did right, others resisted, but that all things fell out essentially for good generally, and for the good of the Church particularly. In this he may be accurately representing the tone of the underlying sources, and the culture of the Church at the time of his

---

3. Though it does provide a cursory sixty-nine-page summary of the subsequent period through its publishing (1954).

4. Courtesy of the British Online Archives, SPG Correspondence Collection: "America in Records from Colonial Missionaries, 1635–1928." MSS copy scans: https://microform.digital/boa/collections/11/america-in-records-from-colonial-missionaries-1635-1928.

Appendix 3

writing,[5] but in doing so he reproduces institutional hagiography largely uncritically and rarely deploys a historiographic idiom that diverges in any appreciable way from survivor bias.

The clearest problem this bias creates for *The Anglican Church in New Jersey* appears in the Church's treatment of the enslaved, and specifically enslaved Africans and African Americans. Here Burr cleaves to the *tone* of his sources, which were written by priests who saw slavery as entirely justifiable within a "great chain of being," while ignoring *the actual data about slavery* that the sources contain. Prolific enslavers, like Col. Lewis Morris and Col. Daniel Cox, who helped make draconian slave codes New Jersey law, are described in entirely glowing terms. Burr's whitewash can perhaps best be seen in a subsection title which unironically asserts that "The Church Cherishes the Negro." This brief section (224–28) paints a picture of benevolent concern and solicitude on the part of White Anglican priests. Almost without exception, the priests that he mentions as devoting attention to "the negroes" in this section in fact sought to create, buttress, and benefit from a slave society, while being active enslavers themselves. The letters Burr is working with, as he admits (226), make frequent mention of the enslaved, but he is very selective in his presentation. Included in the New Jersey SPG correspondence are plans for slave-worked plantations governed by priests,[6] reports of how Christianization is useful for suppressing slave revolt,[7] and mathematically challenged insistences that Anglicans are not significant enslavers.[8] But when Burr refers to these aspects of the correspondence, he justifies the enslavers, failing to indicate any appreciation for the crushingly oppressive injustice of the system the Church helped produce. Nor does he articulate precisely how enslavement constituted "cherishing."

---

5. One review from the time it was published (William Warren Sweet, "*The Anglican Church in New Jersey*. By Nelson R. Burr," *Church History* 24.2 [1955]: 188–89) actually suggested that Burr has "refused to set the Church with its ministers and people upon a pedestal of perfection, and records the losses, failures and weaknesses as well as their courage and successes." The bar was set very low indeed to result in such an estimation.

6. T. Haliday to SPG Secretary, 9 October 1717, SPG Correspondence Collection, Book A, Vol. 12, 301–7.

7. J. Sharpe to SPG Secretary, 23 June 1712, SPG Correspondence Collection, Book A, Vol. 7, 214–17.

8. J. Holbrooke to SPG Secretary, 17 November 1727, SPG Correspondence Collection, Book A, Vol. 20, 193–98.

The Anglican Church in New Jersey by Nelson R. Burr

 Burr's approach to the relation of enslaved Black people to the Church appears to be consistent with his convictions regarding race and the Church in general. In *The Anglican Church in New Jersey* he indicates his belief not just that the Anglican (and Episcopal) Church is essentially only for White people, but rather that it is only for a narrow subset of White people. This prejudice can be seen in his commentary on the demographic tables in his conclusion (e.g. Table IV, 483–84) ostensibly explaining the obstacles to Episcopal Church growth in New Jersey presented by immigration from "southern and eastern Europe" (468).

 Burr's text, though useful as a compendium of topically organized references to SPG correspondence pertinent to New Jersey, is less a critical historiography, and more a starry-eyed, but deeply flawed hagiography of the Church. While clearly knowledgeable of the Church's responsibility for slavery and racism from the testimony of the SPG letter archive, Burr manipulates his narrative to keep that knowledge from his readers with a dexterity that approaches prestidigitation.

Appendix 4

Colonial (Anglican) and Antebellum (Episcopal) Parishes, Missions, and Preaching Stations in New Jersey[1]

Preaching station at Acquackanonk (near Passaic)

St. Thomas' Church, Alexandria (Kingwood)

Preaching station at Allamuchy (near Hackettstown)

Christ Church, Allentown

St. Andrew's Church, Amwell (moved to Lambertville, aka West Amwell)

Mission at Andover

Mission at Atlantic City

Preaching station at Barnegat

St. Mark's Church, Baskingridge

Mission at Batsto

1. If a preaching station became a mission or a mission became a parish in nearly the exact same location before the end of the Civil War, in general only the most established status is listed. However, many preaching stations and missions listed in small villages laid the foundation for churches nearby even if not in the exact same location. For a list of the preaching stations in the colonial era specifically see Burr, *Anglican Church in New Jersey*, 655–56.

Colonial (Anglican) and Antebellum (Episcopal) Parishes

Christ Church, Belleville (aka Second River, aka Trinity Chapel, Belleville)

Zion Church, Belvidere

Trinity Church, Bergen Point (aka Holy Trinity, Bergen; now part of Jersey City)

Preaching station at Bethlehem

St. Stephen's Church, Beverly (aka Churchville, aka Willingborough)

Preaching station at Black River (now Chester)

Christ Church, Bloomfield

St. Bartholomew's Church, (Old) Boone Town (aka Boonton)

St. John's Church, Boonton

Christ Church, Bordentown

St. Paul's Chapel, Bound Brook (aka St. Paul's Mission at South Bound Brook)

Mission at Brandsville (aka Walnut Corner in Knowlton)

St. Andrew's Church, Bridgeton (Cumberland Co.)

Holy Child Jesus Chapel and Burlington College, Burlington

St. Barnabas' Church, Burlington (aka Free Mission Chapel of St. Barnabas)

St. Mary's Church, Burlington

St. Mary's Hall and Chapel of the Holy Innocents, Burlington

St. John's Church, Camden

St. Paul's Church, Camden (aka Zion Church)

Mission at Cape May Court House

Mission at Cape May Island

Mission at Carpenter's Landing (now Wenonah / Mantua / Clarksboro)

Mission at Cedar Grove

Preaching station at Chatham

Mission at Cheesequake

St. John's Church, Chew's Landing (aka Timber Creek)

Christ Church, Claremont (aka Bergen)

Appendix 4

St. Peter's Church, Clarksborough (aka Berkeley, aka Sandtown)

Calvary Church, Clinton

St. Paul's Church, Clinton

St. Mary's Church, Colestown (aka Waterford)

Mission at Columbia (in Knowlton Twp.)

Preaching station at Cranbury (aka Cranberry)

Grace Church, Crosswicks (aka St. John's Crosswicks)

St. John's Church, Dover

Mission at East Newark

St. Peter's Mission, Eatentown

Church of the Mediator, Edgewater

Preaching station at Egg Harbor

Christ Church, Elizabeth (aka Elizabethtown)

Grace Church, Elizabeth (aka Elizabethport)

St. John's Church, Elizabeth (aka Elizabethtown)

Trinity Church, Elizabeth

St. John's Free Chapel, Englishtown

Trinity Church, Fairview

Calvary Church, Flemington

St. Stephen's Church, Florence

Church of the Good Shepherd, Fort Lee

Mission at Franklin (aka Quakertown)

Mission at Fredon

St. Peter's Church, Freehold (formerly at Topenemus aka Topenemes)

St. Thomas' Church, Glassborough

Church of the Ascension, Gloucester (aka Gloucester City)

St. John's Church, Greenwich (Greenwich Twp., now in Warren Co.)

St. Stephen's Church, Greenwich-in-Cohansey (aka Greenwich, now in Cumberland Co.)

Mission at Groveville (near Yardville)

Colonial (Anglican) and Antebellum (Episcopal) Parishes

Christ Church, Hackensack

St. James Church, Hackettstown (related to St. Peter's, Mansfield/Hackettstown)

Grace Church, Haddonfield

Mission at Hammonton

Christ Church, Hardwick

Mission at Harmony (now in Warren Co.)

Trinity Church, Hightstown

St. Paul's Church, Hoboken

Trinity Church, Hoboken

St. Luke's Church, Hope

Christ Church, Hopewell (succeeded by St. Michael's, Trenton)

Preaching station at Horseneck (aka Caldwell)

Mission at Howell Works, Monmouth Co. (aka Howell Furnace)

Church of the Holy Trinity, Hudson (now The Heights neighborhood of Jersey City)

Trinity Church, Irvington (aka Irvington Place, aka Camptown, aka Clintonville)

Mission at Jacksonville (near Springfield, Mansfield, and Mount Holly)

Mission at Jamesburg

St. Matthew's Church, Jersey City

Trinity Church, Jersey City (aka Third ward free mission chapel, aka Trinity Chapel)

Christ Church, Johnsonburg (aka Log Gaol)

Mission at Keyport (aka Lockport, aka St. James Brown's Point)

St. James Church, Knowlton (aka Oxford)

Mission at Lafayette (suburb of Jersey City)

St. Andrew's Church, Lambertville (moved from Amwell)

Mission at Leedsville (village in Egg Harbor Twp. near Linwood)

Preaching station at Long-a-coming (now in Berlin Twp.)

Appendix 4

St. James Church, Long Branch

Mission at Lumberton (near Burlington)

Macedonia Mission, Macedonia (Tinton Falls)

Grace Church, Madison

Preaching station at Maidenhead (now Lawrenceville)

Preaching station at Manahawkin (now in Stafford Twp.)

Mission at Manasquan Village (aka Squan)

St. Peter's Church, Mansfield (near Hackettstown)

Mission at Marksborough (near Johnsonburg)

Mission at Martinville (aka Martinsville near Bound Brook)

Mission at Matchaponix (south of Spottswood)

Preaching station at Maurice River (likely downstream of Millville)

Mission at May's Landing (near Atlantic City)

St. Peter's Mission Chapel, Medford

Christ Church, Middletown

Trinity Church, Middletown (Middletown Point)

Christ Church, Millville (Cumberland Co.)

St. Stephen's Church, Millville in Millburn (Essex Co.)

Mission at Mine Hill

Mission at Montague

St. Luke's Church, Montclair (aka West Bloomfield, aka Mount Clair, aka Mont Clair)

Trinity Church, Moorestown

Zion Church, Moravia (Gloucester Co.)

Mission at Morris Plains

Church of the Redeemer, Morristown

St. Peter's Church, Morristown

St. Andrew's Church, Mount Holly

Trinity Church, Mount Holly (related to the Mission in the village of Turpentine)

Colonial (Anglican) and Antebellum (Episcopal) Parishes

St. Stephen's Church, Mullica Hill

Preaching station at Musconetcong (likely near Hampton)

Christ Church, Newark (aka Christ Free Mission Church, Newark)

Grace Church, Newark

The House of Prayer, Newark

St. Barnabas' Church, Newark (aka Roseville)

St. John the Baptist Mission, Newark

St. Mark's Church, Newark

St. Matthew's Chapel on the Hill, Newark

St. Matthew's Church, Newark

St. Paul's Church, Newark

St. Peter's Church, Newark

St. Philip's Church, Newark

Trinity Church, Newark

Preaching station at New Barbadoes Neck (now Kearny and Harrison)

Christ Church, New Brunswick

Church of St. John the Evangelist, New Brunswick

Mission at New Egypt

Calvary Church, New Providence

Christ Church, Newton (aka Newtown)

Mission at Old Bridge

Mission at Oldham (near Patterson)

Grace Church, Orange

St. Mark's Church, Orange (aka Williamsville)

Mission at Pahaquarry (in Hardwick Twp.)

Mission at Parsippany

St. John's Church, Passaic (aka Passaic Bridge)

St. John's Church, Paterson

St. Paul's Church, Paterson

Appendix 4

Grace Church, Pemberton

Mission at Penn's Grove (aka Penns Grove, in Carneys Point Twp.)

St. George's Church, Penn's Neck

Preaching station at Pensaukin Creek (aka Pensauken; near Wrightsville, Bon Air, Maple Shade)

Preaching station at Peppercotten (aka Papakating; near Sussex)

St. Peter's Church, Perth Amboy

St. Luke's Church, Phillipsburgh

St. James' Church, Piscataway (aka Piscatawa; now at Edison)

Grace Church, Plainfield

Trinity Church, Plainfield

Mission at Plattsburgh (now Sykesville in Chesterfield Twp.)

Christ Church, Pompton

Trinity Church, Princeton

Mission at Princeton Basin

Mission at Prospect Plain

St. Paul's Church, Rahway

St. Peter's Church, Rancocas

Preaching station at Readington

Trinity Church, Red Bank

All Saints Memorial Church, Riceville

Christ Church, Ridgewood

Christ Church, Riverton

Rockaway Mission, Rockaway

Rocky Hill Mission, Rocky Hill

Church of the Holy Trinity, Roundabouts (aka Roundabout, a village of South Amboy)

St. John's Church, Roxbury

St. John's Church, Salem

St. Bartholomew's Chapel, Saltersville (aka Bayonnetown)

Colonial (Anglican) and Antebellum (Episcopal) Parishes

Mission at Schooley's Mountain (near Hackettstown)

Mission at Scotch Plains

Preaching station at Shark River (near Wall and Neptune City)

Christ Church, Shrewsbury

St. John's Church, Somerville

Christ Church, South Amboy (aka St. Stephen's Church)

St. Paul's Church, South Bergen (aka St. Paul's, Bergen; now part of Jersey City)

Church of the Holy Communion, South Orange

Mission at South River

St. Peter's Church, Spotswood (aka Spottswood, aka Spotteswood, etc.)

Mission at Springfield (near Mansfield and Mt. Holly)

Mission at Stanhope

Mission at Stockton (near Camden)

Mission at Succasunna (aka Succasunny, aka Succasunna Plains)

Calvary Church, Summit

Trinity Church, Swedesborough (aka Raccoon)

Preaching Station at Tinton Falls (the manor)

Mission at Tom's River

St. Michael's Church, Trenton

St. Paul's Church, Trenton (aka South Trenton)

Trinity Church, Trenton

St. Mark's Chapel, Tuckerton

Preaching station at Turkey (supported from St. John's, Elizabeth)

Mission at Upper Amboy (one mile south of South Amboy)

Grace Church, Van Vorst (aka Jersey City, aka Harsimus)

St. Thomas' Church, Vernon

Mission at Vincentown

Trinity Church, Vineland

Appendix 4

Mission at Washington (aka Port Washington, aka Port Colden, with St. Matthew's Hall Chapel)

Mission at Westfield

St. John's Church, West Hoboken (now Union City)

Preaching station at Whippany

Mission at Wolf Hill (aka West Long Branch)

St. James' Church, Woodbridge

Trinity Church, Woodbridge

Christ Church, Woodbury

Mission at Woodstown

Mission at Woodsville (near Hopewell)

Mission at Wywayanda

Appendix 5

Congregational Giving to the American Colonization Society (ACS) in the Diocese of New Jersey (through 1865)[1]

1834	Trinity Church, Newark	$17.43
1834	St. Peter's Church, Perth Amboy	$14.00
1835	St. Peter's Church, Perth Amboy	$6.68
1836	St. Peter's Church, Perth Amboy	$7.50
1837	St. Peter's Church, Perth Amboy	$6.70
1838	St. Peter's Church, Perth Amboy	$6.30
1838	Christ Church, New Brunswick	$7.00
1839	St. Peter's Church, Perth Amboy	$7.00
1840	St. Peter's Church, Perth Amboy[2]	$5.725
1841	St. Peter's Church, Perth Amboy	$8.00
1842	St. Peter's Church, Perth Amboy	$15.00
1856	St. John's Church, Somerville	$49.00
Overall Total		$150.335

1. As reported in diocesan convention journals (1834–1865).
2. This donation does in fact include a half-penny.

Appendix 6

Congregational Giving in the Diocese of New Jersey to the Africa Mission of the Episcopal Church (through 1865)[1]

1835	St. Peter's Church, Perth Amboy	$2.50
1835	St. Andrew's Church, Mount Holly	$8.88
1835	St. Mark's Church, Orange	$5.00
1835	St. James' Church, Piscataway[2]	$0.09
1835	Trinity Church, Woodbridge	$0.61
1835	St. James Church, Knowlton	$1.07
1836	St. Luke's Church, Hope	$0.62
1840	Christ Church, Shrewsbury	$3.08
1841	Christ Church, Shrewsbury	$5.13
1842	Christ Church, Shrewsbury	$5.25
1842	St. John's Church, Elizabethtown	$21.43
1847	St. Paul's Church, Hoboken	$10.00
1851	St. Peter's Church, Berkeley at Clarksboro	$28.00

1. As reported in diocesan convention journals (1835–1865).
2. Nine cents is not a typo.

Congregational Giving in the Diocese of New Jersey

1852	Christ Church, Shrewsbury[3]	$2.00
1852	St. Peter's Church, Berkeley at Clarksboro	$22.00
1853	St. John's Church, Elizabethtown	$1.32
1853	St. Peter's Church, Berkeley at Clarksboro	$42.25
1854	St. Peter's Church, Berkeley at Clarksboro	$37.23
1854	St. Stephen's Church, Mullica Hill	$9.27
1855	St. Peter's Church, Berkeley at Clarksboro	$36.43
1855	St. Stephen's Church, Mullica Hill	$8.00
1856	St. Peter's Church, Berkeley, at Clarksboro	$46.61
1856	St. Philip's Church, Newark[4]	$5.00
1856	St. Peter's Church, Morristown[5]	$5.00
1856	Church of the Redeemer, Morristown[6]	unspecified amount
1857	St. John's Church, Salem[7]	$62.00
1857	St. Peter's Church, Berkeley at Clarksboro[8]	$142.72
1857	St. Stephen's Church, Beverly	$75.00
1857	Trinity Church, Hoboken[9]	$20.00
1858	St. Peter's Church, Berkeley in Clarksboro	$52.00
1858	St. Stephen's Church, Beverly	$75.00
1858	Trinity Church, Hoboken[10]	$20.00
1859	St. Peter's Church, Perth Amboy	$120.00
1859	St. Stephen's Church, Beverly	$60.00
1859	Grace Church, Jersey City	$2.00

3. Christ Church, Shrewsbury reported jointly with Christ Church, Middletown and Trinity Chapel, Red Bank.

4. Specifically designated for "Mrs. Thompson, Africa." The gift is designated specifically for a Black missionary.

5. Specifically designated for "Leacock Fund, Africa."

6. The annual report by Rev. J. H. Tyng states that the "interest of the Sunday school is devoted to the African Mission" but no specific financial numbers of any kind appear in his report.

7. This giving is designated for "Foreign Miss." and Africa is mentioned, but no specific dollar amount for funds dedicated to the African mission particularly are specified.

8. Specifically designated for "Mrs. Thompson, Africa." So in this unusual instance, the gift from a White congregation is designated specifically for a Black missionary.

9. Specifically designated for "Grace Wright" scholarship in Africa.

10. Again, designated for the "Grace Wright" scholarship in Africa.

Appendix 6

1860	St. Stephen's Church, Beverly	$50.00
1861	Trinity Church, Princeton	$66.54
1861	Christ Church, Bordentown	$17.50
1861	St. Stephen's Church, Beverly	$40.00
1862	St. Andrew's Church, Mount Holly	$1.00
1862	Christ Church, Allentown	$23.50
1862	St. Stephen's Church, Beverly	$30.00
1863	Christ Church, Allentown	$37.00
1863	Grace Church, Crosswicks	$4.00
1863	St. Andrew's Church, Mount Holly	$1.00
1864	Christ Church, Allentown	$47.50
1864	Grace Church, Crosswicks	$9.00
1865	Grace Church, Crosswicks	$7.00
1835–65	Overall Total[11]	$1207.53

11. This table does not include general account Foreign Missions giving during this period, which, at least during the lengthy tenure of Bishop Payne (Liberia) went more to the Liberia Mission than any other mission. Dunn, *History of the Episcopal Church in Liberia*, 96.

Selected Bibliography

"1st draught." Lambeth Palace Archives, Gibson Papers, MSS 941, No. 72.
"An Act for Regulating Negro, Indian, and Mallatto Slaves within this Province of New Jersey." December 12, 1704. In Bernard Bush, *Laws of the Royal Colony of New Jersey*, 28–30. Vol. 2. Trenton, NJ: New Jersey Archives, and Records Management, 1977–1986.
"An Act for Regulating of Slaves, March 11, 1713/14." In Bernard Bush, *Laws of the Royal Colony of New Jersey*, 136–40. Vol. 2. Trenton, NJ: New Jersey Archives, and Records Management, 1977–1986.
"An act for the Gradual Abolition of Slavery." February 15, 1804, Acts 28th G.A. 2nd sitting. https://dspace.njstatelib.org/xmlui/handle/10929/68964.
"An Act respecting Slaves." March 14, 1798, Acts 22nd G.A. 2nd sitting. http://fas-history.rutgers.edu/clemens/NJLaw/slavelaw1798.html.
"An act supplemental to the act entitled 'An act respecting slaves.'" https://www.nj.gov/state/darm/WebCatalogPDF/VanWickle/1812_An%20Act%20Supplemental%20to%20the%20Act%20entitled%20An%20Act%20Respecting%20Slaves_29%20January%201812.pdf.
"An Act to Abolish Slavery." Passed April 18, 1846. https://www.montclair.edu/anthropology/wp-content/uploads/sites/36/2021/06/Slavery-in-New-Jersey-Literature-Review-Appendix-B-Slave-Codes_Remediated.pdf.
"An Act to prevent the Importation of Slaves into the State of New-Jersey, and to authorize the Manumission of them under certain Restrictions, and to prevent the Abuse of Slaves." March 2, 1786, Acts 10th G.A. 2nd sitting. https://digitalcollections.nypl.org/items/510d47e3-f8a3-a3d9-e040-e00a18064a99.
"An act to prohibit the exportation of slaves or people of color out of this State." November 4, 1818. https://www.nj.gov/state/darm/WebCatalogPDF/VanWickle/1818_An%20act%20to%20prohibit%20the%20exportation%20of%20slaves%20or%20servants%20of%20color%20out%20of%20this%20State_5%20November%201818.pdf.
"An Act to prohibit the importation of Slaves into any port or place within the jurisdiction of the United States, from and after the first day of January, in the year of our Lord one thousand eight hundred and eight." Passed March 2, 1807. https://govtrackus.s3.amazonaws.com/legislink/pdf/stat/2/STATUTE-2-Pg426.pdf.

Selected Bibliography

American Society for Colonizing the Free People of Color of the United States. *The Twenty-First Annual Report of the American Society for Colonizing the Free People of Color of the United States, with the Proceedings of the Annual Meeting, December 12, 1837.* Washington, DC: James C. Dunn, 1838.

The Archives of the Episcopal Church. "Consulting the Past Through the Archival Record: A Guide for Researching the Impact of Slavery on Church Life and African Americans." https://www.episcopalarchives.org/church-awakens/files/original/2253 337c254b62e28a5d3b44307faa75.pdf.

Bailey, Anne C. "They Sold Human Beings Here," *New York Times*, February 12, 2020.

Bailey, Sarah Pulliam. "Atlanta Megachurch Pastor Louie Giglio Sets off Firestorm by Calling Slavery a 'Blessing' to Whites." *The Washington Post*, June 16, 2020. https://www.washingtonpost.com/religion/2020/06/16/atlanta-megachurch-pastor-louie-giglio-sets-off-firestorm-after-calling-slavery-white-blessing/.

Barratt, Norris Stanley. *Outline of the History of Old St. Paul's Church Philadelphia, Pennsylvania.* Lancaster, PA: New Era Printing Co., 1918.

Bayker, Jesse, Christopher Blakley, and Kendra Boyd. "His Name Was Will: Remembering Enslaved Individuals in Rutgers History." In *Scarlet and Black, Volume I: Slavery and Dispossession in Rutgers History*, edited by Marisa J. Fuentes and Deborah Gay, 58–81. New Brunswick: Rutgers University Press, 2016.

Bennett, Robert A. "Black Episcopalians: A History From The Colonial Period To The Present." *HMPEC* 43.3 (1974) 231–45.

Berkeley, Francis L., Jr. *Dumore's Proclamation of Emancipation.* Charlottesville: University of Virginia Library, 1941.

Bhutta, Neil, Andrew C. Chang, Lisa J. Dettling, and Joanne W. Hsu. "Disparities in Wealth by Race and Ethnicity in the 2019 Survey of Consumer Finances." *FEDS Notes.* Washington, DC: Board of Governors of the Federal Reserve System, 2020. https://doi.org/10.17016/2380-7172.2797.

Bilmes, Linda J. and Cornell William Brooks. "Normalizing Reparations: U.S. Precedent, Norms, and Models for Compensating Harms and Implications for Reparations to Black Americans." *RSF* 10.2 (2024) 30–68. https://doi.org/10.7758/RSF.2024.10.2.02.

Birch, Samuel. *Inspection Roll of Negroes.* 2 vols. 1793. Mss held at US National Archives. Vol. 1, NAID 17337716: https://catalog.archives.gov/id/17337716. Vol. 2, NAID 5890797: https://catalog.archives.gov/id/5890797.

Blazina, Carrie and Kiana Cox. "Black and White Americans Are Far Apart in Their Views of Reparations for Slavery." Pew Research, November 28, 2022. https://www.pewresearch.org/short-reads/2022/11/28/black-and-white-americans-are-far-apart-in-their-views-of-reparations-for-slavery/.

"Boell, Thomas, of Freehold, Monmouth Co." In *Documents Relating to the Colonial History of the State of New Jersey*, Volume XXII, *Calendar of New Jersey Wills*, Vol. 1. 1670–1730, 44. Paterson, NJ: William Nelson, 1901.

"Book E of Wills, p. 307, Trenton, N. J. Will of Job Throckmorton (Colts Neck), made 23 April, 1748." In *Throckmorton Family History: Being the Record of the Throckmortons in the United States of America with Cognate Branches*, by Frances Grimes Sitherwood, 83. Bloomington, IL: Pantagraph, 1930.

Boyd, Julian P., ed. *Fundamental Laws and Constitutions of New Jersey, 1664–1964.* Princeton: D. Van Nostrand, 1964.

Bragg, George F. *History of the Afro-American Group of the Episcopal Church.* Baltimore: Church Advocate, 1922.

Selected Bibliography

Bray, Thomas. *Rev. Thomas Bray*. New York: Arno, 1972.
Brockmann, R. John. *Commodore Robert F. Stockton (1795–1866): A Protean Man for a Protean Nation*. Amherst, NY: Cambria, 2009.
Brown, Robert. *The Story of Africa and Its Explorers*. Vol. 1. London: Cassell, 1892.
Bruns, Thomas Nelson Carter. *Louisiana Portraits*. New Orleans: National Society of the Colonial Dames of America in the State of Louisiana, 1975.
Buck, Elaine, and Beverly Mills. *If These Stones Could Talk: African American Presence in the Hopewell Valley, Sourland Mountain, and Surrounding Regions of New Jersey*. Lambertville, NJ: Wild River, 2018.
Burgess, George. *List of Persons Admitted to the Order of Deacons in the Protestant Episcopal Church in the United States of America, from A.D. 1785 to A.D. 1857*. Boston: A. Williams, 1874.
Burr, Nelson R. *The Anglican Church in New Jersey*. Philadelphia: The Church Historical Society, 1954.
Burt, Nathaniel. "The First Rectors: 1834–1866." In *Trinity Church Princeton, New Jersey: A History in Celebration of 150 Years 1833 to 1983*, 10–23. Princeton: Barracks, 1988.
"Bush of Oxford to the Mr. Whitfield, 1741 September 17." Box 5, folder 18. MSS held at Stewart M. Robinson Collection of Colonial Sermons, C0513, Manuscripts Division, Department of Special Collections, Princeton University Library.
Calloway, Anne, and Jolyon G. R. Pruszinski, ed. "A History of Trinity and St. Philip's Cathedral: Slavery, Racism, and Renewal in 'God's House.'" *DNJRJR*, September 25, 2023. https://dionj-racialjusticereview.blogspot.com/2023/09/a-history-of-trinity-and-st-philips.html.
Christ Church, Shrewsbury. "Anglican Slavery in New Jersey: A Focus on Christ Church Shrewsbury." January 2019. https://christchurchshrewsbury.org/?page_id=3459.
———. *Parish Register*. MSS held at Christ Church, Shrewsbury, NJ.
Church of England. "Church Commissioners Publishes Full Report Into Historic Links to Transatlantic Chattel Slavery and Announces New Funding Commitment of £100m in Response to Findings." October 1, 2023. https://www.churchofengland.org/media/finance-news/church-commissioners-publishes-full-report-historic-links-transatlantic-chattel.
The Church Pension Fund. "Confession." In *Enriching Our Worship 1*, The Church Pension Fund, 19. New York: Church Publishing, 1998.
Church Pension Group. "Church Pension Group Releases Report on the Origins and Sources of Its Assets." *ENS*, May 8, 2024. https://episcopalnewsservice.org/pressreleases/church-pension-group-releases-report-on-the-origins-and-sources-of-its-assets/.
———. "Report by the Church Pension Group on the Origins and Sources of Its Assets: Resolution 2022-A129: Resolution for a Forensic Audit of the Funds of the Domestic and Foreign Missionary Society." May 2024. https://www.cpg.org/globalassets/documents/publications/resolution_a129_report_from_cpg.pdf.
Chute, William J. "When Perth Amboy Was a Seaport Town." *The Journal of the Rutgers University Library* 17.2 (1954) 32–49.
City of Evanston. "Evanston Local Reparations." https://www.cityofevanston.org/government/city-council/reparations.
Colonization Society of the City of Newark. *A Sketch of the Colonization Enterprise, and of the Soil, Climate and Production of Liberia, in Africa*. Newark, NJ: Colonization Society of the City of Newark, 1838.
Cone, James H. *The Cross and the Lynching Tree*. Maryknoll, NY: Orbis, 2011.

Selected Bibliography

Croes, John. "Address." In *Journal of the Proceedings of the Forty-Seventh Annual Convention, of the Protestant Episcopal Church, in the State of New Jersey*, 7–16. New Brunswick: Terhune & Letson, 1830.

Crummell, Alex. *The Greatness of Christ and Other Sermons*. New York: Thomas Whittaker, 1882.

Darity, William, and Kristen Mullen. *From Here to Equity: Reparations for Black Americans in the Twenty-First Century*. Chapel Hill: University of North Carolina Press, 2022.

DiCamillo, Mark. "Majority of Voters Believe Black Californians Continue to Be Affected by the Legacy of Slavery, Yet Cash Reparations Face Headwinds." Berkeley Institute of Government Studies Poll #2023–18. September 10, 2023. https://escholarship.org/uc/item/5ks5g9f6.

Diocese of New Jersey. *Journal of Proceedings of the Seventy-Fifth Annual Convention in Trinity Church, Newark, on Wednesday, 26 May, 1858*. Burlington: Franklin Ferguson, 1858.

———. *Journal of Proceedings of the Sixty-Seventh Annual Convention: Held in Trinity Church, Newark, on Wednesday 29th, and Thursday 30th of May, MDCCCL*. Princeton: J. T. Robinson, 1850.

———. *Journal of the Eighty-Fifth Annual Convention. 1868*. New York: John W. Amerman, 1868.

———. *Journal of the Proceedings of the Eighty-First Annual Convention Held in Grace Church, Newark, on Wednesday and Thursday, May 25th and 26th 1864*. Philadelphia: J. B. Chandler, 1864.

———. *Journal of the Proceedings of the Eighty-Second Annual Convention Held in St. Mary's Church, Burlington, on Wednesday, May 31st 1865*. Philadelphia: J. B. Chandler, 1865.

———. *Journal of the Proceedings of the One Hundred and Eleventh Convention, Being the Ninety-Eighth Year of the Protestant Episcopal Church, In the Diocese of New Jersey, Held in St. Paul's Church, Camden, Tuesday, May 8th, and Wednesday, May 9th, 1883*. Princeton: C. S. Robinson, 1883.

———. *Journal of the Proceedings of the Seventy Third Annual Convention; Held, in Grace Church, and in Trinity Church, Newark, on Wednesday, 28 May, 1856*. Burlington, NJ: Samuel C. Atkinson, 1856.

Doane, George Washington. *Diocese of New Jersey: The Episcopal Address, The Twenty-Fourth, to the Seventy Third Annual Convention, in Trinity Church, Newark, Wednesday, May 28, 1856*. Burlington: Samuel C. Atkinson, 1856.

———. *Diocese of New Jersey: The Episcopal Address, The Twenty-Third, to the Seventy Second Annual Convention; in St. Mary's Church, Burlington, Wednesday, May 30, 1855*. Burlington: Printed at the Gazette Office, 1855.

———. *Diocese of New Jersey: The Episcopal Address, to the Seventy-First Annual Convention, in Grace Church, Newark, Wednesday, May 31, 1854*. Burlington: Printed at the Gazette Office, 1854.

———. *Diocese of New Jersey: The Episcopal Address, to the Seventy-Third Annual Convention, in Trinity Church, Newark, Wednesday, May 28, 1856*. Burlington: Samuel C. Atkinson, 1856.

———. *Diocese of New Jersey: The Episcopal Address to the Sixty-Fifth Annual Convention; in Grace Church, Newark, Ascension Day, June 1, 1848*. Burlington: Edmund Morris, at the Missionary Press, 1848.

Selected Bibliography

———. *Episcopal Address Delivered at the Convention of the Protestant Episcopal Church, in the State of New-Jersey; May 28, 1834*. Camden: Josiah Harrison, 1834.

———. *The Episcopal Address to the Sixty-Eighth Annual Convention, in St. Mary's Church, Burlington, Wednesday, 28th May, 1851*. Philadelphia: King & Baird, 1851.

Dod, William Armstrong. *Paul of Tarsus: An Inquiry into the Times and the Gospel of the Apostle of the Gentiles*. Boston: Roberts Brothers, 1872.

Douglas, Kelly Brown. *The Black Christ*. Maryknoll, NY: Orbis, 1994.

"Dred Scott v. Sandford (1857)." National Archives. https://www.archives.gov/milestone-documents/dred-scott-v-sandford.

Dunn, D. Elwood. *A History of the Episcopal Church in Liberia 1821–1980*. London: Scarecrow, 1992.

East Brunswick Historical Society. "Van Wickle and Morgan Slave Ring Leaders East Brunswick, NJ (1818)." *Pure History*, November 18, 2011. https://purehistory.org/van-wickle-and-morgan-slave-ring-leaders-east-brunswick-new-jersey-1818/.

Edwards, Abigail. "Trinity's Founding Fathers." Unpublished research paper, 2022. MSS held at Trinity Church, Princeton, NJ archives.

Egerton, Douglas. *Death or Liberty: African Americans and Revolutionary America*. Oxford: Oxford University Press, 2006.

The Episcopal Church. "Racial Justice Audit of Episcopal Leadership: From 2018–2020." The Episcopal Church, January 2021. www.episcopalchurch.org/racial-justice-audit.

Episcopal Diocese of New Jersey. "Province II Slave Trade Lament and Repentance." YouTube video, February 14, 2024. https://www.youtube.com/watch?v=6WawMgopH2s.

Escher, Constance K. *She Calls Herself Betsey Stockton: The Illustrated Odyssey of a Princeton Slave*. Eugene, OR: Resource, 2022.

"Extract from the Instructions to Earl Clarendon when Lord Cornbury & Governor of New York, January 1, 1702/3." British Online Archives, SPG Correspondence Collection. B Series Letter Book, Vol. 1: Appendix.

Fanjul, Stephanie. "St. Wilfrid's Church: Fragments of the Soul of an Urban Church." Capstone Project (2019). MSS held at Rubenstein Library, Duke University. https://hdl.handle.net/10161/18575.

Fauquez, Anne-Claire. "'A Bloody Conspiracy': Race, Power and Religion in New York's 1712 Slave Insurrection." In *Fear and the Shaping of Early American Societies*, edited by L. Henneton and L. Roper, 204–25. Leiden: Brill, 2016.

Fitzpatrick, Regina. "New Jersey State Archives Van Wickle Slave Ring Free Digital Collection." New Jersey State Library, July 18, 2024. https://www.njstatelib.org/news/vanwickleslaveringcollection/.

Freiday, Dean. "Tinton Manor: The Iron Works." *Proceedings of the New Jersey Historical Society* 74 (1952) 250–61.

Fry, Wendy. "California Reparations Task Force to Recommend 'Down Payments' for Slavery, Racism." Calmatters, May 1, 2023. https://calmatters.org/california-divide/2023/05/reparations-payments-california/#:~:text=The%20other%20method%2C%20based%20on,California%20from%201933%20to%201977.

Fuentes, Marisa J., and Deborah Gray White, eds. *Scarlet and Black, Vol. 1: Slavery and Dispossession in Rutgers History*. New Brunswick: Rutgers University Press, 2016.

Garlick, Bernard McKean. *A History of St. Peter's Church, Freehold, New Jersey, 1702–1967*. Freehold: N.p., 1967.

Gedney, Lisa Cokefair, ed. *Town Records of Hopewell, New Jersey*. New York: Little & Ives, 1931.

Selected Bibliography

Geffken, Rick. *Stories of Slavery in New Jersey.* Charleston, SC: The History Press, 2021.

Geisheimer, Glenn G. "Trinity Episcopal Church." *Newark Religion.* http://newarkreligion.com/episcopal/trinity.php.

"Geo. Whitfield 'Concerning my Sermon' To Lord Bush of Oxford, 1741 June 18." Box 5, folder 15. MSS held at Stewart M. Robinson Collection of Colonial Sermons, C0513, Manuscripts Division, Department of Special Collections, Princeton University Library.

"Geo. Whitfield to Lord Bishop of Oxford, 1741 June 9." Box 5, folder 14. MSS held at Stewart M. Robinson Collection of Colonial Sermons, C0513, Manuscripts Division, Department of Special Collections, Princeton University Library.

"Geo. Whitfield to Lord Bush of Oxford, 1741 July 28." Box 5, folder 16. MSS held at Stewart M. Robinson Collection of Colonial Sermons, C0513, Manuscripts Division, Department of Special Collections, Princeton University Library.

"George Washington Doane: The First Professor and a Religious Patron." Trinity College, last accessed October 21, 2024. https://dsp.domains.trincoll.edu/TrinityAndSlavery/george-washington-doane/.

Gerbner, Katharine. *Christian Slavery: Conversion and Race in the Protestant Atlantic World.* Philadelphia: University of Pennsylvania Press, 2018.

"Gibbons v. Morse, 7 N.J.L. 253 (1821)." New Jersey Court of Errors and Appeals, November term, 1821. https://freestateslaveryproject.com/legal-materials/cases/federal/gibbons-v-morse-7-n-j-l-253-1821/.

Gigantino, James J., II. *The Ragged Road to Abolition: Slavery and Freedom in New Jersey, 1775–1865.* Philadelphia: University of Pennsylvania Press, 2015.

———. "Trading in Jersey Souls: New Jersey and the Interstate Slave Trade." *Pennsylvania History: A Journal of Mid-Atlantic Studies* 77.3 (2010) 281–302.

Glasson, Travis. *Mastering Christianity: Missionary Anglicanism and Slavery in the Atlantic World.* Oxford: Oxford University Press, 2012.

Goodfriend, Joyce. "Burghers and Blacks: The Evolution of a Slave Society at New Amsterdam." *New York History* 59 (1978) 125–44.

Grace, Beatrice. *History of St. Peter's Episcopal Church, Spotswood, New Jersey.* Spotswood: St. Peter's Episcopal Church, 1956.

Greason, Walter D. *Suburban Erasure: How the Suburbs Ended the Civil Rights Movement in New Jersey.* Lanham, MD: Rowman & Littlefield, 2013.

Hammond, Joseph W. "Orchard Home: The Story of a Gracious Residence, and of the People Who Lived and Worked There." *New Jersey Studies* 5.1 (2019) 1–100.

Harrison, Chaim. "Three Jewish Reminders for When the World Seems Overwhelming." Reform Judaism. https://reformjudaism.org/beliefs-practices/spirituality/3-jewish-reminders-when-world-seems-overwhelming.

"Harvard & the Legacy of Slavery." Harvard University, September 14, 2022. https://legacyofslavery.harvard.edu.

Hawks, Francis L., ed. "The Memorial of Col. Morris Concerning the State of Religion in the Jerseys, 1700." *Proceedings of the New Jersey Historical Society* 4 (1849–50) 118–21.

Hills, George Morgan. *History of the Church in Burlington, New Jersey.* Trenton: W. S. Sharp, 1885.

Hodges, Graham Russell. *Black New Jersey: 1664 to the Present Day.* New Brunswick: Rutgers University Press, 2018.

Selected Bibliography

———. *Root and Branch: African Americans in New York and East Jersey, 1613–1863*. Chapel Hill: University of North Carolina Press, 1999.

———. *Slavery and Freedom in the Rural North: African Americans in Monmouth County, New Jersey, 1665–1865*. Madison, WI: Madison House, 1997.

Hodges, Graham Russell, ed. *Black Itinerants of the Gospel: The Narratives of John Jea and George White*. New York: Palgrave, 2002.

Hodges, Graham Russell, and Alan Edward Brown, eds. *"Pretends to Be Free": Runaway Slave Advertisements from Colonial and Revolutionary New York and New Jersey*. New York: Garland, 1994.

Holmes, David L. "The Making of the Bishop of Pennsylvania, 1826–1827: Part I: The Nestor's Finest Hour." *HMPEC* 41.3 (1972) 225–62.

Hood, Robert E. "From a Headstart to a Deadstart: The Historical Basis for Black Indifference Toward the Episcopal Church 1800–1860." *HMPEC* 51.3 (1982) 269–96.

Humphreys, David. *An Historical Account of the Incorporated Society for the Propagation of the Gospel in Foreign Parts, to the Year 1728*. London: J. Downing, 1730.

Hunter, Gary J. *Neighborhoods of Color: African American Communities in Southern New Jersey, 1638-2000*. Glassboro, NJ: Rowan University Press, 2015.

"Jacob Van Wickle (1770–854)." Rutgers Scarlet and Black Research Center. https://records.njslavery.org/s/doc/item/1284.

"James Parker Jr. (1776–1868)." Rutgers Scarlet and Black Research Center. https://records.njslavery.org/s/doc/item/1388.

Jarrett-Schell, Peter. *Reparations: A Plan for Churches*. New York: Church Publishing, 2023.

Jea, John. *The Life, History, and Unparalleled Sufferings of John Jea, The African Preacher*. London: Williams, 1800.

"John Croes to Revd. James C. Ward, July 16, 1831." Record ID 108178, Accession number MA 365.121, The Morgan Library & Museum.

"John Holbrook, Will, Northampton County, Virginia—1746." In *Migration of Holbrooks from England to America and Forsyth County, Georgia*, by Willie Tallant, 3–4. Cumming, GA: W. Tallant, 1983.

Johnson, Sylvester A. *African American Religions, 1500–2000: Colonialism, Democracy, and Freedom*. Cambridge: Cambridge University Press, 2015.

Journal of the Proceedings of the Fifty First Annual Convention of the Protestant Episcopal Church, in the State of New-Jersey; Held in Trinity Church, Newark, Wednesday the 28th, and Thursday the 29th Days of May, 1834. Camden, NJ: Josiah Harrison, 1834.

Journal of the Proceedings of the Fortieth Annual Convention of the Protestant Episcopal Church in the State of New Jersey, Held in St. John's Church, Elizabethtown, on the 20th and 21st Days of August, 1823. New Brunswick, NJ: William Myer, 1823.

Journal of the Proceedings of the Forty-First Annual Convention of the Protestant Episcopal Church in the State of New Jersey, Held in St. Michael's Church, City of Trenton, on the 18th and 19th Days of August, 1824. New Brunswick, NJ: William Myer, 1824.

Journal of the Proceedings of the Thirty-Ninth Annual Convention of the Protestant Episcopal Church in the State of New Jersey, Held in Christ-Church, Shewsbury, on the 21st and 22nd Days of August, 1822. New Brunswick, NJ: William Myer, 1822.

Keith, George. *An exhortation & caution to Friends concerning buying or keeping of Negroes*. New York: Printed by William Bradford, 1693. Reprint: Ann Arbor, Text Creation Partnership, 2011. http://name.umdl.umich.edu/A47141.0001.001.

———. "An exhortation & caution to Friends concerning buying or keeping of Negroes." *The Pennsylvania Magazine of History and Biography* 13 (1889) 265–70.

Selected Bibliography

———. *A Journal of Travels from New-Hampshire to Caratuck on the Continent of North-America*. London: Joseph Downing, 1706.

Kelley, Robert M. "Slavery Evidenced in the Parish Register." Christ Church, Shrewsbury, January 2019. https://christchurchshrewsbury.org/?page_id=3459.

Khan, Maysoon. "New York Will Set up a Commission to Consider Reparations for Slavery." Associated Press, December 19, 2023. https://apnews.com/article/new-york-reparations-slavery-commission-18578dfe233c1faeccfc5213050b52d3.

Klein, Mary. "From the Archives: Bishop Whittingham's Questionnaire of 1844—Survey Says . . ." *Maryland Episcopalian*, August 19, 2020. https://marylandepiscopalian.org/2020/08/19/from-the-archives-bishop-whittinghams-questionnaire-of-1844-survey-says/.

"Laity of Salem, New Jersey to SPG." British Archives Online, SPG Correspondence Collection. A Series Letter Book, Vol. 16, 201–2.

Langford, Kristal C. "Inside the Van Wickles' Slave Ring: 'Exposing a Scene of Villainy.'" Lost Souls Public Memorial Project. https://lostsoulsmemorialnj.org/wp-content/uploads/Inside-Van-Wickles-Slave-Ring.pdf.

Laskowski, Elizabeth. "Updated: Robert Morris." Founders and Slavery, April 19, 2015. https://foundersandslavery.wordpress.com/2015/04/19/updated-robert-morris/.

Latrobe, Henry. "Description of the Schuyler Copper-Mine in New Jersey." *The Medical Repository* 6 (November, December, 1802, and January, 1803) 319–21.

"Letter from Mr. Sharpe to ye Secretary. New York. June 23rd, 1712." British Online Archives, SPG Correspondence Collection: "America in Records from Colonial Missionaries, 1635–1928." A Series Letter Book Vol. 7: 214–17. MSS copy scans: https://microform.digital/boa/collections/11/volumes/37/the-a-series-letter-books-1702–1737.

Lewis, Harold T. "Racial Concerns in the Episcopal Church Since 1973." *AEH* 67.4 (1998) 467–79.

———. *Yet with a Steady Beat: The African American Struggle for Recognition in the Episcopal Church*. Valley Forge, PA: Trinity, 1996.

Mack, Jessica R. "Albert Dod." Princeton University. https://slavery.princeton.edu/stories/albert-dod.

Macy, Harry, Jr. "The Van Wicklen/Van Wickle Family: Including its Frisian Origin and Connections to Minnerly and Kranchheyt." *The New York Genealogical and Biographical Record* 128.4 (1997) 241–51.

Marrin, Richard B., ed. *Runaways of Colonial New Jersey: Indentured Servants, Slaves, Deserters, and Prisoners, 1720–781*. Westminster, MD: Heritage, 2007.

McGinnis, William. *A History of St. Peter's Church in Perth Amboy, New Jersey, 1686–1956*. Woodbridge, NJ: Woodbridge, 1956.

McKean, Robert, and Abraham Beach. "Some Early Records for Christ Church, New Brunswick, and Saint James Episcopal Church, Piscataway: Marriages, Baptisms and Burials, 1758–1759 and 1767–1784." *Genealogical Magazine of New Jersey* 91 (January 2016) 3–14.

"Mr. Haliday to the Secretary. Amboy. October 9th, 1717." British Online Archives, SPG Correspondence Collection: "America in Records from Colonial Missionaries, 1635–1928." A Series Letter Book Vol. 12, 301–7. MSS copy scans: https://microform.digital/boa/collections/11/volumes/37/the-a-series-letter-books-1702–1737.

Selected Bibliography

"Mr. Holbrooke to the Secretary. Salem. November 17th, 1727." British Online Archives, SPG Correspondence Collection: "America in Records from Colonial Missionaries, 1635–1928." A Series Letter Book Vol. 20: 193–98. MSS copy scans: https://microform.digital/boa/collections/11/volumes/37/the-a-series-letter-books-1702-1737.

New Jersey Reparations Council. "For Such a Time as This: The Nowness of Reparations for Black People in New Jersey." New Jersey Institute for Social Justice. June 19, 2025. https://www.njisj.org/print/njrcreport.pdf.

"New Jersey Slavery Records." https://records.njslavery.org.

"Northeast Slavery Record Index." https://nesri.commons.gc.cuny.edu.

Parker, James, ed. *Historical Sketches of Parishes Represented in the Conventions of the Protestant Episcopal Church in New Jersey, 1785–1816, and Biographical Notices of Lay Delegates in Those Years*. New York: John Polhemus, 1889.

Pascoe, C. F. *Two Hundred Years of the S.P.G.* 2 vols. London: Society's Office, 1901.

Patterson, William. *Laws of the State of New Jersey*. New Brunswick: Abraham Blauvelt, 1800.

Pennington, Edgar Legare. "Thomas Bray's Associates and Their Work Among the Negroes." *Proceedings of the American Antiquarian Society* 48 (1938) 311–403.

Perry, William Stevens. *The Bishops of the American Church, Past and Present*. New York: Christian Literature Co., 1897.

Pettigrew, William A. *Freedom's Debt: The Royal African Company and the Politics of the Atlantic Slave Trade, 1672–1752*. Chapel Hill: University of North Carolina Press, 2013.

Pingeon, Francis. "An Abominable Business: The New Jersey Slave Trade, 1818." *New Jersey History* 109.3 (1991) 15–35.

Power-Greene, Ousmane K. *Against Wind and Tide: The African American Struggle against the Colonization Movement*. New York: New York University Press, 2014.

The Protestant Episcopal Church. *An Historical Sketch of the African Mission of the Protestant Episcopal Church in the U.S.A.* New York: Foreign Committee, 1884.

The Protestant Episcopal Church in the Diocese of New Jersey. *Journal of the Proceedings of the One Hundred and Eighteenth Convention, Being the One Hundred and Fifth Year of the Protestant Episcopal Church in the Diocese of New Jersey; Held in St. Mary's Church, Burlington, Tuesday, May 6th, and Wednesday, May 7th, 1890. Together with Appendices and the Episcopal Address*. Princeton: The Princeton Press, 1890.

———. *Journal of the Fifty Second Annual Convention of the Protestant Episcopal Church, in the State of New Jersey; Held in St. Mary's Church, Burlington, on Wednesday the 27th, and Thursday the 28th Days of May, 1835*. Burlington: The Missionary Press, 1835.

———. *Journal of the Proceedings of the Fifty First Annual Convention of the Protestant Episcopal Church, in the State of New Jersey*. Camden: Josiah Harrison, 1834.

———. *Journal of the Proceedings of the Forty-Eighth Annual Convention, of the Protestant Episcopal Church, in the State of New Jersey*. New Brunswick: Terhune & Letson, 1831.

———. *Journal of the Proceedings of the Forty-Ninth Annual Convention of the Protestant Episcopal Church, in the State of New Jersey*. New Brunswick: Terhune & Letson, 1832.

Pruszinski, Jolyon G. R. "The Episcopal Mission at the Free Black Settlement of Macedonia, NJ: 1853-1887." *DNJRJR*, May 26, 2025. https://dionj-racialjusticereview.blogspot.com/2025/05/the-episcopal-mission-at-free-black.html.

Selected Bibliography

———. "The History of Slavery at Christ Church, New Brunswick." *DNJRJR*, March 27, 2023. https://dionj-racialjusticereview.blogspot.com/2023/03/the-history-of-slavery-at-christ-church.html.

———. "Public History in the Diocese of New Jersey Racial Justice Review: Research, Reckoning, Education, and Formation." *AEH* 93.3 (2024) 634–44.

———. "Reparations Commission Address, 2024 Diocesan Convention." *DNJRJR*, March 6, 2024. https://dionj-racialjusticereview.blogspot.com/2024/03/video-reparations-commission-address.html.

———. "Rev. Eugene L. Henderson: First Black Priest Ordained in the Diocese of New Jersey." *DNJRJR*, February 17, 2025. https://dionj-racialjusticereview.blogspot.com/2025/02/rev-eugene-l-henderson-first-black.html.

———. "Rev. James C. Ward (1777–1834), the First African American Clergyman in the Diocese of New Jersey." *DNJRJR*, October 9, 2023. https://dionj-racialjusticereview.blogspot.com/2023/10/rev-james-c-ward-1777-1834-first.html.

———. "The Revolutionary Period and Early Black Estrangement from the Episcopal Church." *DNJRJR*, January 16, 2023. https://dionj-racialjusticereview.blogspot.com/2023/01/the-revolutionary-period-and-early.html.

———. "White Supremacist Symbols at the Diocesan Headquarters (1943–Present)." *DNJRJR*, March 5, 2024. https://dionj-racialjusticereview.blogspot.com/2024/03/white-supremacist-symbols-at-diocesan.html.

Pruszinski, Kyra N. and Jolyon G. R. Pruszinski, ed. "Trinity Church, Princeton and Slavery: A Brief Introduction." *DNJRJR*, April 10, 2023. https://dionj-racialjusticereview.blogspot.com/2023/04/trinity-church-princeton-and-slavery.html.

Race, Henry, and William Frazer. "Rev. William Frazer's Three Parishes, St. Thomas's, St. Andrew's, and Musconetcong, N.J., 1768–70." *Pennsylvania Magazine of History & Biography* 12.2 (1888) 212–32.

"Records of the Presbytery of New Castle, 1814–1834." *Journal of the Department of History (The Presbyterian Historical Society) of the Presbyterian Church in the U.S.A.* 19.2 (1940) 93–97.

The Rector, Wardens and Vestrymen of Trinity Church in the Borough of Princeton. "Certificate of Incorporation." May 17, 1833. MSS held at Trinity Church, Princeton archives.

Reichner, L. Irving. "Nicasius de Sille Bible." *Publications of the Genealogical Society of Pennsylvania* 7.2 (1919) 127–35.

Reimers, David M. "Negro Bishops and Diocesan Segregation in the Protestant Episcopal Church: 1870–1954." *HMPEC* 31.3 (1962) 231–42.

Reinken, Dirk and Jolyon G. R. Pruszinski. "A History of Slavery at St. Peter's Church, Freehold." *DNJRJR*, April 17, 2023. https://dionj-racialjusticereview.blogspot.com/2023/04/a-history-of-slavery-at-st-peters.html.

"Removal to Louisiana: The Van Wickle Slave Ring." Rutgers University Scarlet and Black Research Center. https://scarletandblack.rutgers.edu/archive/exhibits/show/hub-city/removal-to-louisiana.

"The Reverend Absalom Jones." Black Presence in the Episcopal Diocese of New York, Winter 2020. https://blackpresence.episcopalny.org/person/the-reverend-absalom-jones/.

"The Reverend Peter Williams Jr." Black Presence in the Episcopal Diocese of New York. https://blackpresence.episcopalny.org/person/the-reverend-peter-williams-jr-3/.

Selected Bibliography

Rodriguez, Joe. "Stations of Reparations Service at St. Augustine's Episcopal Church, Asbury Park on 3/16/2024." YouTube video, April 19, 2024. https://www.youtube.com/watch?v=Z_AvkWiK8ks.

"Rowland Ellis to SPG, October 8, 1715." British Online Archives, SPG Correspondence Collection: "America in Records from Colonial Missionaries, 1635–1928." A Series Letter Book Vol. 11: 118.

Rugemer, Edward B. "The Development of Mastery and Race in the Comprehensive Slave Codes of the Greater Caribbean during the Seventeenth Century." *William and Mary Quarterly* 70 (2013) 429–58.

Saliby, Sophia. "A Grassroots Effort in Michigan Is Raising Reparations—While the Government Lags." National Public Radio, *All Things Considered*, April 26, 2024. https://www.npr.org/2024/04/23/1246682932/a-grassroots-effort-in-michigan-is-raising-reparations-while-the-government-lags.

"Samson Adams Papers, 1767–1794." University of Michigan Library Digital Collections. https://quod.lib.umich.edu/a/adams/index.html.

Scarborough, John. "The Episcopal Address to the One Hundred and Sixth Annual Convention in St. Mary's Church, Burlington, May 6, 1890." In Diocese of New Jersey. *Journal of the Proceedings of the One Hundred and Eighteenth Convention, Being the One Hundred and Fifth Year of the Protestant Episcopal Church in the Diocese of New Jersey; Held in St. Mary's Church, Burlington, Tuesday, May 6th, and Wednesday, May 7th, 1890*, 155–73. Princeton: The Princeton Press, 1890.

Schermerhorn, Calvin. *The Business of Slavery and the Rise of American Capitalism*. New Haven: Yale University Press, 2015.

Schjonberg, Mary Frances. "Historic New Jersey Church Honors Deceased Veterans." ENS, May 28, 2014. https://episcopalnewsservice.org/2014/05/28/video-historic-new-jersey-church-honors-deceased-veterans/.

Scot, George. *The model of the government of the province of East-New-Jersey in America and encouragements for such as designs to be concerned there: published for information of such as are desirous to be interested in that place*. Edinburgh: John Reid, 1685. Reprint: Ann Arbor: Text Creation Partnership, 2022. http://name.umdl.umich.edu/A58781.0001.001.

Sharp, Granville. *The just limitation of slavery in the laws of God, compared with the unbounded claims of the African traders and British American slaveholders. With a copious appendix: Containing, An Answer to the Rev. Mr. Thompson's Tract in favour of the African Slave Trade.—Letters concerning the lineal Descent of the Negroes from the Sons of Ham.—The Spanish Regulations for the gradual Enfranchisement of Slaves.—A Proposal on the same Principles for the gradual Enfranchisement of Slaves in America.—Reports of Determinations in the several Courts of Law against Slavery, &c*. London: B. White, 1776.

Sherwood, Harriet. "C of E Hoping to Create £1bn Fund to Address Legacy of Slavery." *The Guardian*, March 4, 2024.

Society for the Propagation of the Gospel in Foreign Parts. *Abstract of Proceedings, 1750*. London: Edward Owen, 1751.

Society of the American Colonization Society in New Jersey. "Proceedings of a Meeting Held at Princeton, New Jersey, July 14, 1824 to Form a Society in the State of New Jersey to Cooperate with the American Colonization Society." Princeton: D. A. Borrenstein, 1824.

Selected Bibliography

St. Peter's Church, Freehold. "Stations of Reparations—History in Story, Song, and Prayer." YouTube video, March 25, 2023. https://www.youtube.com/watch?v=K1x6bEZOmGU.
State of New Jersey. "Documents at the New Jersey State Archives relating to the Van Wickle Slave Ring." State of New Jersey. https://www.nj.gov/state/darm/WebCatalogPDF/VanWickle/VanWickleTableOfContents.pdf.
———. *Laws of the State of New Jersey.* New Brunswick: Abraham Blauvelt, 1800.
Steen, James. *History of Christ Church, Shrewsbury, New Jersey.* Shrewsbury: Christ Church, Shrewsbury, 1972.
Stockton, Robert Field, and John R. Thomson. "Subscription Book of 1827 to Build a Protestant Episcopal Church in the Borough of Princeton." August 16, 1827. MSS held at Trinity Church, Princeton archives.
Strassburger, John Robert. "The Origins and Establishment of the Morris Family in the Society and Politics of New York and New Jersey, 1630–1746." PhD diss., Princeton University, 1976.
"A Supplement to the act entitled 'An act to regulate the election of members of the legislative council and general assembly, sheriffs and coroners in this state,' passed at Trenton the twenty-second day of February, one thousand seven hundred and ninety-seven." November 16, 1807, §1, Acts 32nd G.A. 1st sitting. https://dspace.njstatelib.org/xmlui/handle/10929/50467.
Talbot, Anne. "The Will of Mrs. Talbot." In George M. Hills, *History of the Church in Burlington, New Jersey*, 246–47. Trenton, NJ: William S. Sharp, 1876.
Thompson, Thomas. *An Account of Two Missionary Voyages: The One to New Jersey in North America, the Other from America to the Coast of Guiney.* London: Society for Promoting Christian Knowledge, 1937. Reprint of 1758 edition.
———. *The African Trade for Negro Slaves, Shewn to be Consistent with Principles of Humanity, and with the Laws of Revealed Religion.* Canterbury: Simmons and Kirkby, 1772.
United States Bureau of the Census. *Fifth Census of the United States, 1830: Population Schedules, Georgia*, Vol. 6. Washington, DC: The National Archives, 1945.
———. *Historical Statistics of the United States, Colonial Times to 1970*, 2 vols. Washington, DC, 1975.
———. *Population Schedules of the Sixth Census of the United States, 1840: New Jersey*, Vol. 4, Mercer County. Washington, DC: The National Archives, 1967.
Van Wicklin, John. "Family of Jacob^5 Charles Van Wickle." Houghton University. https://facultysites.houghton.edu/JohnVanWicklin/Home%20page/Genealogy/FamPages/jacob^5charles.htm.
Washington, Booker T., et al. *The Negro Problem: A Series of Articles By Representative American Negroes of To-Day.* New York: James Pott, 1903.
Wax, Darold D. "Africans on the Delaware: The Pennsylvania Slave Trade, 1759–1765." *Pennsylvania History: A Journal of Mid-Atlantic Studies* 50.1 (1983) 38–49.
Weeks, Daniel J. *Not for Filthy Lucre's Sake: Richard Saltar and the Antiproprietary Movement in East New Jersey, 1665–1707.* Bethlehem, PA: Lehigh University Press, 2001.
Weiss, Harry B. *The Personal Estates of Early Farmers and Tradesmen of Colonial New Jersey, 1670–1750.* Trenton: New Jersey Agricultural Society, 1971.
Wheeler, William. *The Ogden Family in America.* Philadelphia: Lippincott, 1907.
Whitefield, George. *Three Letters from the Reverend George Whitefield viz. Letter I. Written from Georgia, to a Friend in London; wherein he vindicates his Asserting, That*

Selected Bibliography

Archbishop Tillotson knew no more of True Christianity than Mahomet. Letter II. To the same, on the same Subject. Letter III. To the same, dated at New Brunswick in New-Jersey, April 27, 1740. Glasgow: James Duncan, 1740.

Wilder, Craig Steven. "'Driven . . . from the School of the Prophets': The Colonizationist Ascendance at General Theological Seminary." *New York History* 93.3 (2012) 157–85.

Winner, Lauren. *The Dangers of Christian Practice: On Wayward Gifts, Characteristic Damage, and Sin.* New Haven: Yale University Press, 2018.

Woodson, Carter G. *The History of the Negro Church.* Washington, DC: The Associated Publishers, 1921.

WPA. *Inventory of the Church Archives of New Jersey: Protestant Episcopal.* Newark: The Historical Records Survey, 1940.

Wright, M. M. Thompson. *The Education of Negroes in New Jersey.* New York: Bureau of Publications, Teachers College, Columbia University, 1941.

Wu, Sen-Yuan. "New Jersey Population: 1790 TO 2010." New Jersey Department of Labor and Workforce Development. https://www.nj.gov/labor/labormarketinformation/assets/PDFs/dmograph/est/nj1790_2010.pdf.

Yarsiah, James T. *The Episcopal Church—Early Missionaries in Liberia 1821–1871: Positive and Negative Impact of Missionary Activities.* Saarbrucken: LAP LAMBERT Academic, 2014.

Young, Otis E., Jr. "Origins of the American Copper Industry." *Journal of the Early Republic* 3.2 (1983) 117–37.

Index

Abolition, scriptural support for, 45–48, 150–51
Abolition, xxxi-xxxii, 16, 19n5, 23n23, 25–30, 31, 32, 34, 36, 38n38, 39, 60, 78, 90–91, 99, 107, 109, 126, 139, 141, 142
Adams, Samson, 23n20, 98n4
African Methodist Episcopal (AME) Church, 19, 23n21, 38, 97, 98–99
The African Trade..., by Thomas Thompson, 16, 58–66, 79n12, 125 (See also Thompson, Thomas)
All Saints' Church, Atlantic City, 129n8
American Colonization Society (ACS), xxxii, 27, 28, 31, 34, 36, 84, 108–16, 117–18, 126, 140, 165
Anabaptists, 55
The Anglican Church in New Jersey, by Nelson Burr, xxx, 31n1, 98n5, 137, 142n33, 152–55
Anglican Church in North America (ACNA), xxi, xxviii
Annapolis, Maryland, 104–5
Anti-racism, xiii, xvii, xx, 151
Apprenticeship, xxxii, 28, 140 (See also Slavery, euphemism for)
Archbishop of Canterbury, 5, 124
Asbury Park, New Jersey, 73, 77n3, 107, 129
Atlantic City, New Jersey, 129, 130

Bainbridge, Absalom, 83

Baptism, xxxi, 5, 13, 15, 17, 18, 50, 55, 100, 117, 118, 124, 137
Baptists, 7, 23n21, 38, 55, 97–99, 101
Barbadian settlers, 4, 5, 12, 124
Barbados, 4, 5, 12, 16, 17, 43, 48, 52–53, 54n9, 79n11, 124, 136
Beach, Abraham, 17n34, 33n7, 35, 54n9, 81, 126
Belleville (aka Second River), New Jersey, 13
Bishop of London, 11n1
Blackwell, Robert, 17n34, 54n9
Boonton mine, 86
Bray, Thomas, 12n2, 19n4, 104n34
British Archives Online, 49n3, 52n7, 55n12, 104n34, 137, 153n4
Brunswick, Georgia, 36n25, 84, 126

Camden, New Jersey, 70–73, 129, 130, 135n1
Cape Coast Castle, 15, 58–59, (See also Ghana)
Cape May County, 35n21, 82n26
Caribbean, 4n5, 5, 26, 82, 123, 124, (See also West Indies, Barbados, Codrington Plantation)
Catholicity (universalism), xvi, xxviii, xxx, 129
Chapman, George T., 112
Christ Church, Allentown, 9n9, 15, 58, 125, 136n5, 156, 168
Christ Church, Bordentown, 157, 168

Index

Christ Church, Elizabeth, 135n4, 158
Christ Church, Hopewell, 49, 159
Christ Church, Middletown, 9n7, 9n9, 15, 58, 98–101, 112, 125, 160, 167n3
Christ Church, New Brunswick, 9n9, 32n6, 33, 35, 80–83, 103, 103n32–33, 111, 129n4, 161, 165
Christ Church, Newton, 9n9, 103, 103nn32–33, 161
Christ Church, Second River (Belleville), 9n9, 14, 157
Christ Church, Shrewsbury, xvii, 9n7, 9n9, 13, 13n12, 15, 16, 17n34, 22n16, 33n6, 43, 58, 77n2, 99–101, 107, 112, 118–19, 125, 128, 163, 166–67
Christ the King, Willingboro (Levittown), 130
Church Missionary Society (aka Church Mission Society), 102
Church of England (COE), Church Commissioners, xviii
Church of England (COE), xviii, 7–10, 11–17, 21–23, 32, 34, 43, 52, 55, 58, 124, 135
Church of the Ascension, Atlantic City, 129n8, 158
Church of the Redeemer, Morristown, 112, 160, 167
Church Pension Fund, xix
Churches, Colonial-era list, 6, 7–10
Churches, Diocese of New Jersey through Civil War, 156–64
Civil War, xi, xxxii, 29, 34, 83–84, 113, 115, 139, 140, 143
Clarkson, David, 112
Cochran, Richard, 83
Codrington Plantation, 16, 17, 43, 54n9, 79n11, 124
Colemantown, New Jersey, 28
Coleraine Tweedside Plantation, Georgia, 84
Company of Merchants Trading to Africa, 59, 79 (see also its predecessor, the Royal African Company)

Condit, Joel W., 112
Congregationalists, 7
Cooke, Samuel, 17n34, 22n16, 54n9, 80, 125
Cox, Col. Daniel, 154
Croes, Bishop John, xviin5, 23n22, 31, 33, 35, 81, 82, 102, 104–5, 126–27
Crummell, Alexander, 19n6, 27, 38n35, 106n41, 109, 113
Curry, Bishop Michael, xxiii
Cutting, Leonard, 81

Declaration of Independence, 20
Devaines, William, 60, 79n12
Diocese of Maryland, 104–5
Diocese of New Jersey Racial Justice Review, xvii, xviiin13, 72n8, 73n13, 78n4, 80n17, 82n28, 83nn29–30, 85–86n52, 86n55, 88n58, 89n61, 101n19, 105nn39–40, 106n42, 106n48, 107n51, 110n9, 119n47, 129n4, 131, 131n16, 135, 135n3, 149
Diocese of the Northeast and Mid-Atlantic (ACNA), xxi, xxviii
Doane, Bishop George Washington, 16–17, 34, 35–36, 38n35, 67–70, 84, 88n58, 89n59, 106n41, 106n43, 109n4, 110–11, 116, 117n40, 118nn42–43, 127
Doctrine of Discovery, 5n9
Dod, Albert Baldwin, 85
Dod, William Armstrong, 85
Domestic and Foreign Missionary Society, 111
Dore, James, 82
Douglass, Frederick, 109
Dred Scott v. Sandford, xxxii, 28
Duffin, Nicholas, 88, 106n48
Dutch settlement, 3, 5, 7, 123

East Jersey, xxxi, 3, 4, 5, 6, 13, 14, 25, 26, 43, 123, 124
Eatontown, New Jersey, 70, 107
Elizabeth (aka Elizabethtown), New Jersey, 9n7, 9n9, 33n6, 43, 52,

184

Index

103, 103n33, 112, 116, 130, 135n4, 158, 163, 166–67
Ellis, Rowland, 104n34
Emancipation Proclamation, xxxii, 82
Episcopal Church, Black rejection of, 19–24, 32, 34–35, 38–39, 72n10, 96–105
Episcopal Diocese of New Jersey, xxi, xxiii–xxiv, xxvii–xxviii, xxix, 18–24, 31–40, 67–74, 77–95, 120, 123–32, 133–45, 155, 156–64
Episcopal Diocese of Newark, xxi, xxviii, 34, 85–89, 107, 127, 128n2, 156–64
Essex County, 141n31, 160
An Exhortation & Caution to Friends..., by George Keith, 17n33, 43–48, 78n5

Finley, Robert, 108–9
First Presbyterian Church, Newark, 85
Floyd, George, xvii
Fortune, Carrie Smiley, 115
Fortune, T. Thomas, 114
Franklin, Benjamin, 14, 125
Franklin, Gov. William, 14, 125
Frazer, William, 17n34, 54n9, 97–98
Freedman's Commission, 128
Freehold, New Jersey, xxix, 9n9, 15, 43, 44, 52, 58, 77, 78–80, 83n30, 86n52, 125, 158
Frelinghuysen, Sen. Theodore, xvi
Fugitive Slave Act, xxxi, 26, 109n5, 113

Garthwaite, J.C., 112
General Convention Resolution A143, xvii
General Theological Seminary, 19n6, 36, 38, 106n41, 109n4
Ghana, 79 (see also Cape Coast Castle)
"Good news," xv–xvi
Good Shepherd Mission, Atlantic City, 129n8
Gouldtown, New Jersey, 29
Grace Church, Crosswicks, 9n7, 158, 168
Grace Church, Jersey City, 163, 167
Grace Church, Newark, 112, 161

Grace Wright scholarship, 167nn9–10
Gradual Abolition, xxxi–xxxii, 25–30, 31–39, 90–95, 99, 126, 139–40
Gradual Emancipation Act (aka Gradual Abolition Law, "Act for the Gradual Abolition of Slavery"), xxxi–xxxii, 26–27, 29, 32, 91, 99, 126, 139–41
Great Awakening, 15
Guineatown, New Jersey, 28

Haliday, Thomas, 17n34, 52–54, 154n6
Hanson, William, 85
Hare, George Emlen, 84
Hays, Jabez, 112
Henderson, Eugene L., 73
Henderson, Matthew H., 112
Hendrickson, Phebe, 100n14
Hicks, Mary, 81n22
Historically Black Congregations, 88, 127, 129 (see also Christ the King, Willingboro; St. Alban's, New Brunswick; St. Augustine's, Asbury Park; St. Augustine's, Atlantic City; St. Augustine's, Camden; St. Elizabeth's, Elizabeth; St. Monica's, Trenton; St. Philip's, Newark; St. Thomas,' Red Bank; St. Wilfrid's, Camden; and Trinity and St. Philip's Cathedral, Newark)
Holbrooke, John, 55–57, 154n8
Holmdel Baptist Church, 99, 101
Hooghlandt, Hendrich, 50

Innes, Alexander, 17n34, 54n9, 78n6, 80, 125
Integration (forced), 130

Jamaica, 48
Jea, John, 19, 20, 38, 98
Jensen, August, 73, 107
Jim Crow, 127, 129
Johnson, Cornelius, 94
Johnston, Oliver, 95
Jones, Absalom, 19n6, 37, 38, 109
Jones, Gen. David, 20

Index

Justinian, 63

Keith, George, 8, 14, 17nn33–34, 43–48, 54n9, 78–79
Ku Klux Klan, 127, 129
Landin, Daniel, 107
Leacock Fund, Africa, 113n25, 167n5
Leacock, Hamble J., 113
Levittown, New Jersey, 130 (See also Willingboro, New Jersey)
Lewis, Harold T., xxviii, 72n9, 131n15, 148
Liberia, 28, 36, 70, 84, 109–19, 126, 140, 168n11
Lincoln, Abraham, xi
Lindsay, William, 17n34, 54n9
London, 11n1, 53
Long Branch, New Jersey, 129, 160, 164
Lost Souls Memorial Project, 90n66, 93n74

Macedonia mission, 70, 72, 107, 118, 128, 160
Maidenhead, New Jersey (preaching station, now Lawrenceville), 49, 160
Manumission, xi, xxxi–xxxii, 5, 18, 20–24, 25–27, 29, 32, 35, 37, 47, 63, 81–83, 90n63, 91, 96, 98–101, 117, 124, 125, 126–27, 128, 140, 141n30 (See also Emancipation Proclamation, Gradual Abolition, Gradual Emancipation Act, Thirteenth Amendment)
Marginalization of Black Christians, xxviii, xxx, 4–5, 18–24, 32, 34, 38–39, 71, 96, 102, 105, 108–19, 124, 127, 128, 134, 148–49
Mass incarceration, xviii
McKean, Robert, 81
Merchant, Silas, 112
Methodists, 9n9, 15, 19, 23n21, 38, 97, 98
Middlesex County, 32, 36, 90–95, 126, 141n30
Middletown, New Jersey, 9n7, 9n9, 15, 58, 98–101, 112, 125, 160, 167n3

Mission to Africa (Anglican / Episcopal), 15, 28, 102, 110–11, 113, 116–19, 140, 166–68
Missions, Diocese of New Jersey through Civil War, 156–64
Mitchell, Elias, 106n48
Mitchell, George, 88, 106n48
Monmouth County Historical Association, 138n14
Monmouth County, 4n6, 13, 15, 17n34, 58, 78n8, 80, 138n14, 141, 147, 159
Monmouth University, 138n17
Morgan, Charles, 90n66, 91–92, 93n72
Morgan, Sarah, 91
Morris, Col. Lewis (aka Gov. Lewis Morris), 7n1, 12, 56n14, 81n23, 124, 154
Morris, Col. Lewis, Sr. (uncle of Gov. Lewis Morris), 8n5, 12, 56n14
Morris, Lewis (murdered cousin of Gov. Lewis Morris), 13
Morven estate, Princeton, 84, 110, 138n15
Murray, Gov. John, 20

National Episcopal Church Freedman's Commission (see Freedman's Commission)
Nazi-sympathy, 129
Neau, Elias, 50–51
New Amsterdam, 3
New Jersey Anti-Slavery Society, xxxii, 28
New Jersey Slavery Records (database), 138, 141
New Jersey Society for the Promotion of the Abolition of Slavery, xxxi–xxxii, 26
New Netherland, 3
New Sweden, 3, 55
New York City, 3, 20, 28, 36, 49–52, 106n41, 139
New York, xviii, 103, 142, (see also New York City)
New York University, xxiii
Nichols, William, 80
Nicholson, Gov. Francis, 14

186

Index

North Arlington (Belleville) mine, 13, 125
Northeast Slavery Record Index, 138, 141

O'Fake, John, 88, 106n48
O'Fake, Peter, 88, 106n48
Odell, Jonathan, 17n34, 54n9
Odenheimer, Bishop William H., 34
Ogden, Col. Josiah, 85-88, 88n57
Ogden, Uzal, Jr., 17n34, 33n7, 35, 54n9, 126
Old Burying Ground, Newark, 88
Old School Baptist Church, Hopewell, 97
Ordination of Black Christians, 19, 38, 58, 72n8, 73, 101-5, 106-7, 109, 129

Pagels, Elaine, xi-xii, xxiii
Parishes, Diocese of New Jersey through Civil War, 156-64
Parker, James, Jr., 37n30, 126, 142, 145n38
Paterson, Andrew Bell, 85
Payne, Bishop John, 113n24, 115n29, 118, 168n11
Pennsylvania, xxxii, 28, 80n15, 89n59, 101n22, 102-3, 105, 142, (see also Philadelphia)
Perkins, Eliza Greene Callahan, 35n22, 127
Perkins, James, 35n22
Peterkin, Joshua, 85
Philadelphia, 19n6, 38, 48, 60n3, 84n39, 89n59, 92n70, 102, 104, 105, 139
Pilgrim Baptist Church, Red Bank, 101
Plantations, 4, 5, 11n1, 14, 16, 17, 17n34, 32, 47, 52-54, 57, 60, 61, 81n23-24, 83, 84, 86, 91-92, 123, 124, 125, 126, 135, 136, 154
Pledge of Allegiance, xi
Pointe Coupee, Louisiana, 91
Potter, John, 36n26, 83-84, 109
Preaching stations, Colonial-era list, 6, 9, 156-64
Presbyterians, 7, 55, 85, 101-2, 109
Prigg v. Pennsylvania, xxxii, 28
Prime, 83

Princeton Theological Seminary, xviii, xxiii, 138n17
Princeton University, xi, xii, xxiii, 138n17
Province II, of the Episcopal Church, 77n3

Quakers, 4, 7, 16, 19n5, 25, 37, 43-48, 55, 60
Quaque, Philip, 58, 59n2
Queen Anne, 14

Racial uplift movement, 114
Racial wealth gap, xiv, xix, xxx, 67-70, 145n39
Rape, xvi, xxix, 13, 100-101
Ray, Elias (sometimes recorded as "Elias Kay"), 88, 106, 107
Recommended reading, 147-49
Redlining, xviii
Rees, William Henry, 106
Reeves, Charles, 99-101
Reeves, Hannah (née Van Cleif), 99-101
Reformed Episcopal Churches, xxi, xxviii
Reparations Commission (Diocese of New Jersey), xvii, xxiii-xxiv, xxix, 131
Reparations, and Georgetown University, xviii
Reparations, and Princeton Theological Seminary, xviii
Reparations, and the COE Church Commissioners, xviii
Reparations, and the Justice League of Greater Lansing (JLGL), xviii
Reparations, and the New Jersey Reparations Council, xviii, 149
Reparations, and Virginia Theological Seminary, xviii
Reparations, as advocated by Bishop George W. Doane, 67-70
Reparations, in California, xviii
Reparations, in Evanston, IL, xviii
Reparations, in Michigan, xviii
Reparations, in New Jersey, xviii
Reparations, in New York, xviii
Reparations, Normalizing, xix, 148-49
Reparations, Polling on, xix

Index

Reparations, scriptural support for, xxviii, 151

Reparations, xvi-xix, xxi, 67–70, 148–49, 151

Research, xvii, xviii, xix, xxi, xxiv, xxx, 38–39n38, 77, 80n30, 99n8, 107n54, 127–28, 131, 133–45

Revolutionary War, 8, 15, 18–24, 25, 29, 32, 34, 83, 97, 125–26, 139

Rhodes, Jacob, 106, 106n48

Ridgeway, William, 129

Ringwood mine and iron works, 35, 86

Rio Pongas, Gambia, 113

Rowland, John-Hamilton, 33n7

Royal African Company, 4n3, 123 (see also its replacement: the Company of Merchants Trading to Africa)

Rutgers University, 90n65, 138n17

Saddlertown, New Jersey, 28

Salem County, 55–57 (See also St. John's, Salem)

Scarborough, Bishop John, 70–73, 107n53, 128

Schuyler, Col. Peter, 13–14, 35n17, 125

Scotland, 60

Scriptural support, xii, xvi, xxi, xxviii, 61–63, 150–51 (see also Abolition, scriptural support for; Reparations, scriptural support for; Slavery, scriptural support for)

Seabury, Bishop Samuel, 54n9, 81

Second River, New Jersey (See Belleville, New Jersey; Christ Church, Second River)

Segregation, xii, xxix, 17, 29, 71–73, 82, 84, 85–87, 96, 103–5, 107, 116, 117, 118, 119n47, 119n49, 127, 128, 129, 131, 140

Seventh Day Adventists, 55

Sharpe, John, 49–52, 154n7

Shrewsbury, New Jersey, 13n10, 15 (see also Christ Church, Shrewsbury)

Sierra Leone, 102

Skinner, William, 17n34, 54n9

"Slave conspiracies," 5, 49–52

"Slave revolts," 26, 49–52, 154

Slavery audits, xviii (see also *Diocese of New Jersey Racial Justice Review*)

Slavery, as a national sin, 61

Slavery, conversion to Christianity supportive of, 51–52

Slavery, encumbered wealth, 14, 22, 22n18, 35, 39, 124, 125, 126, 127, 136–39, 141, 143–45

Slavery, euphemized as "apprenticeship" or "servanthood," 28, 56, 140, 142

Slavery, geographic externalization of, 15, 36, 83–84, 126, 139, 142–43

Slavery, implied by glebe use, 17n34, 54, 136

Slavery, in mining, 12, 13–14, 86, 125

Slavery, incentives for, xxxi, 4, 5, 12, 124

Slavery, legislation concerning, xxxi-xxxii, 4–5, 16, 22, 25–26, 27, 28, 29, 51, 60, 61, 83, 91, 124, 126, 127, 136, 138, 139–40, 141, 143, 154

Slavery, racialization of, 3, 4, 5, 123–24

Slavery, scriptural support for, 61–63, 150–51

Slavery, tools for researching, 138

Smith, Hanford, 112

Snow Hill, New Jersey, 28

Society for the Propagation of the Gospel, 8, 9, 10, 11n1, 12n2, 13, 14, 15–17, 18–19, 21, 23n24, 31n1, 32, 33, 43, 49–57, 58, 79n11, 104, 124, 125, 136, 137, 153–55

Sourland Region, 96–98

South River, New Jersey, 92, 163

Springtown, New Jersey, 29

St. Alban's, New Brunswick, 82, 129

St. Andrew's, Mount Holly, 33n6, 103n33, 112, 160, 166, 168

St. Andrew's, Ringoes (aka Amwell, moved to Lambertville), 97–98, 156, 159

St. Augustine's, Asbury Park, 73, 77n3, 129

St. Augustine's, Atlantic City, 129

St. Augustine's, Camden, 70–71, 72, 129

Index

St. Elizabeth's, Elizabeth, 135n4
St. George's, Penns Neck, 103n33, 162
St. James Memorial Church, Eatontown, 107
St. James, Atlantic City, 129n8
St. James, Knowlton, 103n33, 112, 159, 166
St. James, Piscataway (aka Piscataqua), 9n7, 9n9, 33n6, 43, 52, 103, 112, 162, 166
St. John's, Camden, 70–71, 129n5, 157
St. John's, Elizabethtown, 9n7, 9n9, 32–33n6, 43, 52, 103, 103n33, 112, 116, 158, 163, 166–67
St. John's, Salem, 7–8n1, 9n7, 55–57, 103, 103n32–33, 162, 167
St. John's, Somerville, 111, 113, 163, 165
St. Luke's, Ewing, 130n14
St. Luke's, Hope, 103n33, 112, 159, 166
St. Mark's, Orange, 103, 103nn32–33, 112, 161, 166
St. Mary's, Burlington, 9n7, 9n9, 14, 15, 17, 33n6, 43, 44, 49, 103, 103n33, 104n34, 125, 157
St. Mary's, Colestown, 43, 135n1, 158
St. Michael's, Trenton, 13, 23n20, 83n31, 98, 119, 125, 130, 159, 163
St. Monica's, Trenton, 130
St. Paul's, Camden, 73, 157
St. Paul's, Hoboken, 112, 159, 166
St. Paul's, Paterson, 103n33, 161
St. Peter's, Berkeley (at Clarksboro), 9n9, 103, 103n33, 112, 158, 166–67
St. Peter's, Freehold, xxix, 9n9, 15, 43, 44, 52, 58, 77, 78–80, 80n17, 83n30, 86n52, 125, 158
St. Peter's, Morristown, 103, 112, 113n25, 160, 167
St. Peter's, Perth Amboy, 8, 9n7, 9n9, 13, 33n6, 37n30, 43, 49, 52, 103n33, 111–12, 113, 119, 126, 162, 165, 166–67
St. Peter's, Spotswood, 9n9, 32, 37, 90–95, 103nn32–33, 117, 126, 163
St. Philip's, Newark, 38, 67–70, 85–89, 106–7, 118, 127, 128, 161, 167
St. Stephen's, Beverly, 157, 167–68

St. Stephen's, Mullica Hill, 112, 161, 167
St. Thomas's, Red Bank, 114, 129
St. Wilfrid's, Camden, 129n9
Stations of Reparations Service, xxix, 77–89
Still, John N., 72n8, 107, 119n49
Stives, William, 97–98
Stockton, Betsey, 85, 119n47
Stockton, Robert, 23n23, 31, 36, 83–85, 109–10, 126
Stokes, Bishop William H., xvii, xxiii
Stoutsburg Sourland African American Museum, 97
Sunday School Society, 103, 117
Swastikas, 131

Talbot, John, 15, 17n33, 54n9, 78n6
Taylor, Joseph, 99–100
Thirteenth Amendment, xxxii, 29, 60, 84, 127, 141, 143
Thomas Boels, 44, 78, 78n6, 78n8
Thompkins, Samuel, 88, 106n48
Thompson, Elizabeth (also spelled "Thomson," of the Africa Mission), 167n4, 167n8
Thompson, Thomas, 15–16, 17n34, 54n9, 58–66, 79, 125
Thomson, James, 115n29
Throckmorton, Job, 80
Timbuctoo, New Jersey, 28
Tinton Falls mine, 12, 13n9, 124
Tinton Falls, 12, 13n9, 72, 107, 118, 124, 128, 160, 163
Topanemus, New Jersey, 78–79
Townsend, John H., 70, 72, 129n5
Toxic positivity, xvi-xvii
Trans-Atlantic slave trade, xviii, xxxi, 4, 22n18, 25–26, 35, 60, 91, 123, 127, 136n8
Trenton, New Jersey, 13, 23n20, 26n6, 83n31, 94n83, 98, 119, 125, 130, 159, 163
Trinity and St. Philip's Cathedral, Newark, 85–89, 106n42, 106n48, (See also St. Philip's, Newark and Trinity Church, Newark)

Index

Trinity Chapel, Red Bank, 112, 162, 167n3
Trinity Church, Elizabeth, 135n4, 158
Trinity Church, Hoboken, 159, 167
Trinity Church, Newark, 14, 32n6, 35, 85–89, 103n33, 104, 106, 111, 112, 117, 125, 161, 165
Trinity Church, Princeton, xii, xvii, 31, 36, 83–85, 105n39, 110, 119, 126, 135n3, 162, 168
Trinity Church, Woodbridge, 9n7, 9n9, 43, 49, 52, 112, 164, 166
Trinity College, Hartford, 36n23
Trinity, Wall Street, 13
Tyng, James H., 89, 167n6

Underground Railroad, 28–29

Van Cleif, Hannah (See Hannah Reeves)
Van Wickle Slave Ring, xxix, 22n17, 32, 36–37, 78, 90–95, 126, 142
Van Wickle, Jacob, 36–37, 90–95, 126
Vannoy, Joseph, 97
Vanois, Catherine, 97
Vaughn (aka Vaughan), Edward, 17n34, 54n9, 125
Virginia, xviii, 14, 20, 32, 57

Ward, James C., 101–5
West Indies, 4 (see also Caribbean, Barbados, Codrington Plantation)
West Jersey, 3, 4, 6, 14, 25, 43, 123
"White blessings," xvi
White flight, 89, 129–30
White privilege, xx, 67–70
White, George, 19, 38, 98
Whitefield, George, 15
Williams, Peter, Jr., 38–39
Williamson, David, 99–100
Willingboro, New Jersey, 130, 157

www.ingramcontent.com/pod-product-compliance
Lightning Source LLC
Chambersburg PA
CBHW031358230426
43670CB00006B/576